The English Garden

The English Garden

A SOCIAL HISTORY

CHARLES QUEST-RITSON

VIKING
an imprint of
PENGUIN BOOKS

VIKING

Published by the Penguin Group
Penguin Books Ltd, 80 Strand, London WC2R ORL, England
Penguin Putnam Inc., 375 Hudson Street, New York, New York 10014, USA
Penguin Books Australia Ltd, Ringwood, Victoria, Australia
Penguin Books Canada Ltd, 10 Alcorn Avenue, Toronto, Ontario, Canada M4V 3B2
Penguin Books India (P) Ltd, 11 Community Centre,
Panchsheel Park, New Delhi – 110 017, India
Penguin Books (NZ) Ltd, Cnr Rosedale and Airborne Roads,
Albany, Auckland, New Zealand
Penguin Books (South Africa) (Pty) Ltd, 24 Sturdee Avenue,
Rosebank 2196, South Africa

Penguin Books Ltd, Registered Offices: 80 Strand, London WC2R 02L, England

www.penguin.com

First published 2001
1

Copyright © Charles Quest-Ritson, 2001

The moral right of the author has been asserted

The Illustration Acknowledgements on pages 268–71 constitute an extension of this copyright page

Set in Adobe Caslon
Typeset by Rowland Phototypesetting Ltd, Bury St Edmunds, Suffolk
Colour reproduction by Dot Gradations.
Printed in Great Britain by Butler and Tanner Ltd.

A CIP catalogue record for this book is available from the British Library

Hardback ISBN 0-670-88768-4
Paperback ISBN 0-140-29502-X

✣ Frontispiece: *detail of the illustration on page 118.*

For E.G.

Contents

Introduction

Garden history has been abducted by the art historians. This book is an attempt to get it back for the social historian. Too much garden history has been concerned with when gardens were made, what they looked like, who made them and how they changed. More interesting by far is what the makers expected from the gardens, and how they and their successors evaluated their investment in gardening and the return it brought them. On the individual level, the story of gardens and gardening is a tale of aspirations and self-fulfilment. Most accounts are concerned with what owners, designers and gardeners did, rather than why they did it. We need to know *why* people garden. We need to discover the costs and the benefits as they have been perceived down the years. And we need to get away from irrelevant arguments about how the picturesque style of gardening differed from the sublime. Garden historians are obsessed with stylistic minutiae of which the principal participants themselves were barely aware.

Mark Girouard argued that the design and management of country houses had altered through the generations in direct response to transformations in English society itself.[1] The same is true of gardens. John Sales recently elaborated the theme:

> we now realize that garden styles mirror the aesthetic, social, technological, economic and political attitudes of the time at least as accurately as any other art form. Even more importantly, gardens intimately reflect the personalities and ideals of individuals. The changing fortunes and ambitions of successive generations are there to see in gardens if you know how and where to look.[2]

There is more to social history than drawing attention to the great gulf which divides the rich from the poor and then whingeing about it. This book is

✻ *Detail of the illustration on page 257.*

concerned mainly with the middle and upper classes, who are more literate and more conspicuous, and have left more traces of their passing. They are more interesting because others aspire to be like them. For historians, at any rate, the rich are always with us. John Loudon made the point – it was such a basic assumption that he did so almost in passing – when he compared gardens formal and informal: 'the Geometric Style was most striking and pleasing, and most obviously displayed wealth and taste while, in modern times, the natural or irregular style, from the sacrifice of profitable lands requisite to make room for it, becomes equally a sign of wealth and taste'.[3]

An individual's standard of living depends upon his income and his expenditure; in the mass, it depends upon the current balance between population and production. A case can be made for regarding the history of England from 1500 to 2000 as one of fairly consistent improvement. The proportion of people for whom economic and political worries were not an overriding concern grew, as indeed did the number who felt able to commit more of their resources to ornamental or recreational gardening. People have been moving up the hierarchy of needs.

Gardens and gardening in England go back long before 1500, though facts become difficult to establish before then and indeed are fairly sparse until the end of the seventeenth century. There is no doubt, however, that there have always been gardeners by trade – people who cultivate plants for reasons which are generally economic, but sometimes social or aesthetic. There have always been people who were willing to employ gardeners to access the benefits of their skills. There have always been nurseries and seedsmen to supply them. There have always been advisers to educate and inspire amateurs and professionals, employers and their employees. The word 'gardener' has always covered a broad range of people with different interests. It means a tradesman, but it may also mean an amateur who enjoys gardening. It is sometimes used to suggest a person with superior horticultural expertise or an interest in plants. In this book I use 'gardener' to denote a man who earns his living by working in gardens; I refer to his employer, or any person who works in his own garden, as a 'garden-owner'.

We lack an account of gardens and gardening which explains the social and financial reasons why they changed and evolved as they did. We need to analyse how the costs and benefits of gardens and gardening have been perceived through the centuries. We need to understand the changing aspirations of garden-owners. At every stage, in every age, we need to ask what owners sought from their gardens. We need to find an answer to the question, what are gardens *for*?

Gardens are defined by the purpose for which they exist. Oldest and most universal are gardens for food – economic gardens where fruit and vegetables are cultivated. Almost as old, and now as widespread, are ornamental gardens which exist principally for growing flowers. Commonly included with the idea of 'gardens' are remoter or less personal amenity areas, everything from deer parks to ornamental woodlands or public parks. Each has a distinct function, each is subject to different expectations and each provides value in its own way. Sometimes owners look for an economic return; costs are then conventionally computed in terms of capital outlay and annual income expenditure, including income forgone. More often, garden-owners measure value in terms of prestige, self-sufficiency, power and even aesthetics. These requirements may then be seen against the background of constantly changing social indices: population changes, changes in industry and trade, changes in country life and changes in social legislation.

Garden history is now an established discipline. When young, it tended to occupy itself with the artistic and architectural development of different styles, monographs on particular designers or gardens, and accounts of phenomena like plant-hunting. Little was achieved until the 1970s, and then research was concentrated upon big themes, big names and big gardens. Recent books and articles have begun to look at secondary aspects of garden history, lesser designers and minor gardens, but the focus is always upon the development of style. There is an assumption that garden history can only be studied as the history of art.

The trouble is that art historians describe the development of garden styles and fashions without adequate reference to the social and economic conditions which engendered them. Here is a recent example of the genre. Apologies are needed for quoting it at such length, but it comes from an in-depth study of gardens in the best tradition of American academia and it is worth reading through carefully:

> the items in the continuum prompt a myriad of more specific questions. Among them are these: What is involved in creating a garden? How are gardens described and notated? What sorts of meanings can gardens possess? What sorts of messages can they convey? Can gardens express deep-felt feelings and emotions? Can they have moral force? What artistic tasks can they perform? What distinctive pleasures can they yield? What patterns of influence linked gardening and her sister arts in the eighteenth century? What philosophical and aesthetic theories supported eighteenth-century gardening practice? The questions just listed vary greatly in scope. They involve the psychology of perception and the history of ideas as well as straightforward philosophical analysis. But they all bear on a fundamental question of aesthetics, namely, 'What is art and what does it do for us?'

I think this is bunk, and pretentious bunk at that. Gardening is social history. It has little to do with the history of art or the development of aesthetic theories – and nothing whatsoever with moral forces, artistic tasks and the psychology of perception. It is all about social aspirations, lifestyles, money and class. Why do

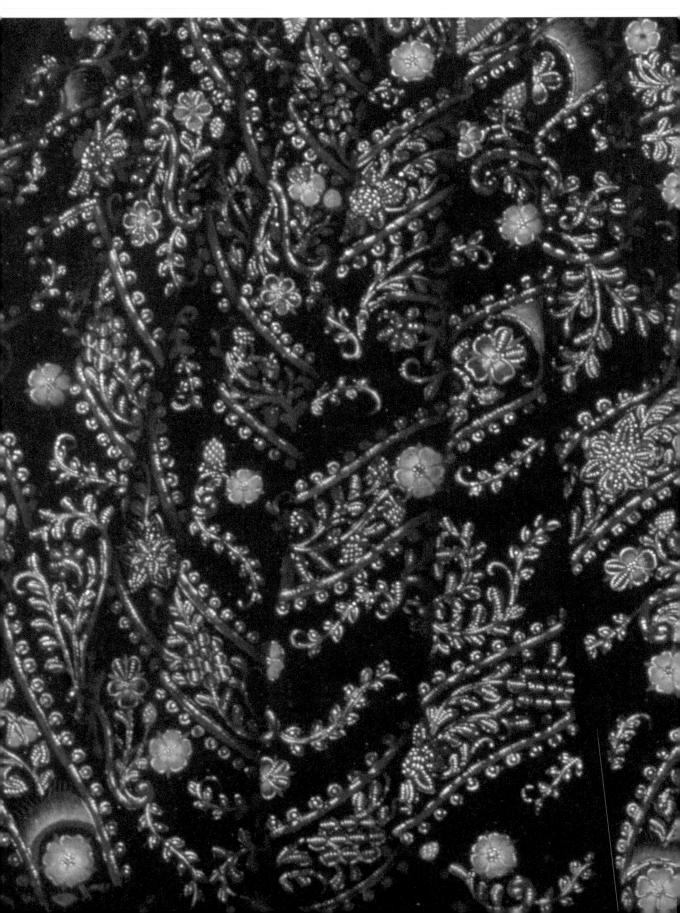

CHAPTER ONE

Early English Gardens
1500–1640

The Background to Tudor Society

Modern English history begins in 1485. The years before the accession of Henry VII were marked by the effects of the Black Death, the Hundred Years War and the Wars of the Roses, which isolated England from the European mainstream and reduced it to economic ruin. The arts of peace could not be practised in England until the establishment of the Tudor dynasty in the years following the demise of Richard III on Bosworth Field. Time and again throughout this book, we will see that the prospects for gardens and gardening declined in times of warfare and improved with the return of peace and prosperity. In 1500 there were fewer than 3 million people in England – not enough to fill the country, exploit its mineral resources or develop large-scale industry. 'The population of this island,' wrote an Italian visitor at the time, 'does not appear to me to bear any proportion to her fertility and riches.'[1] There was, however, a substantial growth in population from 3 million to 5¼ million during the period up to 1650.

Henry VII's first concern was to consolidate his power. As the central government grew in strength, so too did the rule of law and the exercise of justice. Religious, political and social freedoms were severely curtailed in parallel with this. Paradoxically, much political power was given to new men who rose in status through trade, the professions, good marriages, better farming, public office and local administration. And the sixteenth century was also a time of greater general prosperity, arising in part from an increase in overseas trade. With those foreign contacts came foreign cultural influences, especially from France, the Netherlands and Italy.

Prosperity engendered more spending by the better-off on comforts and pleasures, as opposed to necessities and self-defence. More people were better off in 1640 than in 1500; many enjoyed an improved and improving standard of living. The roots of a consumer society were already detectable among the newly rich

❊ *Detail of the illustration on page 38.*

lawyers, landowners, merchants and administrators who did well for themselves during those years. Against this background it is fair to suppose that gardens and gardening were one of the luxuries on which more people were able to spend more money than before and that the spin-offs for those further down the economic hierarchy were also measurable.

Changes in Land-holding

The dissolution of the monasteries sparked a revolution in land tenure as enormous tracts of land passed into new hands. It was not just the monasteries whose land was redistributed; the secular clergy, especially the land-rich bishops, also learned the political wisdom of reducing their land-holdings. In the 1520s, Church lands covered about one-sixth of the kingdom. The confiscations of the 1530s and 1540s, quickly followed by sales and grants to new owners, gave Henry VIII money to pursue his policies of centralization and altered the social balance within England as a whole. Three-quarters of the Church's lands were sold off by 1558, mostly to the gentry classes, who thus became the strongest supporters of the Tudor monarchy, its land reforms and the new Protestant Church. The greatest shift of political, economic and cultural power in the period 1500–1640 was to a substantially enlarged class of gentry.

Many of the families who exercised power and influence in the succeeding centuries owed their fortunes to the commercial opportunities which this great redistribution of land engendered. A minor gentry family which combined social ambition with commercial opportunism as ruthlessly as the Spencers did in Northamptonshire was able to make substantial additions to its land-holdings during the sixteenth and seventeenth centuries. Sir John Thynne was a farmer's son who worked for the first Duke of Somerset, uncle and Lord Protector to Edward VI, and bought the site of an Augustinian priory in Wiltshire called Longleat with sixty-three acres, to which he was able to add a further 6,000 acres over the following years. The overall effect was to increase considerably the proportion of the country as a whole which was owned by the gentry, at the expense of the Church, the magnates and ultimately the crown itself.

Even before 1500 there were men of influence who derived their power not from land or office but from trade, manufacture or finance. Such men mixed freely with the older, more established families whose wealth and power were based on land tenure. Some merchants and traders bought land to establish themselves among the landowning classes. It has been suggested that the new landowners brought with them the skills, disciplines and aptitudes which had enabled them first to flourish in other fields of endeavour and then to convert their energy and investment into the acquisition of land. Now they wanted to maximize their returns, which put them in the forefront of innovation in land use and management. Some landowners gained a reputation for ruthlessness in their pursuit of greater wealth, and were criticized for razing cottages, farms, hamlets and whole villages without regard for the ordinary people who lived there. Most were happy, if the opportunity arose, to invest in new industries on their estates, like mining, smelting and glass-making. They discovered that by flooding the water meadows in the chalk valleys of southern England they could greatly increase the growth of grass and make possible the maintenance of more sheep and cattle. In the sixteenth and, especially, the seventeenth centuries, land reclamation became an economic proposition as never before. This was the time when the heathlands of Wessex and the uplands of Derbyshire were enclosed and the Fens and the Somerset Levels were drained – some 100,000 acres between 1631 and 1653. This was paralleled, in other parts of the country, by large-scale enclosure of the medieval open fields.

This detail from a portrait of Lord Edward Russell, by an unknown artist, in 1573, shows him standing at the centre of a turf maze; the setting is symbolic (and bears the legend Fata viam invenient*) but shows what sixteenth-century gardens contained.*

Prosperity was also enjoyed by the farmers. Production rose, and so did prices. Security of tenure, fixed rentals and fairly stable costs were matched by rising prices for their produce. There was more money about as the sixteenth century progressed; yeomen rose into the ranks of the gentry.

The English rule of primogeniture meant that, right up until the twentieth century and at all social levels, landed property tended to pass intact from father to eldest son. The younger sons of large landowners and well-heeled gentry took the values and education which they had received as members of the wealthier classes into their lives as members of the less well-off. It has, however, been estimated that in each generation some 20 per cent of all families produced no inheriting sons. The daughters who inherited therefore had an attraction as marriage partners which was directly related to their value. Most marriages were between people of the same class, but not necessarily of equal wealth, though a widow with control of her property could use her wealth as a means of moving up the social scale – as Bess of Hardwick did. But political power offered the greatest security to the ambitious, for, when well used, it begat further power. No Elizabethan administrator, Restoration judge or Whig politician regarded his career as purely an act of public service; it was also an opportunity to do well for himself. It could be expensive, too. The diplomat Sir Thomas Hoby had to drop out of royal service in the 1590s because he no longer had the means to support himself at court. Those whose success brought substantial worldly rewards built extravagant prodigy houses and gardens to accommodate Queen Elizabeth I on her progresses or King James I on his hunting trips. Sir William Cecil's house at Theobalds grew so large as a result of playing host so often to Elizabeth I that it came to be regarded almost as a royal palace itself – a fate which turned into fact when Robert Cecil was asked to give it to James I in return for Hatfield. The gardens too were enormous – larger, for example, than Henry VIII's gardens

Robert Cecil, first Earl of Salisbury, *by John de Critz*, c. 1607. *James I so coveted Cecil's house and garden at Theobalds that he made Cecil exchange it for a run-down royal estate called Hatfield.*

at Hampton Court or Nonsuch. But there was also a substantial element of personal competition and self-aggrandizement in such ostentatious and palatial houses and gardens as Holdenby, Theobalds, Hatfield and Wilton.

The Gardens of the Tudor Monarchs

The early history of English gardens and gardening is fraught with problems. The biggest is the absence of 'genuine' Tudor and Renaissance gardens for us to visit and study today. No one has expressed this loss with greater eloquence than Sir Roy Strong: 'Bridgeman, Capability Brown and Repton and their imitators from 1720 onwards were responsible for the mass destruction, on a scale unmatched in any other European country, of the old formal gardens in the Renaissance, Mannerist, Baroque and Rococo styles. There is no English equivalent to the

Villa d'Este at Tivoli or to the palace at Heilbronn outside Salzburg.'² This is a view which has led some writers to describe the great landscapers of the eighteenth century as the most villainous vandals in the history of art.

As a result, the history of Tudor and Jacobean gardens in England has generally been constructed from literary sources, fleshed out by descriptions of some rather grand, larger-than-life gardens whose designs or plantings are especially well documented – to this day, some authors recount the story of gardens and gardening in the sixteenth century as if the only garden-owner in England was Henry VIII. The problem is complicated by the fashion that evolved in the middle of the nineteenth century for the re-creation of olde worlde Elizabethan gardens: the 'Elizabethan' garden at Montacute was laid out in the 1840s, the maze at Hatfield (that most incorrect of 'historic' gardens) dates from 1841, while most of the ancient yews known as 'the Sermon on the Mount' at Packwood were planted after 1850. It is scarcely surprising, therefore, that the customary solution to our ignorance about sixteenth-century gardening is to describe the long-lost gardens of Theobalds and Nonsuch, and to illustrate them with photographs of modern Tudor-style gardens. These are usually reconstructions made either at the time of the Arts and Crafts movement in the late nineteenth century, or in the last thirty years of the twentieth century, when the passion for Tudor Revival gardens based on patterns and plans in obscure French herbals seems to have gripped every well-heeled Englishwoman possessed of a sixteenth- or seventeenth-century manor house.

Roy Strong offers us a charming contrast between civilized Italy and barbarian England at the start of our period: 'while the Medici were enjoying the delights of villa life with its splashing fountains, ordered walks, vine-covered pergolas and clipped topiary box trees, England was a land of the castle and moat still just emerging from the Wars of the Roses'.³

Traditional histories of English culture during the sixteenth and early seventeenth centuries drew heavily on ideas about the Italian Renaissance. After the sack of Rome in 1527, scholars and artists of every discipline tucked their skills and knowledge into their knapsacks and fled the burning city. Dispersed throughout the about-to-be-civilized world, they gravitated to northern Europe and spread their New Learning among peoples who longed to be freed from the shackles of medieval superstition – the English above all others. Here the development of culture was enormously assisted by the Henrician Reformation and, more particularly, by the dissolution of the monasteries. These enabled the writ of Renaissance learning to reach every part of the country and permeate every social level. Within a few years, England could boast splendid prodigy houses with spectacular gardens like Hatfield, Theobalds and Wilton, and a more general flowering of culture which embraced William Shakespeare, Thomas Tallis and Inigo Jones.

Many garden historians pay homage to this tradition. They start by stating that the Renaissance was characterized by a spirit of inquiry, a curiosity about the natural world and man's place within it. Then they go looking for the origins of modern gardens and gardening in the writings of Pliny and Alberti and tell us that a time-lag of at least half a century is perfectly normal between the inception of a new style in Italy and its arrival in England. Such studies can be divided into two categories: those which maintain that Italian garden styles arrived much earlier than previously supposed – it's just that the evidence has been difficult to come by – and those which say that it never arrived at all, or, if it did cross the English Channel, that it came via France anyway. After all, Englishmen had little contact with Italy until the 1590s and little was known of Italian gardens until Inigo Jones returned from his second trip to Italy in 1613. All are agreed that Italian and French gardens passed through phases which should broadly be categorized as Early Renaissance (or Humanist), Mannerist and Baroque, and that the same progression should be found in English gardening. The trouble is that there is little enough evidence to prove it.

We are on much surer ground when we consider the gardens of the Tudor kings: they are comparatively well documented and a delight to read about even today. No one evokes them better than Roy Strong again:

> At the time they must have made a profound impact as expressions of Tudor magnificence. In the mind's eye we need to conjure them up, first from above looking down from the state apartments, opulent with tapestries and glittering with gold and silver, to see them rolled out like some gigantic multi-coloured carpet below us. Within the chequer-board of the formal walks the squares carry patterns, some in intricate interwoven knots, others in swirling arabesques, yet others arranged in the convolutions of the labyrinth. The patterns are delineated by lines of sweet-smelling herbs and the spaces between are filled with coloured sands and earths in the case of the closed knots, or with gillyflowers, primroses, violets or sweet-williams in the case of the open ones. Occasionally these knots must have performed a symbolic function and the allusion would be caught from above. Descending into the garden we need to stroll along its walks. The walls are covered with espaliered pear, apple and damson trees, the roses of York and Lancaster scent the air and everywhere we look there will be a forest of pinnacles bearing brightly coloured heraldic beasts, their gilding catching the sunlight. There will be the marvel of the sculptured figures of men, women, animals and fabulous monsters in quickset and rosemary that seem to inhabit the garden. Perhaps there will be the spiralling walks of a mount to climb or the plashing waters of a marble fountain.[4]

The 'brightly coloured heraldic beasts' were distinctively English and peculiar to royal gardens. Modern visitors to the châteaux of the Loire will remember that

This detail from the background to The Family of Henry VIII, *an oil painting by an unknown artist, c. 1545, shows the king's gardens laden with heraldic devices.*

Louis XII is often represented as a porcupine and François I as a salamander. This late-medieval form of royal brand-awareness existed also among English kings – Richard II, for example, took the white hart as his emblem. The badges of the warring houses were used as declarations of fealty during the Wars of the Roses. Henry VIII and Elizabeth I developed this practice and carried it to great lengths of invention and fancy, so that their houses and their gardens alike were decorated with a menagerie of painted symbols which proclaimed the legitimacy and power of the upstart Tudor dynasty. It was one way of competing with François I and a French court that had imbibed more of the Renaissance than had the English. Gilded greyhounds, lions, leopards, dragons, antelopes, hinds and other beasts were placed in royal gardens on posts that were painted in the family's colours of green and white. Around them were railings tricked out in the same combination of shades. A German called Von Wedel who visited the Great Garden at Whitehall in 1584 confirms this:

> Hence we went into the queen's garden, in which there are thirty-four high columns, covered with various fine paintings: also different animals carved in wood, with their horns gilt, are set on the top of the columns, together with flags bearing the Queen's arms. In the middle of the garden is a nice fountain with a remarkable sundial, showing the time in thirty different ways.[5]

Sundials were another obsession of the Tudor monarchs, foreshadowing the mythology of the Sun King.

Most cultural changes start at the top and filter down, but the gardens of Henry VIII and Elizabeth I had no effect on the gardens or gardening of their subjects. Henry VIII's arcane heraldic allusions were fine for putting François I in his place but they were no more than a short-lived fad which the Tudor monarchs invented as part of the aura of kingship. A few – *very* few – of the richest nobles went some way to copying the royal preoccupation with heraldic beasts: when the Earl of Leicester decorated his garden at Kenilworth with bears and ragged staffs, he was expressing pride in his own ancestry and putting himself on a level with the queen he hoped to marry. It was not a fashion of any relevance to the rich London merchant who wanted an Italianate fountain and a fig tree in the garden of his Cheapside mansion. It is true that the court, especially under Henry VIII at Nonsuch Palace, became a major centre for artistic patronage, but that did not make the king a significant force in the history of gardening.

Provided you search hard enough, it is possible to discern a multitude of symbolic meanings in the designs and plantings of Tudor gardens. Roses and lilies, for example, become emblems which tell of the virtues of the Virgin Queen rather than plants to enjoy for their intrinsic beauty and usefulness. Look closer still, and you will find no end of complicated allegorical cults which appear to extol Gloriana, even if these arcane classical allusions are more obvious to modern historians than sixteenth- and seventeenth-century writers. All gardens, of course, may be read as a statement of the owner's self-esteem, education, power, wealth and loyalties: that is one of the themes of this book. But it is a mistake to underestimate the owner's intrinsic enjoyment. In the sixteenth century, that enjoyment could take the form of pleasure in flowers or fruits, pleasure in walking, pleasure in following the knots, and pleasure in understanding the relevance of garden ornaments. But such objects of pleasure were also enjoyed in a straightforward manner, free of the political message which the spin-doctors of the day put into them. In Tudor times flowers were widely cherished for their beauty, colour and scent; it was in the sixteenth century that the 'garden of delight' developed as something to be preferred to a merely utilitarian vegetable or herb garden. All Tudor gardens need to be taken at face value as places to enjoy.

What were Tudor Gardens Used for?

English gardens in the sixteenth and early seventeenth centuries had three main purposes. First, they were places for exercise and sport; second, they were places to grow fruit, vegetables, herbs and flowers; and third, they were places for entertaining and showing off. These three functions recur from generation to generation as the story of English gardening unfolds.

It would be a mistake to suppose that all gardens copied or resembled in any but the smallest detail such sumptuous creations as Henry VIII's Hampton Court or the vast garden laid out a century later by Isaac de Caus for the Earl of Pembroke at Wilton. These are the gardens about which most is known and written, and the courtly entertainments and extravagances which they witnessed make for enjoyable reading. They were not, however, typical of the country as a whole. Garden history is all too often told from the viewpoint of the rich. That said, grand gardens were intended – as grand houses were – to impress important visitors. These included political allies, dynastic connections, royal judges and high-ranking officials. A visit by the king or queen – Elizabeth I was a tireless progressor – was a valuable opportunity for advancement and the gardens attached to grand houses were places in which the monarch might be entertained. Two generations after building them, the Salisburys found that the house and garden at Hatfield which they made to receive James I were too big and too expensive to maintain. Not until the 1820s, when the second Marquess married the daughter tected from people and animals beyond, but mainly because they came to be regarded as attached to a house – a private area where life was lived. The gardens of the well-to-do were usually walled. There is an extensive example still at Stonor in Oxfordshire which may go back to the twelfth century but was remade in Tudor times, and another at Parham in Sussex, which was built in 1577, at the same time as the house, and extends to five acres. Enclosures also offered protection to fruit trees, which added to their popularity; the shelter they created gave plants a longer growing season. Gervase Markham advised that the pleasure garden and the orchard should be attached to the parlour end of the house 'as well for the prospect thereof to all your best roomes as also because your house will be a devence against the Northerne coldnesse, whereby your fruits will much better prosper'. Further enclosures might be added over the years, so that houses ended up with an irregular arrangement of several walled gardens around them. The more distant enclosures like fruit orchards and nut grounds were usually hedged. Some gardens were surrounded by water, which might be the relic of an old moat or a series of fish-ponds which were used for keeping carp. The garden at Acton Court in Gloucestershire was built shortly after 1500 as a one-acre walled enclosure attached to the house by two bridges over the moat. At Helmingham in Suffolk the garden was established on an older moated site and later enclosed to prevent the deer swimming across from the adjoining park to feed on garden produce.

Knots were a distinctively English passion in the sixteenth century and remained popular in middle-class gardens right through to about 1700. This design comes from Stephen Blake's The Compleat Gardener's Practice, *1664.*

Knot gardens were the most common feature of sixteenth-century gardens. They were an English phenomenon, little known in France or Italy. Knots were square or rectangular patterns made with one or more different types of plant, typically box and santolina. Their lines were interlaced so that they were seen to weave in and out of each other, over and under, in an endlessly fascinating and often complex design. They take their name from their resemblance to the knots one may make with rope or string. The word was used fairly inexactly. Straightforward, simpler patterns were also known as knots, as were geometrical shapes which used only one type of plant. Pictorial designs such as an heraldic crest within a shield were described as knots. The beds enclosed by all these weaving patterns sometimes contained flowers. Often, however, they were grassed or filled with sands and gravels of different colours to enhance the overall complexity of the design. The height of fashion was to have a garden with 'knotts so enknotted, it cannot be exprest'.[8]

Knot-masters were highly regarded craftsmen. There is a record, from 1520, relating to the Duke of Buckingham's garden at Thornbury in Gloucestershire, when 'John Wynde, gardener' was paid 3s 4d 'for diligence in making knottes in the Duke's garden'.[9] Knots continued to develop throughout the sixteenth century and latterly to achieve designs of great elegance and complexity. A new knot garden at Petworth in 1585–7 cost 39s 6d, equivalent to ten months' wages for the head gardener at the time.[10] Knots remained popular right until the time of James I, when they tended to be replaced by the more complicated designs in box which are known by their French name, *parterres de broderie*.

This change of fashion started at the top and took a long time to filter down. Writing in 1613, Gervase Markham regarded knots as proper traditional ornaments for gentry gardens. He was somewhat scornful of the gardens of the 'great ones, since these are given over to novelties' – an early example of middle-class resistance to trendy upper-class fashions. Contrast this with a much-quoted aside in his essay 'On Gardens', where the well-to-do, fashion-conscious Francis Bacon was altogether dismissive: 'as for the making of knots or figures, with divers coloured earths that they may lie under the windows of the house on that side which the garden stands, they be but toys; you may see as good sights many times in tarts'. Nevertheless, Bacon designed and planted knots in his own garden at Gorhambury and knots were still to be found in gentry gardens right to the end of the seventeenth century. They were also copied in recipes for sweetmeats and pastries: a marzipan knot was one of the chief attractions of the dessert offered at banquets.

The most common feature of ornamental gardens in the sixteenth century, apart from the knots, was the gallery. The word 'gallery' was applied not only to long, spacious rooms which stretched the length of a great house on the uppermost floor, such as one sees at Montacute in Somerset. Garden galleries were wooden structures, usually one storey high, which went around the outside of an enclosed garden, sometimes on one side only and sometimes enclosing them entirely, like a wooden cloister. Some galleries were glazed and a few (like one at Thornbury Castle in Gloucestershire) even had an upper storey, but all provided shelter from rain and sun. Like their interior equivalents, the garden galleries were intended to facilitate walking for exercise and to enable the intricacies of the knots to be enjoyed all through the year. In a town house, the gallery would adjoin the parlour, which was the room furthest from the public entrance on the street, so that both the parlour and its garden were reserved for the householder, his family and his closest friends. The business and public reception rooms were always at the front, while the personal quarters were at the back and on the first floor. Such houses were often designed so that the garden could be seen or entered only from the parlour at the back. It was also accepted that the garden should be fully visible from the gallery, from which the patterns of the knots might best be appreciated.[11]

The rose-clad arbour in this engraving of perfect country life, c. 1600, becomes a summer banqueting house.

It is clear that elements of the Italian Renaissance garden of the late fifteenth century were not slow to reach England. Italian gardens were copied from the earliest days, as the three very different West Country gardens of Thornbury Castle, Horton Court and Acton Court indicate. All included a rectangular enclosed garden divided into quarters with a fountain in the middle and knots in the beds – a quincunx. Horton Court was a comparatively modest garden, made by an English diplomat called William Knight, who had been educated partly at Ferrara University and represented both Henry VII and Henry VIII on missions to Italy. The most spectacular garden building at Horton, dating from 1521, is the 'ambulatory', which is an open loggia of the sort fairly common in Italy even to this day. It was designed like a banqueting house to offer a sheltered room for private entertainment and to overlook the formal features of the garden itself. But, as one would expect, it was the richer citizens of London who had greater opportunities to discover the latest fashions in Italian garden style and to copy the essential components in their own town gardens. Early maps of London make it clear that fountains set in stone basins were especially widely appreciated. The country gentry were undoubtedly susceptible to the same cultural influences and aspirations, but they and their gardens were also influenced by an interest in land management and country pursuits. There was already a feeling that country life was superior to town life, because the air was fresher.

London Fashion

The dominance of London in all matters of garden innovation cannot be too strongly emphasized. It was not just a question of supplying the demands of garden-makers and garden-owners in other parts of England; the citizens of London had the education, knowledge, contacts and money to indulge themselves as richly as any of their descendants today. We now know that, even before 1500, wealthy Londoners enjoyed their gardens. Environmental archaeology has revised our ideas on just when new species were introduced into England: oriental exotics like bananas and New World plants from sweetcorn to pumpkins all prove to have been introduced to London earlier than supposed.

Towns in the sixteenth and seventeenth centuries were smaller than one might imagine. In the 1590s, the largest after London was Norwich, with a population in the region of 30,000. London was different. London controlled the commercial life of England as no comparable European city dominated any other nation. Its population rose from 120,000 in 1550 to 200,000 in 1600 and 375,000 in 1650. Indeed, it continued to grow, to 490,000 in 1700 and 675,000 in 1750, by which time it accounted for one-eighth of England's entire population and was the largest city in Europe, larger even than Constantinople. By the middle of the sixteenth century, London was the centre of almost every English economic activity. Its size created a demand for every commodity and service. As London grew and, with it, a sense of the pleasures it offered to the better-off, something akin to the London season started to develop. James I and Charles I resisted it: both encouraged the gentry to spend less time in London and more in the country. For commercial horticulture this meant the establishment of numerous market gardens in and around the metropolis to provision its inhabitants. Orchards were planted in the Home Counties to provide fruit all the year round.

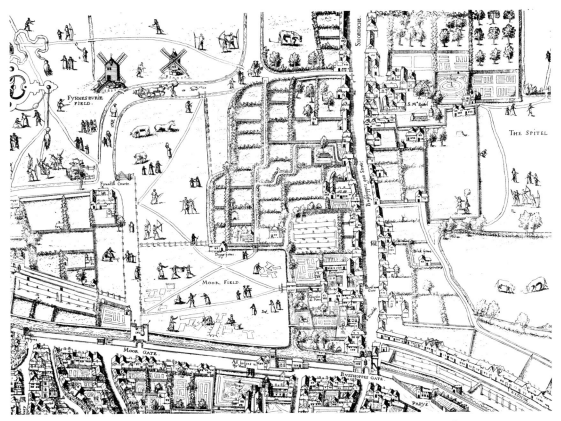

London was still a garden city when this area of Moorgate, from
The Copperplate Map, *was drawn, c. 1553–9. As with modern London gardens, many of
the fashions and features of country gardens have been scaled down and copied.*

Nothing has survived of London's Tudor and Jacobean gardens. At every stage
in its history, pressure on land has led to the disappearance of private and commercial gardens in and around London, though there was still a small orchard in
Fenchurch Street as late as Ralph Treswell's surveys of 1607–14. The larger
gardens in every period tend to be on the edge of the built-up area and at country
properties or villas within easy distance of the big city. The area around
Moorfields, for example, was noted for its villa gardens in the sixteenth and seventeenth centuries, just as the modern development of gardening skills is concentrated in the Home Counties. If 40 per cent of the Royal Horticultural Society's
members now live in London and Surrey, within easy commuting distance of the
money-making opportunities offered by the City, then there is a precedent which
goes right back for 500 years.

London became the centre of the nursery trade and the seat of the leading seedsmen. Horticultural innovation became concentrated not on country estates but in London itself, and this continued until at least the end of the eighteenth century. By the end of the seventeenth century, the London nursery trade was so well established and dominant that country-house gardeners had already begun the practice which has survived to this day of sending off large annual seed orders for plants of every kind, old favourites and new introductions, especially for food plants and ornamentals. During the Tudor and Stuart periods, London nurseries began to develop contacts in Vienna and Italy and, more particularly, with nurserymen in France and the Netherlands, whom they might visit to source plants for a rich patron. Provincial nurserymen certainly existed, but their stock and their custom were limited. It was said that when, in 1604, seeds and garden shears were needed for a Caernarfonshire garden they had to be ordered from London, 'for there is none to be had in this country'.[12] In 1621 it was possible to buy some herb seeds in Carlisle, but for hyssop it was necessary to send as far as York (well over 100 miles).[13] York had some competent nurserymen. Harvey tells of a lease of land in York granted in 1541 on the condition that the lessee 'promyseth to graft and set fruyt treys of the sayd ground and to leyff them growyng of the sayd grownd at the end' of the term. Norwich had some medium-sized nurserymen and it was there that the striped Gallica rose known as 'Rosa Mundi' (*Rosa gallica* 'Bicolor') first occurred in the sixteenth century.[14]

This stylized drawing of a moated pleasure garden in London from Philip Stubbes's Anatomie of Abuses, *1583, portrays the garden as a place for flowers, fruits and courtship.*

London gardeners had their own livery company, though not until the early seventeenth century. Gardening had been an identifiable job or profession in London since at least the fourteenth century. The preamble to the Gardeners' Company's first charter sets out the operations controlled by the company as 'the trade, crafte, or misterie of Gardening, planting, grafting, setting, sowing, cutting, arboring, rocking, mounting, covering, fencing and removing of plantes, herbes, seedes, fruites, trees, stocks, setts, and of contryving the conveyances to the same belonging'. It also states that certain ignorant and unskilful persons who had taken upon themselves to practise the said trade, not having been apprenticed thereto, had sold dead and corrupt plants, seeds, stocks and trees.[15] It was to prevent these cowboys from giving a bad name to the entire profession that the company was founded.

It follows that, when enforcing its newly won privileges, the company was

Royal palaces were surrounded by deer parks: note that the approach down the avenue at Nonsuch Palace, Surrey, in this oil painting dated c. 1620, is fenced off.

have started in 1499, when Henry VII placed his new palace of Richmond within the old deer park of Sheen. In 1507, the Duke of Buckingham began to lay out the garden around Thornbury Castle in Gloucestershire and expanded the size of the surrounding parks until they exceeded 1,000 acres. In the 1520s Cardinal Wolsey surrounded his new palace at Hampton Court with no less than three deer parks. In 1532–3 Sir William Fitzwilliam was licensed to add a further 600 acres of meadow, pasture and wood to his parks at Cowdray in Sussex. Henry VIII (the biggest *nouveau* of them all) was a great collector of parks. His corporate raids on ecclesiastical properties were not confined to monastic lands: from Thomas Cranmer, Archbishop of Canterbury, he acquired Knole, Otford, Burstow and Wimbledon.

From time to time it was suggested that too many new parks were being made or enlarged. Deer parks were traditionally sited on poor agricultural land, so that the better farmland was not lost to hunting. The worry in the sixteenth century was that too much good agricultural land might be converted into parkland by the *nouveaux riches*, especially after the dissolution of the monasteries. The ultimate controls which prevented this happening were economic: the new emparkings of the first half of the sixteenth century were more than matched by the disparkings of the second half. Parks were expensive to maintain and, even in medieval times,

The English Garden: A Social History

there was pressure to make better economic use of the land: agriculture, animal grazing and industry were more profitable. The trend towards the breaking up of parks continued into the seventeenth century. The Devon historian Tristram Risdon remarked in the 1630s that 'many parks were disparked, and converted from pleasure to profit; from pasturing wild beasts to breeding of cattle, sheep and tillage'.[20] Later in the century, Richard Sackville, fifth Earl of Dorset, granted four farmers

> the liberty to plough anywhere in the Park [at Knole] except in the plain set out by my Lord and the ground in front of the house, and to take three crops, and it is agreed that one-third of each crop after it is severed from the ground shall be taken and carried away by my Lord for his own use. The third year, the farmers to sow the ground with grass seed if my Lord desires it, and they are to be at the charge of the seed, the tillage, and the harvest.[21]

Trees too had a value, quite apart from the shelter they offered to livestock, which was conspicuously absent in the kind of large open pastures that were still common in much of the country. When Sir Thomas Barrington bought Watchingwell Park in the Isle of Wight from Charles I in 1631 – Barrington lived at nearby Swainston and wanted to increase his land-holding in order to optimize his rentals – he made it clear that his plan was to fell the remaining trees and convert the whole park into agricultural holdings. The crown decided that the timber should be preserved from felling and promptly bought the estate back from him. Parks near houses, however, tended to be kept unchanged: they were by now the essential setting for a big house.

The main reasons for the decline of parks were always economic or social, though an owner who was able to increase the wealth of his family could also bolster its prestige by expanding the deer park. This helps to explain why deer parks continued to be emparked and stocked until surprisingly late. After the Earls of Worcester acquired Badminton in the mid-seventeenth century, they and their descendants the Dukes of Beaufort continued to extend the park for several generations. Not that they had any need to prove themselves, for they were the only English noble family to be lineally descended in the direct male line from the Plantagenet kings. But many parks followed the fortunes of

Parks were status symbols: William, second Earl of Salisbury, included a hunting scene in the background to his portrait at Hatfield by George Geldorp, 1626.

more ephemeral families, and were made and unmade as a family passed from rags to riches to rags within three generations.

Throughout this period, the entrance to the park from the garden was increasingly marked by a grand gateway; deer parks were part of the greater landscape long before the end of the seventeenth century. And landowners were still applying to the crown for licences to empark – Boringdon Park in Devon, for example, as late as 1699. The economic importance of a deer park – such as it was – declined during the eighteenth century, as the agricultural revolution made it possible to keep other animals alive during the winter. When the landscape movement got under way, many owners reordered their deer parks with lakes and planted clumps of trees in the fashion of the day. By the nineteenth century the deer park was considered no more than an ornament, designed to emphasize or hint at a family's ancient lineage or to give a boost to the status of more newly rich landowners. And they continue to carry a certain cachet, so that even today landowners possessed of a deer park are not exactly backward in admitting to pride of ownership. The growth of refrigeration at the beginning of the twentieth century made them completely redundant, though deer parks had a place once again in time of war – James Lees-Milne described in one of his diaries the perils of eating deer liver as the guest of Lord Sackville at Knole.[22]

Fruit & Fruit-growing

Fruit-growing has had a long history in Britain. An early fifteenth-century account describes the orchards at Raglan Castle in Wales 'full of apple trees and plums, and figs, and cherries, and grapes, and French plums, and pears, and nuts, and every fruit that is sweet and delicious'.[23] But Raglan belonged to the semi-royal Earls of Worcester and such horticultural riches were not so common after the Wars of the Roses. At Thornbury Castle in the 1510s, the Duke of Buckingham planted an orchard some four acres in extent, 'walled about well and thick set with fruit trees of divers kinds of fruit'.[24] In 1533 sixty-seven apple trees were purchased for the Mount Garden at Hampton Court. Figs and apricots began to be more commonly grown. Henry VIII set the lead in the 1530s and 1540s when he sent 'the king's gardener', Sir John Wolf, on several trips to France to obtain apple trees and grafts for the royal orchards. Sir John was himself a Frenchman, as well as a Catholic priest. Several English writers later in the sixteenth century commented on how proficient in fruit-growing were members of French religious orders and bemoaned the loss of such skills which followed the dissolution of the monasteries in England. Sir John Thynne was typical of the obsessives who make fortunes – his attention to detail was relentless – and when he was building Longleat in the 1560s he asked his steward to 'send me word how my cherry stones, abrycocks, and plum stones that I brought out of France do grow'.[25] Sir Philip Sidney brought cherry and quince trees from Brabant to stock the orchard at Penshurst, which was later commemorated by Ben Jonson:

> Then hath thy orchard fruit, thy garden flowers,
> Fresh as the air, and new as are the hours.
> The early cherry, with the later plum,
> Fig, grape, and quince, each in his time doth come:
> The blushing apricot and woolly peach
> Hang on thy walls, that every child may reach.

In 1611 John Tradescant laid out a vineyard on the north-east side of Hatfield House and planted it with 30,000 vines, the gift of the wife of the French ambassador. By 1617 Fynes Moryson could claim that 'England hath such abundance of Aples, Peares, Cherries, and Plummes, such variety of them, and so good in all respects, as no countrie yeelds more or better, for which the Italians would gladly exchange their Citrons and Oranges.'[26] Henry Peacham declared in 1622 that

The frontispiece from William Lawson's A New Orchard and Garden, *1621: Puritans like Lawson compared the grafting of fruit trees to the action of God's grace upon base humankind.*

The English may have had a reputation for meat-eating, but a very wide choice
of vegetables was cultivated from the sixteenth century: artichokes and cardoons are shown
here in John Parkinson's Paradisi in Sole, Paradisus Terrestris, *1629.*

'among flowers we most admire and esteem the rose; among fruit, the pomeroy and queen-apple'.[27] Both queens and pomeroys were types of apple. By the time that he published his *Paradisi in Sole, Paradisus Terrestris* in 1629, John Parkinson could name sixty different apples which he considered worth growing.

Fruit-growing has always been popular in England at every social level and in every century. It is clear that before 1500 even the poorest had access to apples, pears, plums and cherries, and often damsons, medlars and service trees too. In the sixteenth century, people were more adventurous in the fruits they ate, because hunger (rather than taste or fashion) made necessary the consumption of relatively unpalatable fruits like medlars and rowanberries. What we see throughout this period is a constant search for better cultivars and greater variety – in a word, more choice. Cultivars which extended the season were especially valued. Indeed, the history of fruit-growing is largely the introduction of early-fruiting cultivars and others which will keep well for months after they are picked – in some cases, as late as April or May following the autumn harvest. As the range and reliability of fruit cultivars increased, so people discovered that apples were nicer to eat than medlars.

The pleasures of growing fruit and the desire for variety were perhaps the clearest – and certainly the most important – example of horticultural innovation during this period. Among the well-to-do, it amounted to a fashion, and had far-reaching effects on our tastes and diet. Fruit became a status symbol, sought as much by the rich merchant who could import it into London as by the wealthy man who desired it in the gardens attached to his estate.

As with fruit, so with vegetables. The demand for vegetables was one of the most distinctive characteristics of sixteenth-century gardening. And yet the standard histories of diet have long contradicted the horticultural evidence. We are constantly told that the rich sought to eat as much meat and as few vegetables as possible. Contemporary medical opinion was adamant: vegetables provoked melancholy humour and bodily flatulence. The diet of the poor was high in calories and based upon wheat, barley and oats (usually as bread or porridge), plus butter, eggs and cheese. Even the poorest ate little in the way of vegetables, though all consumed fruit in season. Yet this is not borne out by a study of the recipe books of the sixteenth and seventeenth centuries. As early as 1450, John Gardener had praised the virtues of brassicas, and explained how young leaves might be enjoyed in every season by sowing them four times a year. Vegetables were eaten in abundance, either as salads or as the base in which meats were basted or baked. Beans, peas, beets, leeks, parsnips, spinach and turnips were all fairly widely grown by 1500, as were lettuces, radishes and sorrel among salad plants. Writers, estate accounts and modern archaeology all confirm this: everyone ate vegetables.

Flowers

Flowers were widely grown in Tudor and Jacobean times for their intrinsic beauty. They were planted in gardens for ornament and grown in pots on window-sills. The most popular were roses, lilies, pinks, cowslips, marigolds and violets. Flowers were also picked and brought into the house to sweeten the air. One of the duties of the Almoner at Cowdray Park in 1512 was to keep the hall clean 'and sweete with bowes, and flowers, in their seasons'.[28] One hundred years later, the author William Lawson – who was basically a proponent of fruit-growing, with little interest in anything else – wrote that 'flowers are comely and durable for Squares and Knots, and all to be set at *Michael-tide*, or somewhat before, that they may be settled in, and taken with the ground before Winter, though they may be set, especially sown, in the spring' – and he went on to list roses, rosemary, lavender, cowslips, peonies, gillyflowers (pinks) and lilies among the flowers he considered suitable.[29]

Fashionable roses and pansies are richly embroidered on the costume of Edward Sackville, fourth Earl of Dorset, in this portrait by William Larkin, c. 1613.

By Tudor times, many popular garden plants had already been introduced from overseas – hollyhocks, lilies-of-the-valley and peonies among them. William Harrison was clearly awestruck, when he wrote in 1587, 'to see how many strange herbs, plants, and annual fruits are daily brought unto us from the Indies, Americas ... Canary Isles, and all parts of the world'. Then, early in the seventeenth century, some nurserymen began to be known as 'florists' and to be responsible for the development and cultivation of several very specialized types of flowers. These were grown purely for their beauty; their herbal qualities or usefulness in other ways counted for nothing. It was variety that mattered, and soon the 'florist's' flowers also included carnations, ranunculi, anemones and polyanthus. Many of the foremost florists were town-dwellers and the word came to be applied to amateur enthusiasts for a particular genus. Modern members of a specialist plant society, such as today's Royal National Rose Society, would have been known as 'florists' in the seventeenth century.

Florists thrived on competition, and the demand for new and better cultivars. There was a proliferation of variety. Tulipomania in the 1630s was the first (and

Various Tulips, *watercolour by P. van Kouwenhorn, c. 1630. Tulips were the first flower to become fashionable: prices and values escalated in response to 'tulipomania' and then plummeted.*

most extreme) of many such crazes: John Evelyn was told by a French florist in the 1650s that there were by then no fewer than 10,000 different kinds of tulip. Their fashionable popularity waxed and waned abruptly – a pattern which resembled the meteoric rise and fall of an overvalued stock. It was the archetype which was followed by fashions for carnations, auriculas, dahlias and Hybrid Tea roses. As each flower faded from fashion it lost its commercial value and descended the social scale. The same was true of vegetables and fruit. Parkinson commented that the potato had begun as a delicacy for the Queen, but had become so common that even the vulgar despised it. White currants were more desirable than black ones, not just because of their finer taste but 'because they are more dainty and less common'.

The Trade in Seeds & Plants

Nurseries as we know them emerged slowly. At first it was the garden-owners and garden advisers who were the source of new seeds and plants; selling seeds or plants was a side-line for some other occupation. There was a prosperous family called Banbury which traded in seeds and plants at Tothill Street in Westminster from at least 1550 to 1650. When Lord Burghley built his house at Stamford in the 1580s he engaged advisers from France and Flanders for the design of his garden, but most of his plants came from the Queen's gardener at Greenwich. He was told to ask for lavender, spike, hyssop, thyme, rosemary and sage, and to apply to Hampton Court or Richmond if he needed more.[30]

The discrete trade of a nurseryman began to emerge in the second half of the sixteenth century. At first they were still known as 'gardeners'; the word 'nursery-man' is not found until 1672. But most of the professionals around 1600 were engaged in market gardening, supplying fresh fruit, vegetables and salads in season to London and the larger provincial cities. In 1534 the royal fruiterer, Richard Harris, had planted 105 acres of orchards at Teynham in Kent, for which he 'fetched out of France a great store of graftes, especially pippins, before which time there were no pippins in England. He fetched also out of the Lowe Countries cherrie grafts and Pear grafts of diverse sorts.' This orchard supplied the expanding demand for fresh fruit in London, and was a principal source of graft-wood for many years to come. Others took up Harris's initiative, so that by the end of the sixteenth century Kent was known as the 'garden of England'.

New plants had been introduced from abroad for many centuries before the arrival of the Tudor kings. Exotics like rosemary, Madonna lilies, lupins and bay (*Laurus nobilis*) had already reached England by 1485. Cyclamen, snowdrops and

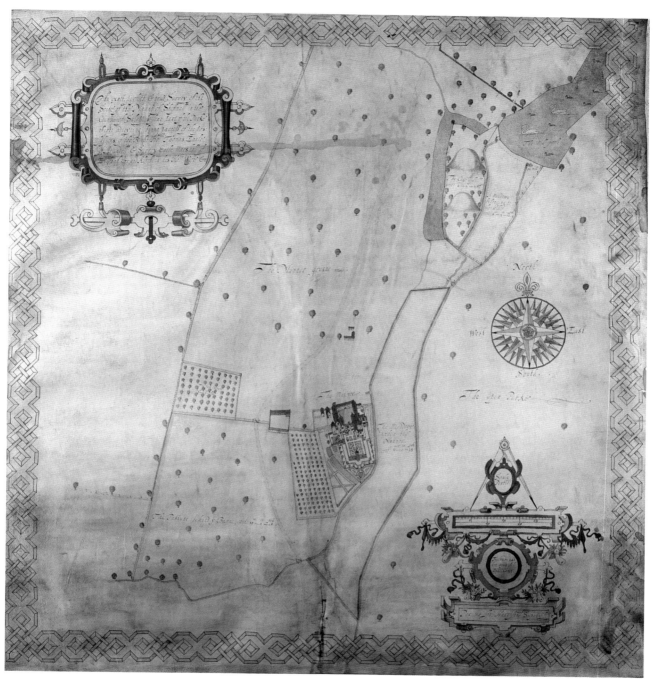

This primitive bird's-eye view of The Manor, Shifnal, in Shropshire, 1635, shows how the formal garden projects into the wider landscape.

Star of Bethlehem (*Ornithogalum* sp.) are all thought to have been introduced during the course of the sixteenth century. It is helpful to reflect that the snow-drops, which have now widely naturalized in every part of England, were probably imported from France and first grown on this side of the English Channel as a winter-flowering curiosity in London gardens less than 500 years ago.[31] Seedsmen came to London from France and Flanders and were often instrumental in the introduction of new plants into cultivation in England. In the 1560s, the garden attached to the Carpenters' Hall bought seeds in London of the following vege-tables and flowers: beet, bugloss, camomile, chicory, clary, endive, gillyflower, hyssop, langue-de-boeuf, lavender, lettuce, marigold, parsley, rosemary, sage, sorrel, spinach, stocks and sweet marjoram.[32] None was originally native to England.

Hakluyt regarded the importation of new and useful plants from overseas as a patriotic duty and achievement, capable of bringing much greater benefit to the country as a whole and to the poor in particular than the building of almshouses or the giving of lands and goods. In due course the introduction of so many plants also enlarged the options and made possible a different kind of gardening. Garden-owners could garden on a grand scale with plants – growing them for their individual interest and variety, collecting them – and principally with exotics, not native plants. Gardening became a statement that one's horizons were inter-national. But that did not happen until after the Restoration.

Jacobean Gardens

At the top end of the market, the seventeenth century saw several significant changes of garden fashion. One was a taste for planting long straight avenues or lines of large forest trees across the deer parks and into the surrounding country-side. Audley End, built by the Earl of Suffolk in 1603–16, had an avenue of double rows of lime trees which led to the great entrance gateway. In 1611 James I replaced an already existing avenue in Hyde Park with one of 200 lime trees. Another was planted at Buxted in 1630, and a map made in 1638 shows three more planted at Wimpole. Designing the park and extending the formality of the garden into it were a form of self-aggrandizement on the part of the landowner. They confirm that people were ready to embrace and control the whole landscape, rather than seeking to protect themselves against it.

Queen Anne of Denmark brought engineers like Salomon de Caus from north-ern Europe to design waterworks and fountains: hydraulic feats were symbols of power. For more modest garden-owners, of course, water remained a necessity, not a statement of style or display. Kings and their richer subjects can usually afford to take land out of production and create an ornamental garden with all the latest fashions. The gentry were more concerned to combine design and productivity, pleasure and profit, with no loss of status or dignity.[33]

At this level gardens in Jacobean times differed but little from Elizabethan ones. Few were designed as part of an integral whole which combined the house, gardens and wider landscape. They grew piecemeal, were modest in size and were dedicated to specific functions – the production of vegetables, fruit and herbal remedies, as well as plants for pleasure. But plants were becoming fashionable. Most people wanted to grow a wider range of everything, most notably fruit and vegetables, and were amazed at the sheer range of new and unusual plants that were being introduced from such places as India and the West Indies. The great status symbol among the richer folk was the ability to grow oranges and lemons; small conservatories were built to protect them during the winter. Gardens became increasingly seen as places to grow plants.

The Elizabethan-style garden, enclosed by railings, was fairly old-fashioned by the time this portrait of William Style of Langley was completed in 1636. The ruins on the hill, however, were much more modish.

More ideas came directly from Italy, too, as diplomatic relations and commercial contacts with England improved. Relatively few people actually travelled to Italy; even the 'Grand Tour' did not really get under way until the start of the eighteenth century. This meant that the civilization of the Baroque, like the culture of the Renaissance and of ancient Rome, was experienced second-hand either through such publications as Thomas Coryate's *Travels* or through visits to northern France. But Italy became smart, and remained fashionable throughout the seventeenth century. Those who did travel to Italy – and especially those who made collections, like the Earl of Arundel – were fêted as great and worthy scholars. There are two famous portraits of Lord Arundel and his wife painted by Daniel Mytens in 1618. Each shows a gallery lined either with statues or paintings, and opening on to a garden which has been much studied to feature in histories of gardening. Unfortunately, neither the galleries nor the gardens can be fitted into the known ground-plan of Arundel House, and

Plants and gardens were just two of the many interests of Francis Bacon, first Viscount St Albans, shown here in a portrait by John Vanderbank, c. 1731. The most important philosopher and lawyer of his day, Bacon's eyes were said to resemble a weasel's.

must therefore 'be regarded as partly fictional in their composition'.[34]

The leading lights of Jacobean gardening were Sir Robert Cecil, first Earl of Salisbury, and Sir Francis Bacon, first Viscount St Albans. As well as being cousins, the gentlemen were possessed of enormous political power, but gardens and gardening were no more than leisure interests in varied and active lives. Cecil was Secretary of State under both Elizabeth I and James I; Bacon was Lord High Chancellor in the early 1620s. Cecil employed John Tradescant the Elder to lay out and plant his gardens at Hatfield and Salomon de Caus to construct his fountains. Bacon wrote one of the best-known and most polished pieces of garden writing, which begins: 'God Almighty first planted a garden: and indeed it is the purest of human pleasures. It is the greatest refreshment of the spirits of man; without which, buildings and palaces are but gross handy-works.' This charming and whimsical essay is little more than a smart piece of journalism, just one of many lifestyle pieces that Bacon wrote after the manner of such writers as Castiglione. It should never have been allowed to become the cornerstone of subsequent accounts of Jacobean gardens. Bacon's description of the ideal garden – a princely paradise – was no more than a fantasy:

> For gardens, speaking of those which are indeed prince-like, as we have done of buildings, the contents ought not well to be under thirty acres of ground, and to be divided into three parts: a green in the entrance; a heath or desert in the going forth; and the main garden in the midst; besides alleys on both sides. And I like well, that four acres of ground be assigned to the green, six to the heath, four and four to either side, and twelve to the main garden. The green hath two pleasures; the one, because nothing is more pleasant to the eye than green grass kept finely shorn; the other, because it will give you a fair alley in the midst; by which you may go in front upon a stately hedge, which is to enclose the garden.

And yet this vision of enchantment has had enormous effect upon the imaginations of subsequent garden-owners. In the second half of the nineteenth century,

Leopold de Rothschild designed much of his garden at Ascott in Buckinghamshire as a fulfilment of Bacon's essay. The fact is that all his essays were popular, quotable works of wisdom intended to entertain and counsel, but not to be taken too seriously or literally.[35]

Francis Bacon was one of the most respectable and unscrupulous men of his times – one of those scholarly psychopaths who are destined from generation unto generation to climb to the very top of the legal profession. He was also as close as any early-seventeenth-century statesman came to being a Renaissance man. Gardens were just one of many fields of endeavour where he felt able to express an opinion. He was above all interested in scientific, philosophical and literary studies and these occupied the major part of his time after his disgrace and dismissal from office. (John Aubrey said that Bacon died from bronchitis or pneumonia as a result of experimenting with deep-freezing a chicken.)

Little is known of Bacon's own garden, and little remains of it. We are on firmer ground with his cousin's pile at Hatfield, whose gardens were laid out between 1607 and 1612, and where the planting continued for some years yet. The house was built in its park, and Cecil bought up more of the neighbouring farms until the entire landscape belonged to him. A French visitor fifty years later commented that it amounted to a 'prospect of nothing but Woods and Meadows, Hills and Dales'.[36]

The grandest of grand gardens at the outbreak of the Civil War was Wilton, where Philip Herbert, fourth Earl of Pembroke, engaged Isaac de Caus to lay out

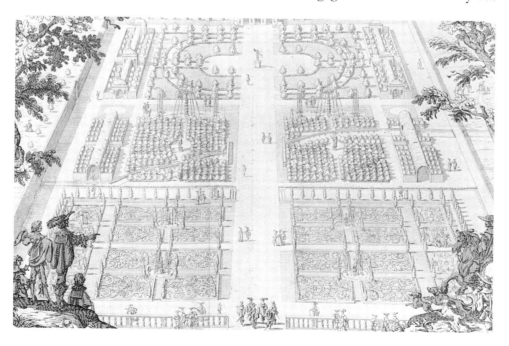

The fourth Earl of Pembroke attracted the international designer Isaac de Caus to lay out his grand gardens at Wilton in Wiltshire. This is a bird's-eye view of the garden from Isaac de Caus's Wilton Garden, *c. 1645–6.*

a vast formal garden in the 1630s and employed Inigo Jones to rework the house. Isaac de Caus had built a famous garden at Heidelberg for King Charles's sister the Electress Palatine Elizabeth. He was related to Salomon de Caus, who had made fountains for Queen Anne of Denmark and was therefore associated with royal patronage. It was quite an achievement for Pembroke to attract such an important international designer to Wiltshire. The garden became famous even in continental Europe. John Aubrey wrote, 'King Charles I did love Wilton above all places and came there every summer.'

Books

Gardening books represent the accumulated know-how of gardeners past and present. There has always been a need for them. This is not a modern phenomenon; the demand for information was strong even before books were printed. Manuscript manuals on cultivation date back at least to the late fourteenth century. Many were translations from French sources: an example was *Le Ménagier de Paris*, written in 1393, which explained how to propagate rosemary when it does not bear seed in cultivation. The answer was to take cuttings, which could then be sent long distances if they were wrapped in waxed cloth, sealed with honey and powdered with flour.

The printed book was an instrument of the Renaissance. From about 1550 onwards, books helped to spread knowledge about gardens and plants as never before. The market for books was driven by need: there was a genuine thirst for practical and useful information about laying out gardens and cultivating plants. Many of the earliest gardening books were plagiarized from one or more sources – a ragbag of other men's experiences drawn together by the energy of the author or publisher. The tendency to crib and recycle wisdom, especially from French sources, continued through to the end of the seventeenth century, but after about 1620 books did rely more upon first-hand experience. The pace of publication increased, too. There were about twenty books on gardening and allied subjects printed during the sixteenth century, and about the same number in the first fifty years of the seventeenth century. In the half-century after 1650 no less than eighty gardening books were published in England. We now have a universe of gardening books which has never ceased to grow and expand.

There were two main markets for garden books in the sixteenth and seventeenth centuries. The stronger, at first, was a need for reliable herbals. Most of the great plant collectors, garden-makers, botanists and writers of the time were principally interested in the uses that plants could be put to in the service of man and medicine.

The first comprehensive herbal was written by William Turner, a nonconformist divine who managed to spend some time as Dean of Wells. Published in 1551, it was a scholarly work, even if some of its recommendations would not find favour with modern medicos and pharmacologists. Turner had many foreign correspondents and was undoubtedly one of the most learned European pharmacist-botanists of his day. Herbals were widely read and used. Lady Mildmay (1552–1620), writing towards the end of her life, commented that she had invariably spent some time every day in reading herbals. Her medical practice was probably based upon Turner's *Herball*.

Better known nowadays is Gerard's *Herball* (1597), a compilation from other sources, mainly French and Latin, with little or nothing drawn from Gerard's own experience. The reason why such a fanciful and useless book enjoyed popular success was simple – people were desperate for ways to cure diseases. Gerard did publish one book, in 1596, which was based on original work and is still of interest – his *Catalogus arborum, fruticum ac plantarum tam indigenarum quam exoticarum* is a list of over 1,000 different plants growing in

William Turner's A New Herball, *1551, is both comprehensive and scholarly – a fount of knowledge about Elizabethan gardening practices.*

his garden at Holborn. It is the first printed *Hortus* in England, and was intended to advance his career by showing him to be a plantsman, botanist, pharmacologist and man of learning. It is tempting to suppose that, once he had established such a reputation, he cashed in on it by writing his popular herbal.

The contribution of herbals to medical progress is best described as neutral. A positive impediment was the doctrine of signatures, which taught that every part of every plant had a useful pharmacological purpose and that its colour or shape made that purpose clear. *Pulmonaria*, for example, was known as lungwort because its leaves were supposed to resemble a diseased lung, a clear indicator that the Almighty intended those leaves to be used in the treatment of pulmonary diseases. The doctrine of signatures was a particular anathema to empiricists like John Rea and the founders of the Royal Society later in the seventeenth century. But pharmacologists in Tudor and Jacobean times were passionately interested in the potential usefulness of new plants imported from India, America and other parts of the world which were then opening up to European shipping. Many of the new plants which now adorn our gardens first came to England so that their medical potential might be studied.

The first book printed in English which concerned itself with gardening, as opposed to herbalism, was Thomas Hill's *A most briefe and plesaunt treatyse*, printed in 1563. He followed it up in 1577 with *The Gardener's Labyrinth*, which he

The tools of the gardener's trade are accurately portrayed in this plate from Thomas Hill's The Gardener's Labyrinth, *1577: we can assume the same for the garden's design, raised beds and sparse planting.*

dedicated to Sir William Cecil, the first Lord Burghley, and published under the none-too-subtle pseudonym of Didymus Mountain. Both books borrowed substantially from French sources and suffered from two common weaknesses which were to dog many gardening books until the eighteenth century. The first was that they refer frequently, perhaps over-frequently, to examples and precedents from classical literature. Indeed *The Gardener's Labyrinth* begins thus:

The worthie *Plinie* ... reporteth, that a Garden plotte in the Auncient time at *Rome*, was none other, than a small & simple inclosure of ground, whiche through the labur & diligence of the husbandman, yeelded a commoditie and yearely revenew unto him. But after yeares (that man more esteemed of himself, and sought an easier life) devised and framed this ground plotte, for the minde, as for pleasure and delight.

Right from the start there was a conflict between the ideal world of classical gardens and the reality of gardening in England in the sixteenth century. This was even more pronounced by Jacobean times, when the better-educated owners, designers and visitors saw their gardens as accurate re-creations of what they had read about in Pliny and other classical texts. This obsession with the writings of the ancients resembled the biblical fundamentalism of the age. The authority of the ancients validated anything modern. On the other hand, the early empiricists saw that much of what they read and believed did not accord with their experience as gardeners in England.

The second weakness was Hill's insistence that all gardening activities should be determined by the moon and its phases. This was a common belief, which was widely accepted until the experimental scientists of the Royal Society showed that the waxing and waning of the moon made no difference either to the germination or to the subsequent growth of plants. Even today, there are some who preach the importance of sowing seeds at the correct phase of the lunar cycle. Nevertheless, the doctrine rather undermined the practical value of Hill's work.

Thomas Hill's A most briefe and plesaunt treatyse, *1563, was the first gardening book to be published in English. Its frontispiece is the embodiment of seventeenth-century aspirations.*

That said, *The Gardener's Labyrinth* is a proper introduction to the art and practice of gardening – how to lay out beds, dig them, dung them, weed them and crop them. It has plans of knots and mazes, and detailed instructions for the cultivation of herbs and vegetables – explaining, for example, that cucumber seeds should be sown early in the year in pans or baskets and put outside on sunny days, or when it rains, but taken in under cover in cold weather until all frosts have passed.

The introduction to Thomas Hill's book told readers that 'bycause thys Arte of Gardening is of it selfe very profitable, and bryngeth most necessarie commodities, therefore in my simple judgment, it deserveth no small commendation and [is] altogyther as necessarie as the others are'. Hill was also aware that flowers are things of beauty. Roses were 'pleasant ornaments in a Garden'. As for the white lily, 'the beautie is affirmed of Plinie to be next to the Rose'. One is left wondering whether he had an independent thought or whether all his judgements on beauty came from the ancients. This need to turn to classical precedent for validation of any personal opinion continued through until the end of the eighteenth century, by which time the empirical science of horticulture had effectively chased away these Renaissance superstitions.

How different – how very different – was Thomas Tusser's *Five Hundred Points of Good Husbandry*, first published in 1573. Tusser may have been educated at Trinity College, Cambridge, but he makes no reference to the classics. His concern is the management of a house, garden and farm, and it was for the lesser gentry, yeomen and husbandmen that he wrote. In truth, the horticultural part of the book forms only a small part of the whole, but its distinctive characteristic is that Tusser wrote from an entirely practical standpoint, which also celebrates the superiority of country life. He offers lists of what to sow and harvest month by month. 'Herbes for the kychen' include cabbage, lettuce and leeks; 'to boyle or to butter' Tusser recommends beans, carrots and parsnips; for salads and sauces he suggests endives, purslane, rocket and sorrell among many others; his garden flowers include columbines, daffodils, carnations, hollyhocks and 'roses of all sortes'.

Tusser too believes in sowing and harvesting when the lunar phases are favourable, but his book is written in a relaxed and relaxing doggerel:

> The Moone in the wane, gather fruit for the last,
> but winter fruite gather, when Mighel is past . . .
> Fruit gathered too timely will taste of the wood,
> will shrink and be bitter, and seldome prove good,
> So fruit that is shaked, or beat of a tree:
> with brusing in falling, soone fauty will bee.

In November:

> Set garlike & beanes, at S. Edmond the king,
> the moone in the wayne, theron hangeth a thing.
> Tencrease of a potte (well proved of some)
> shall pleasure they household, er peskod time come.
> If Garden require it, now trench it ye may,
> one trench not a yard, from another go lay,
> which being well filled, with mucke by & by:
> go cover with mould, for a season to ly.

In January:

> Dig garden, story mallow, now may ye at ease,
> and set (as a daintie) thine runcifall pease.
> Go cut and set roses, chuse aptly the plot,
> the roots of the yongest, are best to be got.

The first book to be devoted entirely to flowers – as distinct from useful and medicinal plants – was John Parkinson's *Paradisi in Sole, Paradisus Terrestris*, published in 1629. Parkinson was a shrewd observer of the botanical scene and a stylish writer. His book describes nearly 1,000 flowers, of which more than three-quarters are illustrated. On the strength of this work, Charles I appointed him Botanicus Regius Primarius.

Implicit in all these gardening books was the understanding that people were free to design and plant their gardens as they saw fit; wealth or the lack of it was the only restraint. Man controlled his environment.

Women

It has been suggested that women took to gardening in the sixteenth and seventeenth centuries because they were denied access to other spheres of activity. It would be more accurate to say that domestic gardening was women's work because the provision of food and medicine was largely their responsibility. Thomas Tusser wrote in 1573:

> In March, May, and Aprill, from morning to night
> in sowing and setting, good huswives delight.

To have in a garden, or other like plot:
to trim up their house, and to furnish their plot . . .
Through cunning with dibble, rake, mattock and spade:
by line and by leavell, trim garden is made.

Tusser was writing for the lesser gentry, yeoman farmers and husbandmen, among whom flowers, vegetables and herbs were considered a wife's province, but even at quite a high social level the women in charge of a household were expected to take responsibility for the raising of vegetables, herbs, salad plants and flowers. Lady Hoby of Hackness in Yorkshire recorded how she had performed her duties – and enjoyed doing so – in her diary entry for 4 April 1600: 'this day I performed my accustomed exercises, I praise God, and was allmost all the after none in the Gardene sowinge seed . . .' And her kinswoman Lady Fettiplace of Appleton in Oxfordshire devoted a page of her personal *Receipt Book* to the problem of how to maintain a supply of fresh herbs and vegetables by making successive plantings and sowings:

The best moneth is aprill in the wane of the moone, at Midsomer in the wane of the moone sow all manner of potherbs, & they wilbee greene for winter; Also Lettice seeds sowne at this tyme and removed when they bee of a prettie bignes at the full wilbe good and hard Lettice at Michaelmas [29 September] . . . Sow red Cabage seed after Allhallowentide [31 October], twoe dayes after the moone is at the full, & in March take up the plants & set from fowre foot each from other, you shall have faire Cabages for the Sumer: then sow some Cabage seeds a day after the full moone in Marche, then remove your plants about Midsomer, & they wilbee good for winter . . .[37]

Writing for the lesser gentry in 1613, Gervase Markham in *The English House-Wife* made it clear that a wife's duties included the care of a garden – sowing seeds of fruit, vegetables, flowers and herbs. He gave detailed instructions for what to sow month by month, and indicated which seeds required to be sown at a particular phase of the moon. However, he was modern and pragmatic enough to override received opinion on sowing times and to add a list of seeds which could be sown 'at all times of the month', including spinach, lettuces, radishes and chives. He also noted which ones resent transplanting (for example, chervil and parsley); which seeds must be sown fresh because they do not keep well; when to sow; when to gather seeds; and how to store them. From the recipes he gives for salads, fruit tarts, jams, conserves and candies, it is clear that a wide choice was available. All this was the domain of the mistress of the house. William Lawson, writing in 1618, went even further. He had no doubt that laying out the pleasure garden was also a job for women: 'the number of Forms, Mazes, and Knots is so great, and men are so diversely delighted,' he wrote, 'that I leave every House-wife to her self' to design it. By 1629 John Parkinson was writing for 'many gentlewomen and others that would gladly have some fine flowers to furnish their gardens, but know not what the names of those things are that they desire' – in other words were ignorant of flowers, but anxious to keep up. Parkinson commended particular species because they were popular among 'the better sort of the gentry', stressing that there was 'no lady or gentlewoman of any worth' who did not like tulips, and emphasizing the importance of rarity and novelty.[38] By 1657 it was acknowledged that hands-on gardening might also be a pleasure for women: 'Gentlewomen, if the ground be not too much wet, may do themselves much good by kneeling upon a cushion and weeding.'

If flower-gardening and kitchen gardens were the responsibility of women, there is no doubt that the tending of fruit trees was considered a man's job. In about 1632 Sir John Oglander wrote a detailed description of the garden he had made around his new house: 'I have with my own hands planted two young orchards at Nunwell: the lower with pippins, pearmains, putles, hornies and other good apples and all sorts of good pears: in the other, cherries damsons and plums. In the upper garden, apricocks, mellecatoons [quinces] and figs.'[39] Nowhere is it suggested that maintaining an orchard might be a job for women. Occasionally, however, one gets an insight into life four centuries ago through some small action or detail which seems to us very modern. Take, for example, Lady Anne Clifford's diary entry for 25 October 1617: 'My Lady Lisle and my Coz: Barbara Sidney [came] and I walked with them all the Wilderness over. They saw the Child and much commended her. I gave them some marmalade of quince, for about this time I made much of it.' In other words, her cousin came to see her and brought a friend, they went for a walk in the garden, her cousin admired the baby, and Lady Anne gave her some jam she had just made.[40]

But women were hired labourers too. At Knole in the time of Charles I, hops were grown, not only around the park, but also in

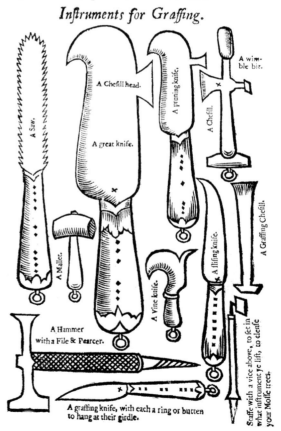

Instruments for Graffing.

A Saw.

A Cheſill head.

A pruning knife.

A Cheſill.

A wimble bit.

A great knife.

A Mallet.

A Vine knife.

A flitting knife.

A Graffing Cheſill.

A Hammer with a File & Pearcer.

A graffing knife, with each a ring or butten to hang at their girdle.

Staffe with a vice above, to ſet in what inſtrument ye liſt, to clenſe your Moiſe trees.

This impressive array of horticultural ironmongery, from Leonard Mascall's Art of Planting and Graffing, *1599, includes instruments for pruning and training as well as grafting. Skill in fruit-growing was highly valued in the sixteenth century.*

it. Women employed to pick the hops were paid 5d a day. Evidently it was a skilled job, because for cleaning and weeding the ground they received only 3d.[41] Weeding was certainly women's work and weeder women were a feature of gardening until well into the nineteenth century, when the all-male hierarchy of Victorian gardening required members of the gentle sex to work at home.

The Cost of Gardening

There is not enough evidence yet available to give us a clear idea of how much gardening cost in Tudor and Jacobean times. It is clear that there were skilled gardeners as well as weeders (invariably women) and labourers.[42] But even the word 'gardener' had a very wide meaning, and embraced such trades and occupations as botanist, florist, forester, fruiterer, fruit-grower, garden-implement dealer, greengrocer, herbalist, horticultural sundriesman, horticulturist, landscape gardener, market gardener, nurseryman, plant merchant, seedsman and sower.[43] We also know, for example, that when John Chapman worked as head gardener for Cardinal Wolsey in the 1510s, his gardeners were paid 6d a day and his labourers 4d a day, but his weeder women received only 3d a day.

We know what these gardeners were paid, but we do not know what their duties were. Sometimes we do know those duties, but not how much the gardeners were paid. There are several mentions of the gardeners' duties in accounts relating to the Earl of Northumberland's households at Wressle and Leconfield in eastern Yorkshire in the same year, 1512. Each household had only one gardener, and there is a suggestion that the post was not always filled: the regulations refer to the gardener 'if there be one'. One of the gardener's duties was to provide herbs for the household. He also had a 'chamber' within the house and received 'Mete ande Drinke within' – that is, his board as well as his lodging. His job specification was to 'attendis hourely in the Garden for Setting of Erbis and Clipping of Knottis and Sweeping the said Garden clean hourely'. The herbs included roses, parsley, primroses, sorrel, mint, dandelions and many others that were made into distillations. Leconfield and Wressle were not among the Earl's more important properties, so the garden's role would be very limited. They were never intended for display, or planted to produce quantities of fruit.[44] But in any event we do not know how the gardeners were rewarded for their services.

It is, however, often difficult to put such figures into context. For example, in 1546, when the king's gardeners at Southwark were receiving 7d a day, the keeper of the garden bought 3,000 'red rossiers' at 3s 4d per 1,000, which seems very inexpensive in comparison to the wages. We do not yet have the detailed costings which will enable us to make a proper financial cost-benefit analysis of gardening in the sixteenth and early seventeenth centuries – the published evidence is as yet too fragmentary. A rich man like Elizabeth's I favourite, Robert Dudley, Earl of Leicester, was able to pay well and command the best of everything. We know that in 1558–9, he paid 9s 10d 'to Oswald for bowes and flowers for the chamber', 3s 4d for lemons, and 8d to the 'keper of the gardeyne at Whight halle in reward for strawing erbes', but we have no way of quantifying the services or goods rendered, nor their quality, nor the period over which they were supplied. The same record tells us that Leicester's agent paid 13s 6d for 'rooses and other flowers for your lordship's chamber by the space of xxvij days at vjd. the day', but once again we have no way of assessing the size of the contract. In 1585, when Leicester ran a much more substantial series of establishments, he paid 18s 'to Thomas the gardner of Wansteed for xlvij potts of gillie flowers at xvjd. the

This illustration from Thomas Hill's The Gardener's Labyrinth, *1577, shows how to design and prepare beds for planting, but the vine trellis in the background hints at the long-term rewards of husbandry.*

pott', and on 20 October 1585 £5 was 'payd by your lordship's commandment to Gouf your lordship's gardener of Wansted of hys quarter's wages from Medsomer to Myckellmas quarter 1585', which makes his annual salary £20. That compares with annual wages of £6 for Lord Percy's head gardener at Syon Park near Brentford, but there is no way of telling what skills were offered by Gouf the gardener or what management responsibilities he discharged which made him worth so much more.[45] Gardeners at Gray's Inn were paid 1s 6d or 1s 4d a day in 1600, and labourers were paid 1s a day. The gardeners responsible for maintenance of the gardens were paid £16 13s 4d annually from 1611 to 1721, but Gray's Inn was a popular and fashionable garden, so these wages may have been on the high side.

The price of plants is also difficult to put into context. When John Tradescant the Elder visited Rouen in 1611 to buy plants for Hatfield, he paid 2s a piece for cherries, mulberries, peaches and pears, at a time when labourers earned 1s a day and women weeders only half that amount. Granted that the cultivars he introduced may well have been unavailable in England – and therefore 'status' plants – the prices still seem high. When Francis Bacon supplied plants to Gray's Inn in

1600, cherry trees were charged at 1s each; birch trees at 1s 6d and woodbines were 6d for 100.[46] It is hard to understand why one birch tree should be worth 300 honeysuckles.

Plantsmen

It is clear that, from at least the middle of the sixteenth century, there were several notable 'plantsman's gardens' in England, owned either by the very rich or by the curious and learned. Some were landowners who became obsessed by plants and wanted to make a fine collection in their gardens; others were educated men who had the opportunity to acquire and study plants from abroad and may also have traded as gentlemen nurserymen. As has been the case with every subsequent generation, few such gardens survived beyond the life of their makers, but the interaction between the rich enthusiasts and the knowledgeable specialists has been an enduring feature of gardening in England ever since.

The vast influx of exotic plants of every kind after about 1500 came not, as one might suppose, first from southern Europe and the Levant, and then from further afield, but from all over the known world simultaneously: African marigolds (*Tagetes erecta*) from Mexico, *Clematis viticella* from Italy, hyacinths from Turkey and oriental planes (*Platanus orientalis*) from Persia. Two plants of great and immediate economic importance which reached England in the sixteenth century were the sycamore tree and the common hop. The sycamore's arrival towards the end of the sixteenth century was of great significance to marginal farmers on the edge of the moors.[47] The shade and shelter offered by sycamores in these bleak areas were matched by the tree's vigour, its speed of growth and its ultimate height, which far exceeded any comparable native tree, even if, years later, its tendency to seed prolifically rendered it one of the gardener's least-loved trees. Hops were first brought to England in 1524; before that date, English beer was brewed without hops.

Contemporaries were aware of the effect these exotics were having upon English gardening, so that from time to time one comes across a comment such as William Harrison's marvelling 'how wonderfully is their [gardens'] beauty increased, not only with flowers ... but also with rare and medicinable herbs sought up in the land within these forty years, so that in comparison of this present the ancient gardens were but dunghills'. And Harrison goes on to mention specifically 'how art also helpeth nature in the daily colouring, doubling and enlarging the proportion of our flowers, it is incredible to report'.[48] It should, however, be said that this is a sentiment which has often been repeated since

The English Garden: A Social History

CHAPTER TWO

The Rise and Fall of the Formal Garden 1640–1730

The Political Background

Garden-making needs peace and prosperity, and there was little of either during the period from 1640 to 1660. The Civil War was expensive for both sides. Taxation remained high during the Commonwealth. The experiment in establishing a Calvinist republic in England was not successful – largely because it was not so harshly imposed as the Reformation had been 100 years earlier. When Parliament invited Charles II to return to the throne of his father, the welcome was genuine and massive. It has been argued that tolerance – as part of the English national character – dates from the individual experience of having to live peacefully with ex-enemies during the years following the restoration of the monarchy. Yet society was still fairly hierarchical. The poll tax, for example, was calculated on a sliding scale which charged nothing of those who received the poor rate, but exacted the maximum contributions from dukes. And, despite the restoration of Charles II, the legacy of the Civil War was that Parliament was ultimately more powerful than the King – a political fact reinforced in 1688.

Whig historians would have us believe that the events of 1688 amounted to a Glorious Revolution. It would be truer to say that the accession of William III was in many ways a disaster for England. Within months, the Dutch king had committed our ancestors to a continental war against Louis XIV. The principal form of taxation which was levied to meet the enormous expense of this war was a land tax; there was less money available for houses and gardens. The same was true of Queen Anne's wars against the French. Nevertheless, these wars coincide almost exactly with the glory days of the fashionable garden designers George London and Henry Wise, who between them dominated the top end of the garden-making market in England between 1688 and 1714. Indeed, one of the most spectacular gardens – now lost – at Canons in Middlesex was designed and overseen by George London and paid for by the first Duke of Chandos out of

❊ *Detail of the illustration on page 91.*

The East Front of Canons, Middlesex, *engraved by Hendrik Hulsbergh after a drawing by John Price, 1720. The first Duke of Chandos pillaged public funds to build his Palladian palace and Dutch garden at Canons.*

monies which, in his capacity as Treasurer, he had siphoned from the war effort. So there is a paradox here: a heavier load of taxation coinciding with conspicuous spending.

This is also the period in which political parties began to emerge – essentially the same interests that dominate English domestic life today. Following the accession of William III and (with a few exceptions) throughout the eighteenth century, England was governed by a small group of Whig magnates. The 1720s and 1730s were the golden era of Whig oligarchical rule – peace abroad, stability at home, legal and executive efficiency and a one-party government. Some of the gardens that leading Whigs made in this period may be seen as political statements. Sir Robert Walpole, first 'Prime Minister', amassed a fortune from his office. His younger son, Horace Walpole, has been widely cited as a reliable authority for the history of gardens and gardening of the age.

This is the period in which there emerged a society which is recognizably modern, one in which we can identify fairly easily with people's attitudes and way of life. A constantly expanding economy led to the sustained prosperity which we take for granted, together with the social and lifestyle improvements which followed – better education, better health, better transport, better laws and better government. Yet one of the paradoxes is that after 1650 the size of England's population was at best stagnant or actually falling back, until it finally took off again after 1730. Another paradox is that agricultural production increased during this period, so that England became a net exporter of grain, and grain became cheaper at home, which meant that farmers made less money and landowners received less in the way of rents. Yet there was money enough for gardening still. Landlords began to feed turnips to their cattle to overwinter their stock – the beginnings of the agricultural revolution which seemed at the time no more than just another improvement in farming practices. Yet it was not until the middle of the nineteenth century that improved communications put an end to the frequent occurrence of severe but local famines.

Civil War, Commonwealth – & the Apple

Since the 1950s English political history has been dominated by such questions as whether there was a 'General Crisis' in seventeenth-century England. All manner of events have been adduced as evidence of such a crisis and in order to define its salient characteristics. Many of the participants in this debate have cited social and economic changes to support their contentions. Fortunately, the social and economic history of gardens and gardening can usually be told without reference to the political concerns of Whig and Marxist historians.

Most people, at all levels, were fairly unaffected by Charles I's problems until after the outbreak of Civil War in 1642. Certainly, no one wanted war. In the event, it brought disruption to trade, high taxation, the requisitioning of property and animals, primitive revenge attacks like the burning of crops, and the heedless destruction which always follows in the wake of an army living off the land. As a royalist living in London, John Tradescant the Younger's reaction to the Civil War was to disappear as quickly as he could, and he took himself off for a little more plant-hunting in Virginia. John Evelyn, another royalist, remained a few months in London before going down to stay with his brother at Wotton in Surrey. He then slipped across to France and spent some ten years travelling abroad, though he later wrote that his main concerns during the 'interregnum' had been 'to continue educating himself and to preserve and manage his estate'. In fact, it was during this period that he started to write about gardens. The Shropshire gentleman-gardener John Rea, by contrast, referred to the Commonwealth as 'our long Winter' and did not feel able to write about flowers and his enjoyment of them until after that winter was over.[1]

It was a common reaction. In 1649 the House of Lords was abolished, which deprived the great landowners of a constitutional role. Many of the nobility and gentry went to live abroad, where they had ample opportunity to study French and Dutch styles in all the decorative arts. Then they began to drift back home again to make some form of accommodation with the Puritan government and to occupy their leisure with the management and improvement of their estates. The richer classes, by and large, kept their wealth and property, but not their political power. During the Commonwealth the established county families who had run local affairs and exercised power on behalf of the king were eased out of their positions. Control passed to committees drawn from the lesser gentry and even from members of the artisan classes who were known to be sympathetic to the Puritans. The memory of this short-lived social revolution remained with the reinstated ruling classes long after the Restoration, and helped to secure the economic, social and political stability of England in the eighteenth century. That stability was, of course, conducive to the practice of such an art as gardens and the development of such a science as gardening.

Meanwhile, the immediate cost of the Civil War fell heavily on adherents of both sides. High taxation was accompanied by sequestrations, but in some cases these were offset by an increased revenue from better farming and it is probably fair to say that little long-term damage was done to gardens and gardening in England as a result of the tribulations of the period 1640 to 1660. Edward Lloyd of Llanforda in Shropshire was typical of the chastened royalist, once a keen gardener, who returned home in 1645 to find his estates sequestered and the money he had once spent upon beautifying his garden wasted. He saw that his overriding need was to rebuild his family's fortunes. He wrote to his mother in 1645, 'I have been charged with folly for my gardens and walks, for my wilderness and fountain and . . . the charges: 'tis true . . . there is not such a noble and gentleman-like vanity . . . as gardens and walks.' Henceforth, he vowed to worship God in his garden.[2] Prominent royalists had to lie low. John Pincent, Rector of Talaton in Devon, spent the Commonwealth propagating and growing the best trees that he could find.[3] Yet even before the Commonwealth, people who had fought on opposite sides during the Civil War were corresponding with each other on matters of shared interest like gardens and plants.

Meanwhile, the Puritans sought to build the New Jerusalem, and this meant a radical change in the way mankind made use of God's creation. One of the most influential Puritan thinkers was a keen horticulturalist – the educationalist and social reformer Samuel Hartlib. Hartlib was a Prussian who came to England in his twenties as an agricultural improver, preaching the need to introduce the modern horticultural practices of Brabant and Flanders, which included the greater planting of potatoes. Hartlib's reputation as an educationalist rested upon his professed aim to see the establishment of the Protestant religion in every school in England, and there is a good deal of tiresome religiosity in much of his writings. Here, for example, he attributes bad harvests to man's sinfulness:

although the Husbandman hath been laborious and diligent in his calling these last years; yet our crops have been thin and scarcity and famine hath siezed [*sic*] on all parts of this Land. And, though I desire the Husbandman to be diligent and laborious in his calling, yet I counsel him to *break off his sins by Repentance* ... and to pray daily to Him for blessings, who *giveth freely to them that ask, and upbraideth not.* For the Country-man hath a more immediate dependance on Him than any other: for if the Lord with-hold His *fat dew from Heaven, it is in vain* that the Husbandman *rise up early, and go to bed late, and eat the bread of carefulness.*[4]

During the Commonwealth, Samuel Hartlib and a group of like-minded reformers proposed a new law to make the planting of fruit trees compulsory – an obligation on every landowner. Hartlib's own contribution was set out in his

Design for Plentie By a Universall Planting of Fruit Trees 'for the benefit and public relief of this whole Nation ... for the relief of the poor, the benefit of the rich, and the delight of all'.[5] Hartlib considered apples, pears, quinces and walnuts to be the fruits most suitable to our climate. Landowners would each plant a specified number of trees. This requirement would be enforced by public authorities empowered to ensure that the plantings took place, that the orchards were duly cultivated and that defaulters were fined. Objections were brushed aside. Even wastelands and commons should be planted with these fruit trees, so that all England became the 'Garden of God'.

Hartlib's concern for horticulture – as with all his interests – was inseparable from his religious beliefs and political activities. He considered it a duty to make God's earth more fertile and productive. In so doing, a man might feed his fellow men, create employment and strengthen the commonwealth of all believers. Hartlib's treatise was subtitled 'The best way of Improvement of Lands' but some of the justification for planting fruit trees was also doctrinal. Adam was employed to keep and order the garden of fruit trees; God put him in the Garden of Eden to dress it and keep it; plants were the first animate bodies that God created and fruits were the first food that was given to man;

The frontispiece to John Worlidge's The Mystery of Husbandry, *1669, reminds us that apples, and their usefulness, were a constant theme of seventeenth-century gardening: cider was promoted as an English rival to French wine.*

King Solomon made gardens and orchards and planted them with fruit trees. But Christian precedent was not enough, even during the Commonwealth. Hartlib also cited the praises of ancient writers for fruits and fruit trees as justification for more plantings – a long list of authors was quoted in detail. Finally, he argued that fruit was useful to the husbandman because he profits from its sale, it brings him good health, it brings long life and so on. Any such activity had to be justified in this way during the Commonwealth – biblically, classically and economically. It was not a good time for pleasure gardens and flower gardens.

Though his proposals were never enacted, it is worth noting how Hartlib was treated as a result. Cromwell thought highly enough of him to give him a pension of £100 a year. He was a hero of the Puritan republic. Yet this was also the time – in the 1650s – when he became a friend of the devout Anglican and royalist John Evelyn. Despite their very different political and religious beliefs, they shared two major interests – education and the improvement of husbandry. Such private relationships were not uncommon during the Civil War and the Commonwealth. Even Evelyn could write that the purpose of gardens and gardening was to re-create the Garden of Eden, that 'delicious place' called 'Paradise'. However, Hartlib's fall from grace when Charles II was restored to the throne was immediate and total. Hartlib was reduced to begging from royalists like Evelyn whom he had befriended. The same was true of many Puritan writers on husbandry and gardening.

The main economic reason for suggesting a move from agriculture to fruit-growing was to spread the risks, but there was also the possibility of increasing revenues. This was a point which intrigued both the Puritans and their opponents: was horticulture more pleasing to God than agriculture because it made better use of His world? Apples could be intensively cultivated on dwarfing stocks and show a greater return per acre than agricultural crops or livestock. Perhaps all England should be turned into a market garden. The Puritan clergyman William Lawson pointed out that 'no ground a man

Apple trees like these in John Laurence's The Gentleman's Recreation, *1716, were pruned to tiny rounded heads and planted in regular lines. The controlling hands of gardeners tightened their grip on nature.*

occupieth (no, not the Corn-field) yieldeth more gain to the purse, and house-keeping, quantity for quantity, than a good orchard'.[6] He was firmly 'of the opinion, that it were better for *England* that we had more Orchards and Gardens, and more large'.[7] He also believed that fruit trees existed to delight mankind 'as God has given man things profitable, so hath he allowed him honest comfort, delight and recreation in all the works of his hands', which was a view not always shared among his brethren. Perhaps a more typical Puritan view of gardens and gardening is expressed by the preacher and cleric Michael Jermin, who maintained that the one purpose of a garden should be to use it as a place to contemplate the misery which Christ suffered for mankind. A garden full of flowers was a garden full of vanities. 'Let those to whom God hath afforded these delights, have in their gardens as *Joseph* had, a Sepulcher, that is, let them in their pleasures, remember their death, that will bee a good measure to keep away the sinne of pleasure from them.'[8] Compare this with the enthusiasm of the royalist Dean Thomas Fuller, for whom market gardening was a source of wonder: 'Oh, the incredible profit by digging of ground!' – as opposed to ploughing it – 'what a profitable use of land and labour it is. 'Tis incredible how many poor people in London live thereon, so that in some seasons gardens feed more poor people than the fields.'[9] But even Fuller expounded a theological reason for the cultivation of flowers. A flower 'in the morning, when it groweth up, is a lecture of Divine Providence', he wrote. 'In the evening, when it is cut down and withered it is a lecture of human mortality.'[10]

The economics of market gardening and fruit-growing were much clearer. Until about 1650, grain was always a profitable crop. The principal way in which a farmer or landowner could make more money would be to enclose more land and convert it from sheep pasturing to arable. But after 1650, supply exceeded demand and England became a net exporter of grain. This meant that farmers looked for alternative sources of income and some with smallholdings turned to market gardening, where the returns per acre were substantially greater. Thomas Fuller believed that market gardening had started in Surrey and Kent about seventy years previously:

> for we fetched most of our cherries from Flanders, apples from France; and hardly had a mess of rathe-ripe pease but from Holland, which were dainties for ladies: they came so far and cost so dear. Since gardening hath crept out of Holland to Sandwich in Kent, and thence into this county [Surrey], where though they have given six pounds an acre and upward, they had made their rent, lived comfortably, and set many people on work.[11]

Fuller was wrong about the origins of market gardening, which go back much further than the end of the sixteenth century, but he was right about the rewards.

Fruit

Andrew Marvell wrote seductively about the pleasures of fruit in his poem 'The Garden', written in about 1650:

> What wond'rous life is this I lead!
> Ripe apples drop about my head;
> The luscious clusters of the vine
> Upon my mouth do crush their wine;
> The nectaren and curious peach,
> Into my hands themselves do reach;
> Stumbling on melons, as I pass,
> Insnar'd with flow'rs, I fall on grass.

The quality and range of fruit at a man's table were status symbols, a measure of wealth. Melons became popular during the course of the seventeenth century. 'Every gardner nowadays knows how to raise melons, but few to govern them,' declared an anonymous writer in 1699.[12] Alexander Pope was triumphant when he succeeded in growing melons – and pineapples, too. By the early eighteenth century, the pineapple was the most prestigious and highly esteemed of fruits. The fruit lasts in good condition for several weeks, so a fine specimen would often form part of the table decoration for as much as a month before it was finally eaten. Much effort in the eighteenth century was dedicated to growing 'pines' as large as possible.

Many English horticulturists and garden-owners sought to plant vines and make wine, arguing that England's latitude and geography made them eminently suitable. William Hughes, for example, published a book called *The Compleat Vineyard* in 1665, which was reprinted in 1670 and 1683 – a remarkable measure of popularity in those days. *The Compleat Vineyard* 'set forth the ways, and all the Circumstances necessary for the Planting [of] a Vineyard; with the election of the Soil; the Scituation thereof; the best way for the Planting of the Young Plants; the best time and manner of Proining; . . . the fashion of *Wine-presses*; the manner of bruising and pressing *Grapes*; and how to advance our *English* wines'. And Sir William Temple, whose garden at Moor Park in Surrey was famous for its fruit, wrote in 1685 that he had 'had the honour of bringing over four sorts into England', including 'the Arboyse from the Franche Comte, which is a small white grape, or rather runs into some small and some great upon the same bunch; it agrees well with our climate, but is very choice in soil, and must have a sharp gravel; it is the most delicious of all grapes that are not muscat'.[13] But none of the outdoor grape cultivars then available proved suited to the English climate. The mild English winters were an advantage, but the weak summer sun was not enough to ripen the grapes.

The same was true of pears. Everyone tried to grow pears because they were more highly esteemed in France than apples and most books about fruit-growing relied heavily on French sources. In 1665 John Rea maintained correctly that all the best cultivars came from France and listed, by way of example, twenty-seven 'choice Pears, lately obtained out of France by the diligence of Sir Thomas Hanmer'. Batty Langley in 1729 praised the beauty of pear trees in blossom, but recognized that a lot of fruit-growing promised more than it delivered, and that unless the season produced favourable weather the quality of the fruit would be a disappointment. Pears need a warm wall or the protection of buildings in towns to ripen well. But people persisted in trying to grow pears that would match the fruit which was imported every autumn from France. Alexander Pope in 1735 asked Philip Miller at the Chelsea Physic Garden to try to procure him budwood of several French cultivars of pear.

Englishmen took up with the apple instead. It was the English fruit par excellence and its cider was a match for any French wines. No lesser man than John Evelyn championed the making of cider, which he saw as a specifically English beverage which could rival the best wines of France or Spain. He added an appendix to *Sylva* on the cultivation of apples and the making of cider.

It is true that the English climate was particularly suited to the cultivation of apples, but a significant reason for their growth in popularity was the association of apples with Protestantism – and Calvinism in particular, that brand of the new religion which symbolized the integrity of the English nation. We have seen that many of the leading pomologists of the day were Calvinist divines. When Ralph Austen published his treatise on fruit trees in 1653 he added a spiritual essay in which he maintained that at the fall of Adam men had been separated from the good apples of the Garden of Eden and condemned to know only bitter crab apples. It was the Christian's duty to regain that lost Eden by cultivating only the best. Fruit trees were, moreover, the most rewarding of all trees to grow because the profits and the pleasures went hand in hand.

But the truth is that, in the latter half of the seventeenth century, the lead in developing fruit-growing came from France and, in particular, from a Catholic priest called Antoine Le Gendre, who had worked in Louis XIII's gardens. Le Gendre developed a technique for training fruit trees against walls to allow more sun and warmth to ripen the fruits and to improve their colour, flavour and sweetness. Before this time, many fruit trees had been pruned like topiary plants into dense mopheads which were quite unsuitable for producing high-quality designed in conjunction with Chandos's Italian architect Galilei was double doors to protect the plants from direct contact with the cold air outside.

However, one should not doubt that by the 1660s most glasshouses were constructed and heated well enough to bring their contents through the English winter. Indeed, it was possible by then to grow tropical plants in England – those which need minimum temperatures of 20 degrees centigrade throughout the year. There is a famous painting which is thought to show the royal gardener John Rose presenting a pineapple to King Charles II in about 1670. Largely because they were hard to grow, pineapples became the ultimate symbol of a gardener's

This famous painting, attributed to Hendrik Danckerts, is said to show the royal gardener, John Rose, presenting Charles II with the first pineapple grown in England, c. 1670. Pineapples were the ultimate symbol of a gardener's horticultural skills and (since they were always expensive) of his employer's magnificence and wealth.

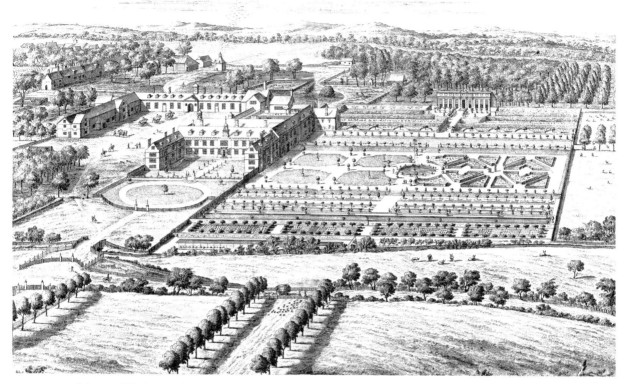

Johannes Kip's overview of Southwick, 1707, shows that the focus of the garden was not the old-fashioned house (to the left) but the smart new orangery at the top.

horticultural skills and – since they were always expensive – of his employer's magnificence and wealth.

John Evelyn was the first man to use the word 'conservatory' to indicate a glasshouse where heat was conserved for the benefit of plants during the winter months. A 'greenhouse' was originally so called because it was used to conserve and display exotic evergreen plants. A plantsman-cum-nurseryman like John Tradescant the Younger was already growing pelargoniums, jasmines, plumbago and hibiscus in his greenhouses in 1656. By the latter half of the seventeenth century, oranges and lemons were increasingly being grown by nurserymen and by the owners of more modest gardens. The well-to-do then began to stock their orangeries with other plants, usually ornamental evergreens like jasmines, pomegranates and oleanders. As they began to be heated by increasingly plentiful supplies of coal, and fitted with more glass, it was discovered that some plants could be induced to grow right through the winter months.

Orangeries, greenhouses and conservatories were designed as ornamental buildings, owing more to architecture than to the demands of horticulture. They were

The Rise and Fall of the Formal Garden 1640–1730

useful garden features which could provide a focal point at the end of an axis or command a view like the old banqueting houses. The orangery at Southwick near Southampton dominated the central axis of the huge formal garden, which was laid to the side of the house. It was therefore a more important element of the design than the house itself. William Talman's greenhouse at Chatsworth, built in 1698, was a grand and spacious structure almost as long as the house itself and looked down over a large sunken pool. The orangery which William Blathwayt built at Dyrham in 1701 was joined to the house and used as a place of entertainment in the summer when the plants were all outside. Queen Anne used to eat her supper in the greenhouse at Kensington Palace; it was built for her by Vanbrugh in 1704 and, like the orangery at Dyrham, is still standing. Glasshouses began to function as enlarged banqueting houses. By 1739 Lady Hertford could describe the Earl of Bathurst's greenhouse at Riskins in Buckinghamshire with its 'collection of orange, myrtle, geranium, and oleander trees' as 'a very agreeable room; either to drink tea, play at cards, or sit in with a book, in a summer's evening'.[18] Orangeries in the classical style, dating from the first half of the eighteenth century, are found throughout England still; later structures from Victorian days, with much more glass and metal or timber frameworks, have tended to disappear.

Avenues

After the Restoration, gardens remained formal and usually enclosed, but their prospects were much more extensive. Walks and avenues had begun to appear before the Civil War, but they were now much more widely planted and they stretched out into the surrounding countryside in a way that embraced the wild landscape beyond. These avenues were statements of confidence in the future. They also showed that a landowner had consolidated his land-holdings and enclosed them. While common rights of grazing and taking wood were still exercised over it, there was no incentive to improve the land in any way. Now it was safe for the landowner to landscape it with trees.

A gentry house would have just one avenue, running out from the main façade of the house or – seen from the other direction – focusing on it. This avenue was planted as much to provide an impressive frame for a view of the house as to improve the prospect from the house itself. One common trick with avenues was to widen them as they moved away from the house. Seen from the far end, this produced the false perspective of converging lines, and would make the avenue seem longer than it really was, and the house larger. When the Duke of Chandos built his sumptuous palace at Canons, he positioned the avenue to make the house

All the elements of wealth and its enjoyment surround this view of Charlecote Park in Warwickshire, painted by Jan Stevens (d. 1722): pride of possession, family entertainments, and labourers in the garden.

appear double its true size. Daniel Defoe explained that 'the Avenue is spacious and majestick, and as it gives you the View of two Fronts, join'd, as it were, in one, the Distance not admitting you to see the Angle, which is in the Centre; so you are agreeably drawn in, to think the Front of the House almost twice as large as it is'.[19]

Not only did a long avenue glorify the house on which it focused, it also asserted the landowner's unfettered ownership of the land – freehold, enclosed and consolidated. A large landowner would plant several avenues and cross-avenues. One of the most extensive was the layout planted by the first Duke of Beaufort at Badminton to complement his magnificent new house. It was never fully planted, but a good idea of it can be gained from the drawings and engravings by Knyff and Kip. Celia Fiennes admired it from the leads of the roof – the highest point from

The long avenues at the very edge of Canaletto's painting of 1748 give scale to the vast layout at Badminton.

which to appreciate it – and noted that she could 'look 12 ways down to the parishes and grounds beyond all thro' glides or vistos of trees'. It is a vast assertion of confidence and glory, with a serious message which Mark Girouard sums up thus: 'When the Duke of Beaufort dined in state in the saloon behind the central frontispiece at Badminton, he was at the hub of a web of converging avenues stretching far into the distance into the surrounding countryside, underlining the fact that all the local avenues of power and influence converged on him.'[20]

The central avenue, aligned on the centre of the main façade of the house, was usually the broadest, at least as wide as the façade of the house itself. It was often the longest too – at Rougham in Norfolk, the lime avenue planted in the 1690s was nearly a mile long[21] – and the principal element of design, with parterres and orchards symmetrically arranged on either side. Avenues were still being planted, both for gentry houses and larger ones, as late as the 1740s. Planting avenues was also considered good economic practice – it was a long-term investment in the

Railings separate the gardens from the deer park at the front of the house, and a new ha-ha at the rear. Meanwhile, a new side-entrance through a detached service wing is projected in these views of Belton House in Lincolnshire from Vitruvius Britannicus, *1761–71.*

future – and it received a boost from John Evelyn's insistence that all landowners should plant more trees.

Avenues were usually of elm or lime but sometimes of beech, horse chestnut or plane – seldom of oak, which was more often thought of as a forestry tree, where dense planting ensured long straight timber. Moses Cook, head gardener to the Earl of Essex at Cassiobury and a founder of the Brompton Park Nursery, maintained that a gardener needed a knowledge of mathematics to plant them. It was important not to 'mask a fine Front, nor vail a pleasant Prospect (as too many doe) by making the walks too narrow'.[22] This principle was nicely expressed by the doggerel written by an anonymous female visitor to Ashridge in Hertfordshire in 1699:

> The stately beech, exactly in a row
> On both the sides, in full proportion grow:
> Their lofty tops so even and verdant are
> You'd think them spacious pastures in the air.[23]

Grand Gardens – French & Dutch

Many nobles and gentlemen went abroad during the Commonwealth, often to be close to Charles II in France, and when they came back they brought with them French ideas of how a house and garden should be designed. When Charles II returned, in 1660, he employed the Mollet brothers, André and Gabriel, to redesign St James's Park. The long French-style canal which they made there, together with the 'Long Water' at Hampton Court, were the first long canals to be built in England. Actually, Charles asked his cousin Louis XIV whether Le Nôtre could come over and advise him on Hampton Court and Greenwich, but it seems that the great designer never made the journey, though Louis did give him permission to go. Both the Mollets were dead by 1666 – probably victims of the plague – when John Rose was appointed 'chief gardener in St James's park'. Rose too had studied and worked in France. He was in due course succeeded by George London, another pupil of Le Nôtre's, so that the connection with French gardens was maintained by the King throughout his twenty-five-year reign. Indeed, right through into the reign of Queen Anne, French-style gardens were the one and only fashion to follow.

Louis XIV did not begin to lay out his mega-garden at Versailles until after 1660; Le Nôtre's garden extensions at Versailles predated the enlargement of the palace. Canals, bosquets, fountains, pavilions and parterres stretched for miles out from the palace. No garden exercised such an influence upon the French King's contemporaries. Not only was unruly nature tamed, but the sheer scale of Versailles impressed everyone – as it was intended to do – by its declaration of power. Louis XIV himself wrote the guide to the gardens at Versailles. An English visitor described them in 1698:

> The Splanade towards the Gardens and Parterres are the noblest things that can be seen, vastly great, with a very large Basin of Water in the middle, walled round with white Marble, on which are placed a great number of incomparable Brazen Vasa, and large Brass figures *couchant*, of the best Masters in Sculpture; it were endless to tell all the Furniture of these Gardens of Marble Statues, and Vasa of Brass and Marble, the multitude of Fountains, and those wide Canals like Seas running in a streight line from the bottom of the Gardens, as far as the eye can reach. In a Word, these Gardens are a Countrey laid out into Alleys and Walks, Groves of Trees, Canals and Fountains, and everywhere adorned with ancient and modern Statues and *Vasa* innumerable.[24]

And he goes on to describe the 2,000 orange trees (some dating from the time of François I), the 700 cases of figs and the fountains which were 'ordered to Play for the Diversion of the *English* Gentlemen'.

Charles II was not an exceptionally keen gardener himself, but William III and Queen Anne were both interested in gardens and, to some extent, led the fashions of their day. Hampton Court was William III's answer to Versailles, and he took a personal interest in its development. William's own gardens at Het Loo were designed by Daniel Marot, a pupil of Le Nôtre, but Hampton Court was a more private garden than Versailles, and not intended as a vast setting for the glorification of the monarch. William's most extensive alterations were to the 'privy garden'. Just as the king had a cabinet, closet or privy chamber for his own seclusion and the entertainment of his closest friends and grandest visitors, so too he developed a privy garden which was his alone to enjoy and to whom only the favoured few might be admitted.

Dutch gardens were smaller than French gardens and made more use of ornamental canals. They were a regional accommodation of the grand French garden, adapted to the constraints of the landscape of the Netherlands – too much water and too little space. The Dutch also made more use of tidily trimmed topiary and planted a greater variety of plants within the parterres – French parterres usually relied upon gravel and grass. Dutch gardens were self-contained and introspective. They seldom stretched out into the surrounding forests and seem positively domestic when compared to Le Nôtre's expansive designs. Many English gardens combined a mixture of features that were in origin either Dutch or French – Dutch topiary was particularly popular at first, as were French avenues.

A View of Hampton Court, *oil painting by Leonard Knyff, c. 1700. Hampton Court was William III's answer to Versailles. Both the parsimonious Queen Anne and the unrefined George I were sufficiently impressed to retain Henry Wise as their royal gardener.*

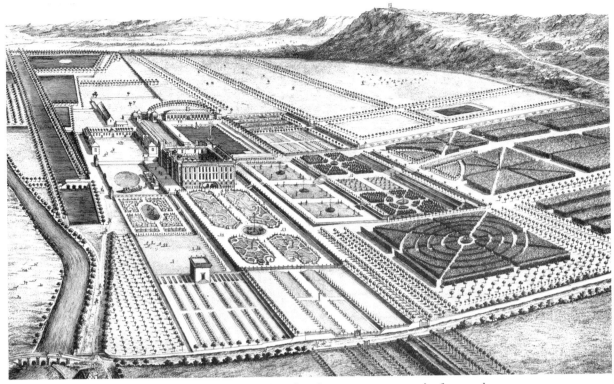

Extensive gardens in the French style were smart accessories for grand houses. This is Chatsworth, Derbyshire, by Leonard Knyff and Johannes Kip from Britannia Illustrata, *1707.*

Queen Anne made some alterations at Hampton Court. It was said, in particular, that she took out all the edgings because she disliked box, but her successor George I was no gardener – unlike his mother the Electress Sophia of Hanover, who described the magnificent gardens she made at Herrenhausen as 'my lifetime's achievement'. Thereafter, the leaders of fashion or 'taste' in England from 1714 were the great Whig politicians – at least as far as gardens and architectural style.

During the first years of Charles II's reign, several landowners laid out their gardens in the grand new style. In 1669, the Earl of Chesterfield started his garden at Bretby on the model of Versailles. Fruit was one of his interests. He grew seventeen different lemon cultivars and twenty-three oranges, planting them directly in the ground and supplying them with temporary shelters to protect them from the Derbyshire winter. As with nearby Chatsworth, Bretby was famous for its complex parterres and for Grillet's waterworks, which included a series of fountains. This was a time when streams were sometimes embanked to make a formal rectangular canal or series of canals. Waterworks were rare, expensive and a tremendous status symbol. The Earl of Kent built grand canals in the French style at Wrest Park in Bedfordshire in the 1680s. But by then almost all the design and planting of grand gardens were the monopoly of one firm, London and Wise of Brompton Park Nursery.

London & Wise

Far and away the most important garden designers of this period were George London and Henry Wise. Their gardens represent the apotheosis of the formal style in England. Their advice was sought by everyone who was anyone. Between them, they dominated English horticulture for nearly fifty years, and the two leading garden designers of the next phase of history, Charles Bridgeman and Stephen Switzer, were both trained by them. The only other designer to have enjoyed such success as London and Wise was the man who undid much of their work in the eighteenth century – Capability Brown.

Despite the fame and fortune they enjoyed as designers, London and Wise were first in partnership as nurserymen. Yet they were each so possessed of energy and industry that within a few years their Brompton Park Nursery dominated the entire English nursery trade. Brompton Park Nursery was the first of several nurseries over the centuries to achieve a position of apparently unassailable pre-eminence – as Veitch of Exeter did in the nineteenth century and Hillier of Winchester in the twentieth. Henry Wise was not one of the four original partners when the Brompton Park Nursery was founded in 1681, but George London was, albeit rather a junior partner to begin with. The most senior partner was Roger Looker or Lucre, who was gardener to Queen Catherine of Braganza at Somerset House in the Strand. The others were John Field, who was head gardener to the Earl of Bedford nearby, and Moses Cook, who was a garden-writer and head gardener to the Earl of Essex at Cassiobury. It was at Cassiobury that Cook developed the idea of making a French-style park of thick woodland cut through with rides. This required many trees, and it may have been the experience which inspired Cook and London to found the Brompton Park Nursery, convinced that there would be a market for a large number of trees. However, Looker died in 1685 and Field in 1687; Cook sold out in 1689. Meanwhile, Henry Wise had joined in about 1687 and the partnership between London and Wise continued until London's death in 1714.

Brompton Park Nursery lies underneath nineteenth-century Albertopolis – the museums of South Kensington. It extended to 100 acres, which made it by far the

Henry Wise rose from humble origins to become royal gardener, the subject of a portrait by Thomas Gainsborough (1727–88) and a very rich man.

largest in England, and had everything that anyone could possibly need for their garden. Switzer reckoned that the value of the Brompton Park Nursery in the 1710s was 'between 30 and 40000 l., perhaps as much as all the Nurseries of France put together'. At one point the Brompton Park Nursery offered twenty-eight peaches, thirty-five plums, thirty apples and seventy-two different pears. This was indeed an achievement, when barely a generation before it had been essential for any keen plantsman in search of unusual plants in reasonable quantities to send an emissary to scour the nurseries of northern France. As with their stock, so with their services: the skills the partners offered were truly comprehensive – their all-in service included garden design, earth-moving, canal-digging and garden maintenance.

George London was a man of enormous energy and strong constitution. He was also remarkably personable, which made him an excellent salesman. He had been apprenticed to John Rose, Charles II's royal gardener, who died in 1677, and then worked in France before taking up a post as head gardener to Henry Compton, Bishop of London, at Fulham Palace, in 1675. It was not a full-time job, because London also worked for John Evelyn's friend the Earl of Arlington at St James's Park and acted as a garden consultant to at least two other gardens. London's close relations with Bishop Compton did, however, give him ready access to the new exotic plants, many from North America, which Compton was introducing into England through his clerical network.

The partners' first big commission, in 1682, was to advise Viscount Weymouth on the improvement of the gardens at Longleat in Wiltshire. This was an important contract and, in the initial months, all four of the original partners in the Brompton Park Nursery visited Longleat and oversaw the works in turn. Lord Weymouth was an able and ambitious politician who had inherited Longleat unexpectedly, following the murder of a young unmarried cousin. He was also extremely wealthy. The new gardens were enormous: a vast and rather formless progression of parterres, statues, orchards, topiary and waterworks which marched relentlessly up the hillside to the side of the house. It ended at a viewpoint right at the top of the hill, with a separate avenue running up towards the bluff known as Heaven's Gate.

George London travelled the country surveying clients' gardens and giving advice. He journeyed indefatigably by horse, riding fifty or sixty miles a day if necessary. This sort of expedition would not have been possible fifty years previously, because the roads, the maps, the whole infrastructure of communications were simply not good enough. So George London was a new phenomenon: a garden consultant based in London who was able and willing to travel the whole country and advise his clients on site, not just in letters and with plans, but by looking at the gardens and assessing what might be done. He brought the remoter parts of England, like Yorkshire and Westmorland, firmly into the ambit of metropolitan gardening.

George London and Henry Wise were not designers of any great originality but they had studied the fashionable gardens of France and they supplied everything necessary to fulfil the demand for French-style magnificence. They were facilitators. Joseph Addison – so often cited as one of the prime movers of the landscape movement – referred to them as 'our heroick Poets'. Their gardens were made to accompany grand houses, most of them new houses built by

The first Viscount Weymouth engaged Messrs London and Wise to make and maintain the most splendid formal garden of the day at Longleat, here seen in a fashionable bird's-eye view by Johannes Kip, c. 1707.

new men with new money. They interpreted the fashions of France and Holland for a clientele that was dazzled by the Sun King's gardens. They were gardens for the ostentatious, the self-consciously fashionable. It could be said that there was a sameness about their gardens, but that was exactly what the clients wanted. And London and Wise were very competent: each site had different technical problems to overcome – a steep slope, or boggy ground, for example. Complex parterres in the French style were one of their specialities. These were comparatively rare, as most owners had replaced the intimate knot gardens of the sixteenth century with larger but simpler formal gardens – quincunxes, squares or rectangles of grass set in gravel with perhaps some topiary, statues or plants in pots at the corners. In contrast, London and Wise promised royal patterns of swirling box, and the plants could all be supplied from Brompton Park Nursery.

Another early client of the Brompton Park Nursery was the first Duchess of Beaufort, a very keen plantswoman and collector of exotics – Switzer said that gardening took up two-thirds of her waking day. Badminton was one of the most ambitious gardens of the period. It was famous for its vast complex of avenues and the great number of formal gardens, orchards and mazes which surrounded it, as well as the Duchess's collection of rare plants. The principal avenue at the front of the house was more than two and a half miles long.

In 1688 George London started working for the first Duke of Devonshire (then the fourth Earl), designing the complex 'western' parterre at Chatsworth. This was followed six years later by a second design on the southern side of the house – twice the size and known as the 'great' parterre – together with extensive plantings of trees and thickly planted geometrical wildernesses through which rides and walks were cut. The whole design needed a lot of plants from Brompton Park Nursery and was labour-intensive to maintain, but there was nothing to match it in the north of England.

In 1689 London and Wise laid out a garden in the Dutch style for William III's new palace at Kensington and planted two subsidiary avenues out across the deer park on the eastern side of Hampton Court Palace. These stood at 45 degrees from the Long Water, which the Mollet brothers had dug for Charles II. They also began to lay out complex parterres in the French style. William stopped work on them when Queen Mary died in 1694, but started again in a hurry in 1699. The privy garden was enlarged and replanted as it looks today.

Royal patronage brought more business to London and Wise, especially from the Whig magnates who did well for themselves out of the Dutch king. But London and Wise had an even more ardent champion in John Evelyn, who regarded them as extremely knowledgeable, energetic and reliable. In 1693 he published a translation of Jean de la Quintinie's *Instruction pour les jardins fruitiers et*

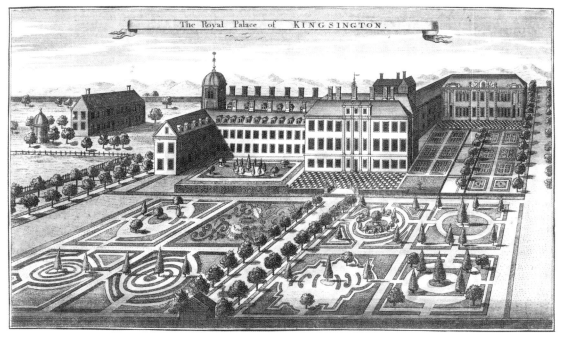

The Royal Palace of KINGSINGTON.

Both William III and Queen Anne employed Messrs London and Wise, and spent lavishly on the garden at Kensington, shown in this engraving of c. 1715.

potagers as *The Compleat Gard'ner* and included a long frontispiece which – quite spontaneously – extolled their praises. Here is a *short* extract from it:

> I Cannot conceive but it must needs be a very acceptable Advertisement, and of Universal Concern to all Noble-men, and Persons of Quality, lovers of Gardens, and Improvers of Plantations (of all Diversions and Employments the most Natural, Usefull, Innocent and Agreeable) at what Distance soever from a Place of so easy and speedy Correspondence and which is so nere this great City, to give this Notice. That of all I have hitherto seen, either at Home or Abroad; or found by Reading many Books publish'd on this Subject, pretending to speak of Nurseries and Plantations for store and variety; Directions for the Designing, or as they term it the Skillful Making, Plotting, Laying-out, and disposing of a Ground to the best Advantage: In a word, for whatsoever were desireable for the Furniture of such a Ground, with the most excellent, and Warantable Fruit (I say Warantable; because it is peculiarly due to their honnest Industry, and so rarely to be met with else-where), and other Accessories to Gardens of all Denominations, as in that Vast and ample Collection which I have lately seen and well consider'd at Brompton Park near Kensington: The very sight of which alone gives an Idea of something that is greater than I can well express, without an enumeration of Particulars; and of the

exceeding Industry, Method and Address of those who have undertaken and Cultivated it for publick Use: I mean Mr. George London (chief Gardner to their Majesties) and his Associate Mr. Henry Wise: For I have long observ'd (from the daily practice, and effects of the laudable Industry of these two Partners) that they have not made Gain the only mark of their Pains; But with Extraordinary and rare Industry endeavour'd to improve themselves in the Mysteries of their Profession, from the great Advantages, and now long Experience they have had, in being Employ'd in most of the celebrated Gardens and Plantations which this Nation abounds in; besides what they have learn'd Abroad, and where Horticulture is in highest Reputation.

And thus it continued at considerable length. Evelyn was a man of universal influence and his recommendation helped to increase the fame and renown of the Brompton Park Nursery yet further. London and Wise then published their own rather abridged edition of De la Quintinie's *Instruction* in 1699, in which they incorporated Evelyn's long dedication again. The book was very popular, not only because it satisfied a need for information about how to cultivate fruit and vegetables but also because London and Wise were themselves so fashionable by then that everyone wanted to be associated with them by buying their book. London and Wise were, quite simply, the best. They excelled at everything.

As the study of estate history has got under way in recent years, it is becoming clear that London and Wise were making and advising on gardens to many more people than previously supposed and, above all, to members of the Whig establishment. They built a handsome conservatory and extensive waterworks for Lord Ferrers at Staunton Harold in Leicestershire; they supplied fruit trees to the Earl of Dorset at Knole; they designed gardens for Sir John Harpur at Calke in Derbyshire, Viscount Cholmondeley at Cholmondeley Castle in Cheshire and the Early of Lindsey at Grimsthorpe in Lincolnshire. They probably had a hand, too, in the third Earl of Rochester's extensive woodland plantings at New Park in Surrey, and the new gardens of Lord Ossulston at Dawly in Middlesex and Brome Hall in Suffolk for Lord Cornwallis.

London and Wise were also very good at working with their clients. At Melbourne in Derbyshire they made a ten-acre garden for Thomas Coke in imitation of Versailles which is often described as the most perfect example of a late-seventeenth-century garden in England. One might have supposed that the scale was so different that such an imitation would be impossible, but Coke had studied the architecture and garden design of Versailles, and George London had himself revisited Versailles in 1698 and met Le Nôtre. Coke was an interesting example of a civilized and knowledgeable owner. He drew his own designs for

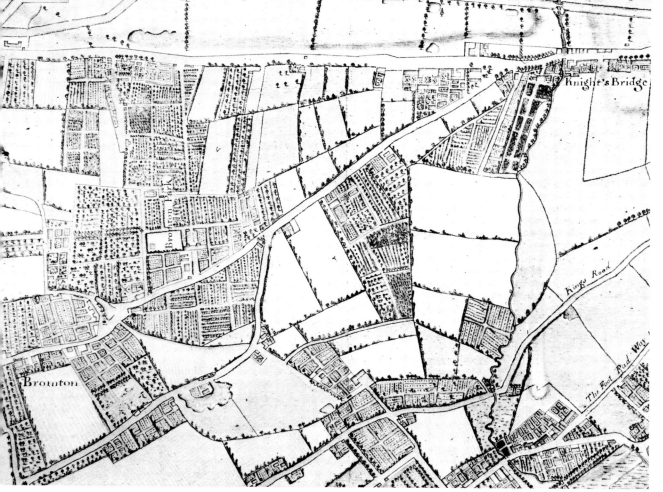

Henry Wise's house, Brompton Park, is completely surrounded by the growing-on beds of his Brompton Park Nursery in this map of 1717.

every stage of his garden development, but then sent them to London and Wise for comment. The same applied when London worked for the Earl of Carlisle at Castle Howard in 1699. Carlisle had strong ideas and it was important that London should work well with him as well as Vanbrugh and Hawksmoor. The final design for Ray Wood was the result of a composite decision.

In the same year, Henry Wise was called in by William III for further advice at Hampton Court. Wise's estimate for the work amounted to £6,638 14s 3d – a vast sum in those days, most of it attributable to digging out part of the semi-circular canal rather than planting. Wise continued to be associated with the garden at Hampton Court right through until the death of George I in 1727 and even built himself a house nearby so that he could be on hand to advise and over-see the gardens. He did the same at Blenheim when working on the Duke of Marlborough's gardens.

Shortly after Queen Anne's accession, Wise was engaged by her as Master Gardener and carried out extensive work at Hampton Court, Kensington Palace and her favourite residence, Windsor Castle. William III had consistently overspent his budget and left his sister-in-law, Queen Anne, with heavy debts when he died in 1702. She started her reign with a determination to cut back on royal expenses, deciding, for example, that the annual maintenance budget for the royal parks, which had cost £5,000 in the last years of William III's reign, should be reduced to £3,360 a year. The parsimonious influence of her favourite, the Duchess of Marlborough, was undoubtedly a factor in these early years of her reign. But Queen Anne was an enthusiastic plantswoman and could not deny herself the pleasures of gardening for ever. By the end of the fourth year of her reign, she had already spent over £25,000 on Kensington alone. Wise's work there received unqualified praise from such an unlikely critic as Joseph Addison in *The Spectator*. However, the Queen's reputation for parsimony then took another form and she became notorious for delays in settling her accounts. It was not unknown for crown contractors like Wise to wait as long as four years for their accounts to be paid. Tilleman Bobart, whose job was to maintain the grass and gravel walks at Hampton Court, claimed for nine years' arrears of salary in 1707.

Wise's biggest commission was to lay out, maintain and later extend the gardens at Blenheim, which were built by a grateful nation to add honour and glory to the name of Marlborough. House and garden alike were to be a monument to military prowess. Marlborough was an enthusiast for both strategy and detail. He wrote to his wife from the battle-front in 1707, urging her to try the fruits of all the fruit trees 'so that what is not good might be changed', adding that 'on this matter you must advise with Mr Wise'. But Wise had chosen well and ensured that the fruit gardens at Blenheim flourished. Nine years later Vanbrugh declared that 'the Kitchen Garden, now [that] the trees are in full vigour and full of fruit is really an astonishing sight. All I ever saw in England or abroad of the kind are trifles to it.' The renown of the fruit gardens at Blenheim was to last right through the eighteenth century. The scale of the flower-plantings at Blenheim was enormous too. In 1707, the Brompton Park Nursery supplied 18,500 yellow crocus (at 1s 6d per 100), 4,600 tulips, 5,100 hyacinths and 5,600 double white narcissus for the Duchess's flower garden alone. By the time Henry Wise died in 1738, he was worth over £100,000 – perhaps £10 million by today's values, and quite an achievement for a man whose origins were so modest that even his place of birth is unknown.

Gentry Gardens

The middle classes and the gentry have almost always made substantially different gardens from those of the landed aristocracy. Until quite recently the super-rich have usually been the trailblazers of fashion – men of power and influence, with large estates. The gentry could not afford to follow the same fashions, at least not on the same scale; their gardens had to fit with an entirely different lifestyle.

One result of the peace which came to England in 1660 was that all landowners felt able to make long-term investments in their land, undertaking improvements to buildings and spending money on tree-planting. They were helped by laws which stipulated that real property – meaning freehold – passed to a landowner's eldest son. These enactments were bolstered by the development of strict settlements which ensured that the 'tenant for life' was restricted in his powers of alienation. This meant that landowners, great and small, could plan for several generations ahead – and not just large landowners, but gentlemen and farmers of every size, provided their holdings were freehold. The main concern of country gentlemen has always been to run their estates as profitably as possible.

This detail from a seventeenth-century English School embroidered hanging shows an unidentified formal garden decked with orange trees. Put out in pots for the summer and over-wintered in the orangery, oranges were great status symbols in the seventeenth and early eighteenth centuries.

that people knew him and sought his advice on a wide spectrum of problems. And, in all he did, he showed an overriding willingness to discuss, encourage, commend and intervene. Evelyn had not enjoyed the Commonwealth years, but used them to

travel, study, assist the royal family in exile and latterly to write. Early in the 1650s he wrote a month-by-month calendar – his *Kalendarium Hortense or Gard'ners Almanac* – which listed jobs to do (and fruit and flowers in their prime) month by month, in the orchard, kitchen garden, formal garden and flower garden.[34] To this he added a note on hardiness, listing plants in three categories or degrees of hardiness. It was the first gardener's calendar published in England.

Evelyn's main concern towards the end of the Commonwealth was the relentless despoliation of the English woodland, which had continued for so many centuries that parts of the country – most notably the Midlands – were almost treeless. He took objection to the Parliamentarian policy of despoiling woods and forests: during the Commonwealth 'it was more the Custom to cut down, than to plant and repair Plantations'.[35] It was this habit of felling timber (and the need for

John Evelyn, seen here in the frontispiece to his Sylva, *1664, dominated the English garden scene in the latter half of the seventeenth century. His books on trees and fruit-growing were classic reference books for several generations.*

royalists to do so too, to pay for their compositions) which inspired Evelyn to understand and articulate the need for replanting. His study of the problem was published in 1664 as *Sylva*. It became a very influential book because, for the first time, people saw the planting of timber as a means of increasing the value of their estates, and ultimately their income too. Planting came to be regarded as a patriotic duty; there was, moreover, an association between Charles II and oak trees. One of the main purposes of Evelyn's efforts to repair English forests was to provide good oak for the Royal Navy and it is said that many of the plantations which were made by his readers grew to maturity in time to help Nelson and the British fleet to victory over Napoleon.

Daniel Defoe, writing in the 1730s, held up the example of Theobalds as typical of many estates at this time:

[it] was a very beautiful Place, when K. James resided at Theobalds ... but it has suffered several Depredations since that, and in particular in the late Time of Usurpation, when it was stript, both of Game and Timber, and let out in Farms to Tenants for the Use of the Publick. After the Restoration it was laid open

again; Woods and Groves were every-where planted, and the whole Chase stocked with Deer.[36]

Sylva ran to no fewer than four editions in Evelyn's own lifetime. The poet Robert Southey (1774–1843) said that it was 'one of the few books in the world which completely effected what it was designed to do'. Evelyn himself wrote that it had been

the occasion of propagating many millions of usefull timber-trees thro'out this nation ... His late Ma[jes]ty Cha. the 2d. was sometimes graciously pleased to take notice of it to me, & that I had by that booke alone incited a world of planters to repair their broken estates and woodes, which the greedy rebels had wasted & made such havoc of.

John Evelyn was enormously influential. His opinion was sought on every subject and he was much quoted by other writers: he was the great authority. But he had shortcomings, too, which deprived us of the major work on plants and

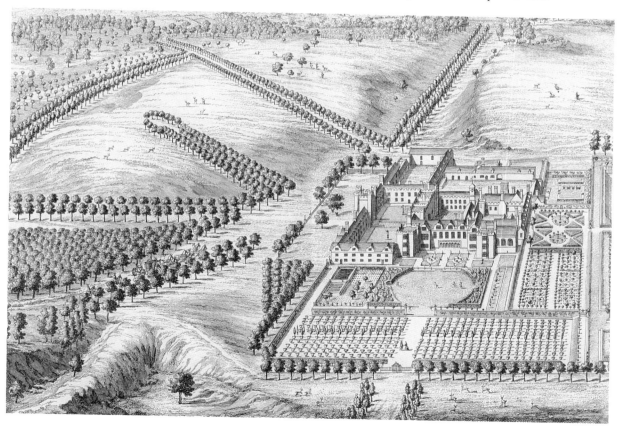

The South Prospect of Knole, *a bird's-eye view, engraved by Johannes Kip, c. 1705. Knole was typical of the many country houses made grander still by planting long new avenues.*

gardens which he planned under the draft name of *Elysium Britannicum*. For a number of reasons, he never felt able to organize and complete it.

As a very old man in 1699, however, Evelyn did remind us, in true Ciceronian prose, of how even the greatest men might decide after a lifetime of public service to retire to the country and absorb themselves in gardening. It was a more fulfilling way to end their days and years:

> How much might I say of Gardens and Rural Employments, preferable to the Pomp and Grandeur of other Secular Business, and that in the Estimate of as Great Men as any Age has produc'd! And it is of such Great Souls we have it recorded; That after they had perform'd the noblest Exploits for the Publick, they sometimes chang'd their Sceptres for the Spade, and their Purple for the Gardiner's Apron. And of these some were Emperors, Kings, Consuls, Dictators, and Wise Statesmen; who amidst the most important Affairs, both in Peace and War, have quitted all their Pomp and Dignity in Exchange of this Learned Pleasure: Not that of the most refin'd Part of Agriculture (the Philosophy of the Garden and Parterre) only but of Herbs and wholsom Sallets, and other plain and useful Parts of Geoponicks, and wrote Books of Tillage and Husbandry; and took the Plough-Tackle for their Banner, and their Names from the Grain and Pulse they sow'd, as the Marks and Characters of the highest Honour.[37]

It was a potent evocation of the ancient Roman lifestyle and an assertion of the superiority of country life. In all this, John Evelyn was thinking and writing as a classicist and philosopher himself. But he was also strongly aware of the shortcomings of ancient gardens and a committed believer in the superiority of modern gardening. By the 1690s, he was prepared to say that the gardens of the ancients 'had certainly nothing approaching the elegancy of the present age'. Gardens of the ancient Romans were no more than plots of ground with shady trees arranged in walks and surrounded by porticos, pillars and architectural decorations. The ancients cared little for flowers and had less variety in their fruits and vegetables.[38]

Science versus the Classics

On 28 November 1660, the Royal Society was founded with the aim of promoting 'physico-mathematical experimental learning'.[39] Horticulture is a science and for over 100 years the work of the Royal Society was crucial to the development of gardening in England. The early success of the Royal Society showed how widespread was support for its perceived aims.

There is always a slight dichotomy between the legal statutes of a body like the Royal Society and the way it actually conducts its business. The society's statutes declared that 'the business of the Society in their Ordinary Meetings shall be . . . to view, and to discourse upon, rareties of nature and art; and thereupon to consider, what may be deduced from them . . . and how far they may be improved for use'. That was fine for the conduct of meetings, but the thinking behind the society's foundation went much deeper. Francis Bacon had certainly been a considerable influence. Bacon was convinced that knowledge was power and that by harnessing nature men could derive great benefit for mankind. Nature could be tamed only by experiment and the application of natural laws.

There are various accounts of what the Royal Society was really *for*. John Evelyn described its purpose as 'the Augmentation of Science, and universal good of Mankind'. 'Science' had a fairly technical meaning at the time – it conjured images of philosophy, wisdom and truth. The best summary of the Royal Society's purposes comes from one of its early secretaries, Thomas Sprat, later Bishop of Rochester, who declared that its aim was 'to make faithful *Records*, of all the Works of *Nature*, or *Art*, which can come within their reach: that so the present Age, and posterity, may be able to put out a mark on the Errors, which have been strengthened by long prescription'.[40]

Those errors of long prescription were twofold: superstition and the classics. Henceforth, science – and this included horticulture – was to be based on experiment and observation. In common with all the natural sciences in the early seventeenth century, gardening was still dominated by Aristotelian philosophy. Sound practices were undermined by ancient superstitions like the habit of sowing seeds at times which coincided with particular phases of the moon. As late as 1676, Moses Cook was warning his readers to avoid erroneous ideas like boring a hole in a tree and pouring honey into it to make its fruit sweet, or watering seeds with coloured water so that they would produce flowers of that colour.[41] Henceforth, garden-writers would continue to refer to classical authors only so long as these references reinforced their own empirical knowledge. They would drop their references to the doctrine of signatures and the phases of the moon. Botany and plantsmanship would no longer be seen as a medical science: plants would be studied and grown for their own sake. Horticulture would no longer be practised according to the rules laid down by Pliny and Virgil: modern authorities would take precedence over ancient. The Royal Society began 'the process of creating new sciences in which an organized body of related inductive knowledge, capable of continuous, unlimited development, could be built up, for the long-term benefit of mankind'.[42] In short, the modernizers had won the battle for the soul of English science.

The upshot can best be traced in the books about gardening which were published during the second half of the seventeenth century and beyond. The most impressive was John Ray's *Historia Plantarum*, which was published in three volumes between 1686 and 1704 and amounted to a complete and systematic list of all plants in the world – a world botany, something which could now be attempted only with the most modern databases. It also contains information on the propagation and cultivation of plants and essays on morphology and taxonomy, all of which read as if they might have been written today.

John Ray the Essex botanist should not be confused with John Rea the Shropshire gentleman-gardener. Rea was a passionate plantsman and plant-collector for whom the chief pleasure of gardening was the pleasure of cultivating plants. Rea's *Flora* was also of enormous importance. His opening words say it all: 'Forty years are now completed, since first I began to be a Planter, and to dedicate more time than I could have spared for Diversion, to that lovely Recreation.' His book includes practical advice on how to set out a garden, dividing the flower garden from the fruit garden and edging the beds with box; how and where to plant things as different as roses, clematis and primroses; how to prepare a nursery bed; the choice and use of garden tools; how to take cuttings; and how to make a hot bed. Rea cannot be faulted on practicalities: every gardener would agree, for example, that 'the best Soil, is that, which is neither Clay nor Sand, but partaking of both'.[43] And he emphasized that the information in his book was 'not taken out of simple Books (the Publishers and Retainers of many Untruths) but learned from my own Practical Experience'. It is the voice of the new empirical gardener.

Rea's *Flora* is an enormously detailed and competent book which aimed to describe every worthwhile plant then in cultivation in England. He saw it as an updated Parkinson's *Paradisi in Sole, Paradisus Terrestris*: the lists of tulips, carnations, ranunculi, anemones and irises are particularly long. It is difficult even today to better many of his descriptions of plants. Take this account of the Crown Imperial *Fritillaria imperialis*, for example:

> The *Crown Imperial* hath a great round Fox-scented root, from which springeth up a tall and strong stalk, garnished from the ground until the middle thereof, with many long shining green leaves, from whence it is naked upwards, bearing at the top a tuft of small green leaves, and under them eight or ten flowers, according to the age of the Plant, hanging down round about the stalk, in fashion like unto a *Lily*, consisting of six leaves [petals], of an *Orange* colour, with many veins of a deeper colour on the backsides of the flowers; next the stalks every leaf thereof hath a bunch or eminence of a sadder *Orange* colour than the rest of the flowers, and on the inside those bunches are filled with sweet-tasted clear drops of water, like unto Pearls, each flower having in the middle a stile compassed with six white chives tipt with yellow pendants.

He then goes on to describe two variant forms: the double-flowered and the yellow-flowered forms. Throughout Rea's book there is no reference to lunar planting or to God Almighty or to the noble writers of classical times; he based his writings purely upon observation.

Quite different was the sort of hands-on gardening manual which started to appear. A typical example is William Hughes's *The Flower Garden*, published in 1672, a tiny, practical pocket-book packed with useful information for the working gardener. Hughes himself said that he wrote for 'Flowrists, Gardeners, or others ... but chiefly for more plain and ordinary Country men and women as a perpetual Remembrancer ...' Here is an extract from the first two pages:

> Whosoever they are that intend a Flower Garden, ought to have either a Nurserie, or else some convenient place in the Kitchen Garden, both for the making of hot Beds whereon to raise tender Plants (by Seeds) that will not endure the Winter; as also to have other necessary beds therein of good earth, fit to sow such Seed on that requires not so great a heat as the other: which seedlings when they are grown up, may be immediately removed into the Flower-Garden, or else set in some order in the same place, or on a fitting Bed in that Garden, to remain until such time they bear Flowers; and then those which are double, and such other as are acceptable, may be transplanted into such places of the Flower-Garden as you see convenient; and the rest may be cast away as little worth.

Note that the advantage of using a hot bed to germinate certain seeds is clearly understood: detailed instructions follow for its construction, mainly from fermenting dung and straw. Note also that Hughes writes for women as much as for men. Note again the assumption that we can control the growing conditions of plants in any way that we wish. Hughes recommends hot-bed treatment for four flowers, all of them tender in the English climate: amaranthus, French marigolds, nasturtiums and Marvel of Peru.[44] Then he goes on to list those plants which may be raised without a need for heated compost. Note finally that there is no suggestion that any of these plants have to be sown in accordance with the phases of the moon – rational observation has overtaken superstition at last. Hughes then goes on to list the plants which can and should best be raised from cuttings, slips, offsets and layers. Roses, for example, 'are increased by Layers; they ought to be cut with the Sheers after they have done bearing; these may also be increased by Suckers or Inoculation'. The book is also full of useful cultivation tips – short, accurate and based upon hands-on experience. For example:

> Those who have good *Tulips* [should] arch the bed over with sticks or Cooper's Hoops, when they are budded and almost ready to Flower, that so they may be

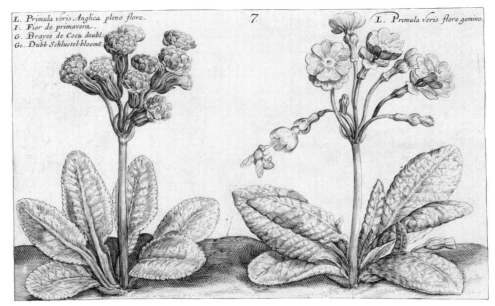

All primulas – and especially auriculas – were fashionable in the seventeenth and eighteenth centuries. This engraving by Crispijn de Passe from Hortus Floridus, *1616, portrays the double and hose-in-hose forms of* Primula veris, *the common cowslip.*

covered in the night to defend them from Frost, Hail, great Rains and high Winds, and also from extream heat, especially when they are fully blown, for then a little Sun is enough for them; and so ordered they may last in Splendour the longer.

From now on there was really no excuse for fanciful regimes of cultivation, improbable mixes of compost (deer dung and chicken's blood), trimming the operations of gardening to accord with astrology or astronomy, or any other pseudo-science. Horticultural practices must be based on the experience of gardeners, both the individual and the accumulated knowledge of others over the years. 'Primroses, both yellow and red, which are most of all esteemed and planted in Gardens … are increased by parting the roots about *October* or *November*.' Plants are best transplanted in wet weather; ranunculi prefer sandy soil and can be propagated by splitting the roots when you replant them; lilies are best propagated from offsets or bulbils; arbutus (strawberry trees) come best from slips or layers rooted in the protection of a south-facing wall. The advice is correct even today.

Hughes was interested in plants, and the introduction of new ones.

So wonderful are the works of Nature, that the least grass doth not only deserve our contemplation, but admiration; much more admirable then are the various beautiful

Flowers, and evergreens (far surpassing all Art) in a good and well-ordered Garden; which are already reconciled to this our colder Climate, and doubtless many more in time will be, especially if those learnèd of the Royal Society, whose fancies run this way, would be pleased to imploy their further indeavours herein.

So Hughes was a firm follower of the Society and its scientific approach. But he still explained his love of plants in terms of religious awe for God's creation: God had made Man from the dust of the earth 'and put him in an undoubtedly pleasant garden, but he, by reason of his disobedience, being turned forth, it is impossible for us his posterity ever to attain unto the like here below; yet doubtless by industry and pains taking in that lovely, honest, and delightful recreation of planting, we may gain some little glimmering of that lost splendour'.

A third example of the new type of practical gardening book that was beginning to emerge was Moses Cook's *The Manner of Raising, Ordering and Improving Forrest-Trees*, published in London in 1676. Cook is important because he was head gardener to the Earl of Essex, a great plantsman, and because he (Cook) went on to become one of the founders of the Brompton Park Nursery. He explained that he was writing for those who 'take delight in Planting or Gardening, or to raise and improve Forrest-trees, or to make Walks, Avenues or Lawns'. Cook clearly had no problem reconciling science and religion. The same was true of all the leading 'scientists' of the day, including John Evelyn. Cook held that it was God's intention that the Sons of Men 'should take care of those [plants] which are tender, lest they should be lost': this feeling that man has care of God's creation is an early example of understanding and concern for the natural world as a whole – what we would call 'the environment'. Cook also explained the way he had learned about plants and gardening:

I always took Notes of what [I] did set or sow, the Time, and on what Ground, and when it proved well, I noted it so; but when ill, I did endeavour as much as I could to know the Reason; which when once I found, I noted it well: I also alwayes was very wary of taking things upon trust; and if any man told me any thing, unles he had sufficient Experience of it, or could give some very good Reasons why it was so, I was always incredulous of it, unless my Judgement told me it was so, or he by Discourse made it plain to me.

Cook had a pragmatic and non-dogmatic approach to gardening practices. One of the most lively debates at this time was between the modernists, who thought that all technical and philosophical activity should be based upon empirical, practical experience, and the classicists, who preferred to emphasize the importance of the wisdom of the ancients. The most remarkable thing to our modern eyes is the absolute necessity of putting current horticultural practices in the context of classical writers. There were notable exceptions – like John Rae – but an obsession with classical precedent was to dog English horticultural thinking almost to the end of the eighteenth century. Most writers of the seventeenth century give credence to the works of Virgil, Pliny and every other ancient whose extant writings could in any way be said to have a bearing on horticultural practices.

John Evelyn resolved this by maintaining that one should refer to the ancient classical authorities on matters of beauty and to modern contemporary sources for scientific questions. Men should acknowledge the example of the ancients and Englishmen might even think of themselves as the new Romans, but they should understand that they lived in a world where modern scientific knowledge was of increasing importance. John Worlidge, writing in 1681, insisted that 'the excellency of a Garden is better manifested by Experience' than from ancient books.[45] Stephen Switzer in 1718 maintained that 'the Precepts of the Cultivating part of Gardening, depend on Observation and Experience; but this of *Designing*, on a noble and correct Judgement and Taste of Things'. Taste was an eighteenth-century preoccupation; for the time being it is enough to note that the style of many seventeenth-century writers on gardening was simple, direct and functional.

Plantsmen & Florists

After the restoration of Charles II, there was a considerable growth of interest in acquiring and cultivating plants – what we would now call plantsmanship. Writing in 1691, John Aubrey was convinced that there had been an explosion of enthusiasm for gardening and exotic plants:

> in the time of King Charles IId, Gardening was much improved and became common: I doe beleeve, I may modestly affirm, that there is now ten times as much gardning about London as there was in Anno 1660: and we have been since that time much improved in foreign plants: especially since about 1683, there have been exotick Plants brought into England, no lesse than seven thousand.[46]

Although this may be an exaggeration – and does not do credit to earlier plantsmen like the Tradescants – it should be remembered that men of culture and intellect at this time were collectors of curiosities: John Evelyn refers to cabinets 'both of Art & Nature'.[47] And one of the characteristics of a gentleman which distinguished him from a man who was merely rich and successful was that he should be a connoisseur, someone who had acquired scientific skills and artistic understanding through study and collecting. For many, it might take the form of collecting prints or books. Others collected plants and grew them for the general good or as embellishments to their own lifestyles. These displays distinguished their owners as civilized members of the upper classes.

John Rea was the most competent all-round plantsman in the early years after the Restoration. He was reputed to have the largest collection of auriculas and tulips in the country. He was never a conspicuous or widely known man. Indeed, John Evelyn, who knew everyone important, had never heard of him until Rea published his book *Flora* in 1665. We need not attach too much significance to this. It is best at every historic period to think of the gardening world as made up of a series of groups which overlap only slightly, so that some members will know each other well and others not at all. Rea was certainly a friend of the Welsh plantsman Sir Thomas Hanmer, who was in turn a friend of John Evelyn.

We have already encountered Rea's *Flora* as an example of empirical scientific writing. It was complemented by similar, but shorter works called *Pomona* and *Ceres*, published all as one. *Ceres* deals with 'such pretty Plants and fine Flowers as are yearly, or every other year raised from seeds' – that is, annuals and biennials. *Pomona* is an enthusiastic treatise on fruit and fruit-growing. But their relative importance is made clear in the frontispiece to *Flora*, which shows Flora crowned as a queen, attended by her lesser maids of honour, Pomona and Ceres.

Our concern here is with Rea as a plantsman who set out 'to inform all such as desire to be Florists, how they may do as I have done, [and] make their own Garden themselves, assisted only by ordinary labourers'. Rea knew that a plantsman's garden is best maintained by the owner with a little unskilled help with jobs that do not require horticultural knowledge. He then pointed out that 'fair Houses are more frequent than fine Gardens' because the former are built by 'artificers', while the latter require 'more skill in the owner, few Gardens being found well furnished out of the hands of an affectionate Florist', meaning a keen plantsman. He also maintained that

> it is impossible for any Man to have any considerable Collection of noble Plants to prosper, unless he loves them ... A choice Collection of living Beauties, rare Plants, Flowers and Fruits, are indeed the wealth, glory and delight of a Garden, and the most absolute indications of the Owners ingenuity, whose skill and care is chiefly required in their Choice, Culture and Position.

Rea also sold plants, which may explain why he was fairly scathing about the time-wasters who sometimes came to his garden. 'I have known many persons of Fortune pretend much affection to Flowers, but very unwilling to part with anything to purchase them; yet if obtained by begging, or perhaps by stealing, contented to give them entertainment.' Modern plantsmen will readily recognize this type of garden visitor – the sort you conduct about your garden, offering them plants which they gladly accept (even the most common), but who do not make an effort to buy, breed or offer similar treasures themselves.

One of the leading plantswomen towards the end of the seventeenth century was Mary, Duchess of Beaufort, the first person to fruit pawpaws and guavas in England. She corresponded and exchanged plants with the leading botanists of her day, including the Bobarts, father and son, at the Oxford Botanic Garden, and Sir Hans Sloane of the Chelsea Physic Garden. She also employed two watercolourists to paint all her exotic plants, just as a modern plantsman might set out to make a photographic record of his garden plants today. Her sister Elizabeth, Countess of Carnarvon, was also a keen botanist and a competent flower painter. Together the sisters were the first English plantswomen of real distinction. One of their brothers was the Earl of Essex of Cassiobury, of whom John Evelyn wrote that 'no man was more industrious than the Earl in planting' – mainly trees, but also exotic plants under the guidance of his head gardener,

Mary Capel, Duchess of Beaufort, and her sister Elizabeth, Countess of Carnarvon, painted by Sir Peter Lely, c. 1658, were knowledgeable and passionate about plants – as were their brothers, the second Earl of Essex and Lord Capel of Tewkesbury.

Moses Cook. The Kip drawing of Cassiobury shows that he planted so many trees that his estate resembled a French or German one, with rides cut out of the woodlands and forests. Their other brother, Lord Capel of Tewkesbury, was a noted cultivator of fruit. His house at Kew had two conservatories attached to it, for the cultivation of oranges and 'myrtiles'. A love of plants, moreover, bridged the social, political and religious divides that cut so deeply into society at the time. The keen amateur plantsmen in John Evelyn's circle included two Catholics – the philanthropist Robert Berkeley of Spetchley and Henry Mordaunt, second Earl of Peterborough (1624–97), a keen genealogist. Alexander Pope, a Catholic and a Tory, was an intimate friend of the Protestant Whig Lord Burlington.

England never suffered from 'tulipomania' to the extent that it gripped the Netherlands. The most popular florists' plants in the seventeenth century were auriculas: colour forms in almost every shade were developed from white and yellow through to brown, crimson, red, purple, violet and various striped combination. Green-edged and white-eyed flowers followed in the middle of the eighteenth century and the tradition of breeding show auriculas continued well into the nineteenth century. Novelty drove the market: a new cultivar would appear, enjoy a few years of glory and then sink into obscurity, to be replaced by another. At the height of its fashion, when first introduced, a new cultivar could command a very high price. 'Some few years ago,' remarked Richard Bradley in 1717, 'a single auricula root sold for 20 guineas.'

Garden tools have changed little over the years. In *Flora*, John Rea advised that the following tools were necessary:

> a Skreen, a Wier-Ridle, two Spades, a bigger and a lesser, likewise Shovels, and Howes of several sizes, a Pruining-hook, Grafting-knives, a Saw, a Chisel and Mallet, and also a small penknife for Inoculating, and laying of Gilliflowers, a Line and Rule, Trowels of several sizes, a handsom Hammer, with two pair of Garden-shears, and two Iron Rakes, a

Most of the tools in John Evelyn's Elysium Britannicum *are clearly identifiable today: the piece of lattice was for planting bulbs at regular intervals.*

bigger and longer in the head, and a shorter with the Teeth thicker set, with several Baskets of Twigs, and Besoms, to sweep and carry away the cleanings of the Gardens.

He also recommended stoves or hearths to keep the temperature up against frosts, a series of manure heaps, a water supply, and three watering cans:

one with a head full of small holes to water plants in summer; one with just a pipe to water pots with rank water wherein the Dung of Sheep, Poultry & etc hath been steeped, that it may be put to the roots without staining the leaves; the third one with a small neck but a bottom full of holes which you control by putting your thumb over the hole at the top & letting in air to let out the water – for gentle watering of young & tender sedlings without washing the earth from them, for by the motion of your thumb you may cause the water to fall gently upon them, more or less as you shall desire.

Most of these tools had been in existence for centuries, though watering cans date back no further than the 1540s. The main omissions are hand-forks (a nineteenth-century invention) and scythes to cut the grass. But mowing was not a task to be undertaken by gardeners. It was the province of specialist mowers, who scythed the grass but ranked below gardeners in the hierarchy of domestic service and were treated as semi-skilled labourers.

Professionals

Towards the end of the seventeenth century, top-flight garden designers like London and Wise began to emerge. They sold high fashions and matched them with high fees. They also spawned a host of imitators who operated in less exalted markets. Stephen Switzer insisted that money was well spent on good design and that owners who failed to plan their gardens properly would regret their omissions and end up the poorer for it. He was particularly scathing of 'several *Northern* Lads which . . . by the help of a little Learning, and a great deal of Impudence . . . invade the *Southern* provinces and . . . pretend to know more in one Twelve-month, than a laborious, honest *Southern* Countryman does in Seven Years'.[48]

It is a common trait among all professionals and tradesmen to decry their business rivals and insist that patrons should be prepared to pay for quality. But for a man to be successful he needs to hold out more than criticism of his competitors. The best designers, like London and Wise, offer something which is seen to be innovative and better than anyone else's. They also have an agreeable social manner which enables them to anticipate and sympathize with the requirements of their clients. They move forward on a wave of personal recommendations from satisfied clients. This was as true of London and Wise in the seventeenth century as of Capability Brown in the eighteenth, William Nesfield in the nineteenth and Gertrude Jekyll and Norah Lindsey in the twentieth. Against that, it must be remembered that only a small fraction of gardens are ever designed by professionals. Most are worked out on paper by their owners, and brought into being with help from gardeners, tradesmen and labourers. Alexander Pope was certain that every man should be his own gardener: 'I have long been convinced that neither Acres, nor Wife; nor any publick Professors of Gardening, (any more than any publick Professors of Virtue) are equal to the Private Practisers of it,' he wrote.

The salaries and wages paid to gardeners in around 1700 differed at all levels from region to region and from garden to garden – much more than we would expect nowadays. Henry Wise, the royal gardener, was paid £200 a year in 1702 by Queen Anne to oversee the maintenance of all the royal gardens – Hampton Court, Windsor Castle, Kensington Palace and St James's. In 1722, the Duke of Chandos's head gardener at Canons, Middlesex, enjoyed an annual salary of £100. This can be compared with the Duke's other principal servants: his chaplain was paid £75 and his chief steward £50. Keith Thomas relates that 'in 1683 the new gardener asked £80 per annum for looking after the grounds at Lyme Hall in Cheshire; he was beaten down to £60, equivalent to the income of a well-to-do clergyman. On Easter Day he appeared in a suit with gold buttons, "better worth than two of my best suits", wryly commented his employer, Richard Legh.'[49] At Stow Bardolph in 1712 the gardener was paid £50 per year and was also allowed to dispose of surplus vegetables for his own profit. On the other hand, he had to supply and pay for his own team of labourers out of that salary.[50]

We need therefore to know what the gardener's duties included. In the case of Stow Bardolph he was expected to keep all 'the gardens, courtyards, orchards and walkes ... according to the best of his skill and knowledge'. He had to 'maintain and keep and furnish ... Stow Hall with all necessary and sufficient kitchen garden stuffe ... raise inlay graft and plant as well all sorts of wall fruit, vines and other Fruit ... also all sorts of Greens (as climit will allow) pinkes, tulips and other flowers'.[51]

We also need to know what level of education and special technical knowledge were required of a gardener. A head gardener was certainly expected to be able to read and write, to be capable of keeping accounts and to have some knowledge of geometry for laying out beds and planting them. He would probably possess a small practical handbook to refer to for solutions to problems and to remind him fruit as I suffer or desire them, and as well tasted as are commonly brought over'.

Temple was also one of many observers who maintained that gardening in England had 'grown into such vogue, and to have been so mightily improved in His Majesty's reign, that perhaps few countries are before us, either in the elegance of our gardens, or in the number of our plants'.[57] This is a view that recurs throughout the history of English gardening – the certainty that, when a person looks back over the last few years, he will find that things are much improved.

This was the period when the excellence of their gardens and the skill of their gardeners became part of the English national identity. Pepys believed, 'We have the best gravel walks in the world, France having none nor Italy; and the green of our bowling alleys is better than any they have.'[58] Pepys, of course, never visited Italy. John Worlidge, in 1677, believed that a delight in gardens applied to Englishmen of all degrees: 'The noble in his country seat, the shopkeeper with his plants and the cottage dweller with his garden ... Neither is there ... scarce an Ingenious Citizen that by his confinement to a Shop, being denied the priviledge of having a real Garden, but hath his boxes, pots, or other receptacles for Flowers, Plants & etc.'[59] John Evelyn was more fastidious about the taste –

Hendrik Danckerts painted the Duke and Duchess of Lauderdale walking in the garden at Ham House, c. 1675. Throughout the seventeenth century the grassy areas outside the formal garden were increasingly used for walking and recreation.

or lack of it – which the labouring town-dweller showed for plants and gardens. In a letter to Sir Thomas Browne, written in the stylized prose which both adopted for such correspondence, he testified to his own 'abhorrency of those painted and formal projections of our cocknet gardens and plotts, which appeare like gardens of past-board and march-payne, and smell more of paynt then of flowers and verdure'.

Even in the seventeenth century, people visited gardens, as they would visit houses, to see exciting novelties such as a new garden building or a new plant. Here is an example which John Evelyn noted in his diary on 27 August 1678:

> After dinner I walk'd to Ham, to see the house and garden of the Duke of Lauderdale, which is indeede inferior to few of the best villas in Italy itself; the house furnish'd like a great Prince's; the parterres, flower gardens, orangeries, avenues, courts, statues, perspectives, fountaines, aviaries, and all this att the banks of the sweetest river in the world, must needes be wonderful.

From about 1700 onwards, garden-visiting – and more especially house-visiting – became a national pastime among the well-to-do. It was up to the housekeeper to decide whether to entertain such callers and normally the visitor would give her some pecuniary recognition by way of thanks. Novelty was what drew them; the old was old-fashioned, and held no charms. This is noticeable in Celia Fiennes's diaries. When she visited the Earl of Chesterfield's house at Bretby in Derbyshire in 1698, she found the Jacobean mansion somewhat lacking in modern features but commented that 'that which is most admired – and justly so to be – by all persons and excite their curiosity to come and see' were the gardens, which were still in the process of being laid out with magnificent waterworks by the French engineer Grillet.

Novelty was valued too among plantsmen – and still is today. Samuel Gilbert, in 1682, omitted what he called 'obsolete and overdated flowers' from his *Florists Vade Mecum*. John Rea regarded his *Flora* as an update of Parkinson's *Paradisi in Sole, Paradisus*

Polygala and Blue Convolvulus, *from the Duchess of Beaufort's* Florilegium *by Everhard Kik, 1703–5. The first Duchess of Beaufort was an avid plantswoman. Two watercolourists painted her entire collection of plants, just as a modern plantsman might take photographs.*

CHAPTER THREE

The Age of Elitism
1730–1820

The Influence of the Classics & the Grand Tour

The basis of all education in England until well into the twentieth century was the classics. Renaissance humanists – and that meant anyone with intellectual pretensions or credentials – looked to the classical world for the universal truths that governed contemporary human affairs. Their influence in England grew steadily, to reach a peak in the middle of the eighteenth century. The classics informed a man's tastes and directed the way he led his life; a classical education was designed to set a man apart from lesser breeds.

It also explained the political alignments within the English social system. Cicero taught that rich men had an obligation to take part in public life, while the lesser landowners – the gentry – could concern themselves with the proper management of their estates. This doctrine reinforced the Whig aristocracy's search for power and wealth from public office, and the Tory gentry's concern to secure and improve their inheritance. In the course of the seventeenth and eighteenth centuries, it became increasingly important that the ruling classes should be not only classically educated but cultivated, too. They should manifest their superior qualities through their command of culture. Houses and gardens became advertisements for the ruling classes. Virtuosos and dilettantes reinforced the message: the upper classes were collectors of books, works of art and other symbols of learning. They served to enhance the owner's prestige. So indeed did plants and gardens.

Taste mattered enormously. It was the mark of a gentleman. If you wanted to insult someone, you said that he had no taste. In 1722, the Earl of Oxford, seeking to offend his political rival, described Robert Walpole's house at Houghton as 'neither magnificent nor beautiful. There is a very great expense without either judgement or taste.' But, since taste is nothing more than fashion, it is surprising how much the eighteenth-century thinkers laboured to analyse and elucidate it.

✳ *Detail of the illustration on page 164.*

The philosopher Lord Shaftesbury, for example, wrote that the beautiful and the grotesque were opposites: 'on one side, Gothic architecture, Dutch paintings, Italian farce, Indian music: on the other, Attic numbers, Ionic and Corinthian orders, and the Greek models of every kind'.[1] Any educated man of taste 100 years later would study these lists with incredulity.

But classical tastes – classical fashions – spilled over into every aspect of gardens and garden-making. Garden-writers, for example, continued to be obsessed with precedents worthy to inspire and copy from the ancient writers. Even Philip Miller felt constrained to preface his great empirical work *The Gardeners Dictionary* with an essay which argued in true rhetorical style that his readers should learn from the ancients, and referred at excessive length to the gardens of Cyrus.

From about 1720 onwards, the larger English gardens began to fill up with classical buildings of every kind. Classical sculptures, too, were more widely displayed in gardens. Both were valued for their inspirational allusions, which could not be appreciated by the uneducated masses. Part of the attraction of the classical world was its ability to suggest educated associations between things: the deities, temples, orders and architectural forms all evoked ideas. Classicism also received a boost from the arrival of Palladianism, a stylized development or reinterpretation of classical and Renaissance architecture largely promoted by Lord Burlington. Palladian architecture was mainly for the very rich but it helps to explain the pro-

The Ruins at Shugborough, *oil on canvas by Nicholas Dall, 1775. The landscape and artificial ruins at Shugborough in Shropshire were made for Thomas Anson in the mid-eighteenth century.*

fusion of classical temples and garden buildings at the time. This Palladianism is traditionally seen as flowing from the growing popularity of the Grand Tour.

The Grand Tour arose out of a desire to visit Italy. It was a feature of English life which lasted roughly between 1600 and 1800, though it was by no means an exclusively English phenomenon – the French, Germans and other nationalities also did Grand Tours. The phrase 'Grand Tour' was first used in 1670. Young men travelled abroad with their tutors to complete their education. It was not a leisure activity; it was supposed to aid learning through contact with great art and history. Then, in the 1700s, the nature of the tour began to change as a slightly different type of person started doing it. They were not so much the academically earnest – though these continued to go – but rich young men out for a good party, the *jeunesse dorée* of the Augustan age. By the 1720s, travel to Italy came to be seen as a social accomplishment and a rite of passage. The typical young Englishman's tour was formalized into a set itinerary: by boat to France, by carriage to Paris and down to Marseilles, thence by boat to Leghorn or Civitavecchia, overland to Rome and Naples, then back via Venice, Switzerland, Germany and Calais again. As it became institutionalized, so the Grand Tour became even more of a social experience, with lots of English-style entertainments on the way.

The received wisdom is that England was fundamentally changed as a result of what these young bloods saw and did in Italy – that they were so inspired by love for the arts which they imbibed as young men that they returned to re-create their experience of classical civilization in such landscapes as Stowe, Rousham and Shotover. Palladian villas sprang up all over England, set in Claude-like gardens, strewn with imitation Temples of the Sibyl, and filled with copies of ancient and modern Roman sculpture.

The truth is that most of these young men went abroad not to improve themselves but to live it up with fellow playboys – carousing, wenching and networking. Most returned home with confused memories, and a firm conviction that their own country was vastly superior to any other they had seen. Only a minority added to our heritage by their collections and fewer still found anything in Italy to inspire their own endeavours in English parks and gardens. None brought home an Italian garden designer to lay out the land around their English seat. And Bridgeman never went on a Grand Tour. Nor did Switzer, or Shenstone, or Brown, or Repton.

However, the failure to acquire any lasting benefit from the Grand Tour did not affect the fashion for classicism at home. The cultivated lifestyle existed to demonstrate the wealth and power of the educated classes. The construction of a great country house and its embellishment with a classically inspired garden were assertions of patrician superiority.

In fact, some of the more charming details that emerge from the accounts of the Grand Tour relate to small individual actions. The young Lord Nuneham, for example, sent melon and broccoli seeds home from Florence in 1756. Similarly, the Earl of Rochford brought some cuttings of the Lombardy poplar back to St Osyth Priory in Essex in 1755, the first to be established in England. But he was in his late thirties – the age at which men become more interested in gardening. And, besides, he was not a real Grand Tourist – he was actually our envoy in Turin.

Grand Tourists have also been credited with starting the fashion for landscape gardening. The argument is that, during the seventeenth century, artists like Claude, Poussin and Salvator Rosa began to study and appreciate the landscape of the Roman Campagna. In the 1720s, long after all three were dead, their work became both collectable and collected. The young men who bought their paintings were so influenced by the beauty of their purchases that when they came home to England they started to turn their gardens into three-dimensional Claudes and Poussins. After all, Henry Hoare predicted that his creation at Stourhead would be 'a charm[in]g Gasp[ar] picture'.

The truth, however, is more complicated. The young men on their Grand Tours were looking for souvenirs. They could not acquire Old Masters like Raphael without enormous problems with export licences: the Italians were never going to let their best paintings leave the country. And important works of art were very expensive. So there was a short-lived fashion for the seventeenth-century landscape painters, as a more reasonably priced alternative. And, in fact, many tourists just commissioned copies of their favourite Old Masters from local artists; most were of religious subjects – Madonnas by Correggio, for example. The most copied of all was Guido Reni's *Aurora*. And there is no connection between what they brought home from Italy and what they did at home. It is true that the greatest collectors also built the most magnificent Palladian houses and glorious classical gardens – including Henry Hoare at Stourhead in Wiltshire, Thomas Coke, first Earl of Leicester, at Holkham in Norfolk, and William Weddell at Newby in Yorkshire. But these were men of exceptional intellectual ability, who distinguished themselves as politicians, scholars or professional men. And they all shared one common characteristic: they were *nouveaux riches* with lots of money to buy their way into social respectability.

The Origins of the Landscape Movement

It is when considering the rise of the landscape garden that art historians show the least understanding of the importance of social and economic factors. They insist that the great and uniquely English cultural phenomenon which attaches to the names of Kent, Brown and Repton owes all its inspiration, direction and development to the literary criticisms, the artistic tastes and the philosophical musings of an educated élite, an aristocracy of enthusiasm and their scholarly intimates. Nothing could be further from the truth.

Of course landscaped parks may be beautiful artistic creations that give expression to the deepest aesthetic needs of the noblemen and gentlemen who make or commission them. But that is not principally how they seemed at the time. Parks were not just a pretty setting for a house; nor were they just a beautiful prospect to be enjoyed from the main windows. They owed more to economic and social considerations: farming, forestry, sport. The landscape historian Tom Williamson explains it quite clearly: 'The landscape park grew out of the lifestyle of its owners and creators: it developed where and when it did because of changes in the nature of that lifestyle, and in the organization of society as a whole.'[2]

The eighteenth century was a period of Whig sleaze. A system of patronage was developed which kept political and financial power in the hands of a self-interested oligarchy. After the Hanoverian succession, political power shifted from the crown into the hands of the landed aristocracy, which tended to be based in the country for much of the year. This simple equation of country life and comfortable living gave a great impetus to the development of horticulture, landscaping and skills of cultivation. Members of the gentry were always hands-on in everything they did; household management, estate management and gardening all occupied them to a much greater degree than they concerned the greater landowners. The latter were more involved in national politics and international cultural activities in a way that the gentry were not. But slowly the aristocracy and the gentry began to realize that in their countryside interests they had much in common. This was important for gardens. Large formal gardens were divisive, and intended to emphasize the differences between the upper middle classes and the really rich. The landscape garden, by contrast, offered a formula that every landowner could copy, whatever the size of his estate. It had a unifying function.

After about 1700, large gardens started to become more simple. There was a gradual loss of the details which had characterized French and Dutch gardens and a consequent disintegration of the whole design. Topiary grew to a size where it cluttered the views, obstructed the paths and was out of proportion to the rest of the garden and difficult to maintain. It would be cut down but not replaced. It is very noticeable in the 1730s how plain the formal gardens are: squares of grass set in gravel and with only a few statues for ornament. Gardens also grew larger as more of them started to look out to the countryside beyond. Even after it had definitely arrived, not all owners – least of all the more modest ones – were instantly enamoured of the landscape style. Thomas Goldney III of Clifton exca-

A View of an End or Secondary Front of Lord Berkeley's New House,
The Durdans, Surrey, *oil on canvas by Jacob Scmits, c. 1689. The deer park was
the precursor of the English landscape park.*

vated a formal canal in the Dutch style as late as 1759. Geometrical gardening died
a long slow death – right through to the end of the eighteenth century.

Many writers, owners and designers have been credited with genius for inventing the landscape movement. Great claims, for example, have been made for Batty
Langley – a designer who appears to have made practically no gardens at all but
wrote a book called *New principles of Gardening* which is available for us to read.
Langley was fairly critical of the older formal gardens and asked, 'is there any
Thing more *shocking* than a *stiff regular garden*; where after we have seen one quarter thereof, the very same is repeated in all the remaining Parts, so that we are

tired, instead of being further entertain'd with something new?' Then he blamed it all upon Messrs London and Wise, 'who, being then suppos'd to be the best Gardeners in *England*, were employed by the *Nobility and Gentry of England* to lay out and plant their Gardens in that *regular, stiff and stuft up Manner* in which many yet appear'.[3] Langley then proposed a simpler style, with parterres of plain grass and no plants, which he said was '*entirely New*, as well as the most *grand* and *rural*'. Actually, it sounds very similar to Switzer's 'extensive or forest gardening'. All the plans that Langley adduces to support his argument seem to us absurdly formal and stilted. And, like Switzer, the first part of his book is jammed with long technical explanations of how to make geometrical shapes: examples start with such helpful phrases as 'to describe a Rhomboides, equal to the given lines and Angle' or 'to describe a Nonagon, or Enneagon, whose Sides shall be each equal to a given Line'.[4] Presumably Langley thought it was important to state his adherence to the natural style, because that was the way that taste was going, but since he does not seem to have designed real gardens or discussed his ideas with influential friends, we can dismiss him as an unimportant (but charming) name in the history of the landscape movement.

Who were the true founders of that uniquely English phenomenon the landscape movement? Despite what we are told by Horace Walpole we can ignore the claims of Alexander Pope and Joseph Addison. Pope may have commanded us to 'consult the genius of the place' but it was scarcely a new idea. John Evelyn had written, back in the previous century, 'at no hand therefore let our Workman enforce his plot to any particular Phantsy, but, contrive rather how to apply to it the best shape that will agree with the nature of the Place'.[5] In any case, the trouble with Pope's injunction is that the spirit of any given place is largely determined by man-made factors – above all, the farming landscape.

When Alexander Pope enjoined his readers to consult the genius of the place, he was giving them licence to make whatever sort of garden they wanted, provided it showed some evidence of a classical education, that all-important common factor among the well-to-do in the eighteenth century. In short, it was quite permissible to do whatever one wished in one's garden and on one's estate. Pope was influential, but only among a small coterie of self-conscious intellectuals that included such designers as Kent and such patrons as Burlington. Nevertheless, as the eighteenth century progresses, Pope's injunction to consult the genius of the place turns up time and again in contemporary writings about landscapes and landscape-making.

Horace Walpole has been a strong influence on our perceptions of how the landscape movement developed. But Walpole had his own agenda. He sought to prove that the English had created a unique, modern, natural style of laying out a garden, and that this could only have been brought about by the English. The art form was 'totally new, original and indisputedly English'. He linked it to the English political liberties which were such a part of his own heritage as a son of the greatest of Whig ministers, Sir Robert Walpole, who laid out the vast house and gardens at Houghton in Norfolk in the 1720s. Modern gardening was a result of 'the growth of the English Constitution' and all the 'happy combinations of an Empire of Freemen'; English gardens were demonstrably different from anything in all those nasty, repressive, autocratic, Catholic countries like France. Walpole does not allow any antecedents earlier than Addison and Pope. The writings of John Evelyn and Sir William Temple, which might have suggested the development of a landscape style of laying out pleasure grounds, he firmly ignores. Nevertheless, Walpole did discern the connection between the old deer parks and the modern landscaped parks: 'it is more extraordinary', he wrote, that 'having so long ago stumbled on the principle of modern gardening, we should have persisted in retaining its reverse, symmetrical and unnatural gardens'. He then sets up William Kent as the all-important painter-cum-landscaper who 'leaped the fence and saw that all nature was a garden'.

Walpole was not alone in seeing Kent as the inventor of natural landscape gardening. Philip Southcote – whose *ferme ornée* we shall examine shortly – once said to Joseph Spence that Lord Burlington and William Kent were 'the first introducers of the fine natural taste in gardening'. Spence then asked, 'which was the first of them that thought of it?' and Southcote replied that 'both pretended to that'. Burlington was a great patron, dilettante and collector. Robert Castell dedicated his *Villas of the Ancients Illustrated* to him. He was the embodiment of Palladian fashion and taste, but it was not a taste that everyone shared. Lord Hervey mocked Lord Burlington for building a house 'without a room to sleep or eat', while others questioned the suitability of Italianate architecture for the English climate. The lordly Whigs replied that Italianate architecture was Baroque (too foreign, too authoritarian and too Catholic), but Palladian architecture was classical. Certainly for new English houses and gardens Palladian classicism dominated the years between 1720 and 1760.

Designs for grand houses were published by Colen Campbell in his three-part *Vitruvius Britannicus* (London, 1715–25). Some were houses where he had been the architect, but most were based upon the work of Andrea Palladio (the '*Ne plus ultra* of his Art') and Inigo Jones (who had 'out-done all that went before') a century earlier. Campbell wanted to show his readers that the styles and skills derived from classical Rome were alive and well in England, where competent architects were able to offer the most modern and fashionable of houses. After Campbell's death, two further volumes were published by Badeslade and Rocque in 1739, many of whose elevations show these splendid Palladian mansions in the setting of their parks and gardens.

William Kent was a competent painter who lived in Rome between 1709 and 1719 and studied painting and architecture. He was patronized by three Englishmen: Burrell Massingberd, Thomas Coke and Lord Burlington. To Massingberd Kent sent copies he had made of paintings by Guido Reni, Annibale Carracci, Veronese and Poussin. He acted as a bear-leader for Coke, helping him to buy paintings and statues, and copying paintings – mainly Correggios. But Burlington and Kent got on so well that they returned to England together and Kent spent the rest of his life as an ornament to Burlington's household.

Gardens of Chiswick House from the West, *painted by Pieter Andreas Rysbrack (1690–1748), would suggest that the basis of Kent's reputation as the founder of the landscape movement is not always obvious.*

Horace Walpole considered Kent a great landscaper, the first to see that gardening might be inspired by landscape painting. But most of Kent's garden work was architectural. His first commission was the Temple of Venus at Stowe in 1731, followed shortly afterwards by a hermitage. Kent was seen to be so competent that he was then asked to landscape Vanbrugh's temple and belvedere at Claremont. Back at Stowe, in 1733, he built the Shell Bridge and had a hand in landscaping and planting the Elysian Fields, where he designed the highly original Temple of British Worthies in 1734. This made him so famous that

William Kent's classical training is apparent in this design sketch,
c. 1730–33, for Lady Burlington's flower garden at Chiswick. The black gardener
was a contemporary fashion statement.

he was asked by Frederick Prince of Wales to design a rotunda for Carlton Garden in Pall Mall. He also turned his hand to some landscaping for Henry Pelham at Esher Place, which shows a remarkable move away from the still rather formal gardens of Chiswick House, so that as early as 1734 Sir Thomas Robinson could write, 'there is a new taste in gardening just arisen after Mr Kent's notion of gardening, viz. to lay them out, and work, without level or line'.

Walpole also suggested that Kent had had such a profound influence upon Capability Brown, who was head gardener at Stowe and laid out the Grecian Valley there, that Brown owed all his later success to the example which Kent had given him. Kent was very fashionable. He was also a fat and indolent man who disliked travel and talked a lot but did rather less. Nevertheless, his contemporary George Vertue wrote that 'no nobleman's Gardens were thought to be of Taste, unless Mr Kent had dispos'd or planted [them]'.[6] Chiswick was much visited and considered one of the most natural gardens of the 1730s, but that naturalness consisted of little more than threading the wooded areas with wiggly paths instead of straight rides. It is important not to follow Walpole into believing that Kent was the precursor of Brown. He needs to be downgraded and seen as a classicist who experimented with pictorial effects in planting. Most of these consisted of contrasts between trees with light, shiny foliage and others with dark, dull leaves. Capability Brown was not interested in this sort of planting and seldom set out to create artistic contrasts.

Burlington and Kent were highly political garden-makers. So was Lord Cobham at Stowe, whose quirky and unusual garden buildings attracted so much attention, like Kent's Temple of British Worthies (with statues of Alfred the Great, the Black Prince, Queen Elizabeth, John Milton and twelve further historic persons). Here was a political message with no relevance to everyday garden-making. Other famous gardens which at some time have been credited with initiating the landscape movement are Stourhead in Wiltshire and Painshill in Surrey. But both were garden circuits, set around a lake, and completely detached from the house. They were themed walks or rides, admired and enjoyed by visitors, but little copied and in any event not typical of the smooth parklands that became so popular from about 1760 onwards. Henry Hoare intended Stourhead to emphasize his newly acquired status as a landowner. Charles Hamilton, a much poorer man, spent so much on making Painshill that eventually he was constrained to sell it.

The Elysian Fields with the Temple of British Worthies, *drawing by Thomas Rowlandson*, c. *1805*.

John Warde and Family on Horseback Surveying Squerryes Court, Kent, oil on canvas by John Wootton, c. 1735. John Warde, a successful cloth merchant, acquired the Squerryes estate in Kent in 1731 and commissioned this painting to record his family's entry to the landed gentry.

The landscaped park grew out of the old deer parks. Horace Walpole credited Bridgeman with inventing the ha-ha, though it can be argued that there was a ha-ha at Althorp as early as 1697, when Bridgeman was still a teenager.[7] Ha-has are embanked ditches, usually faced with brick or stone, which are dug out of the boundary between the garden and the park. Walpole described the ha-ha as the 'capital stroke, the leading step to all that has followed', a crucial advance in the development of designed landscapes. Ha-has became popular during and after the 1720s, and were first built to open a prospect of the deer park, which continued to be the archetypal status symbol. More than ever, venison became a sign of wealth or favour – this was the period when the sale of venison on the open market was proscribed by statute. When William Bowes, a glass-maker from London, bought Burford House, near Tenbury Wells, in the 1720s he was led to believe that the estate included a deer park. Six years of litigation followed the discovery that he had been duped. His fury may be explained by the supposition that he was moving out of trade into the life of a country gentleman.

Parks had long been regarded as objects of beauty. Back in 1616, Gervase

Markham had spoken of the 'beauty and gracefulness of the parke', contrasting the tall timber trees on the hills 'which are commonly called the views or discoveries of parkes' with the 'lawndes' or grazing grounds and the valleys which were 'coverts or places of leave for wild beasts'. Thus, continues Markham, 'you see the parke must consist of view, lawnde and covert and the situation of hill, valley and plaine'.[8] 'It is more extraordinary', wrote Horace Walpole in his essay *Modern Gardening*, that 'having so long ago stumbled on the principle of modern gardening, we should have persisted in retaining its reverse, symmetrical and unnatural gardens.' So parks started as living larders and graduated through the centuries into being first an important part of the surroundings for a gentleman's house and eventually its only acceptable setting. The ha-ha alone prevented the animals from coming up to the very windows of the house itself.

The *ferme ornée* was a development of the trend towards more natural landscaping, and of the plea for 'rural and extensive gardening' which Stephen Switzer had made. It had a short-lived fashion and was particularly associated with two names: William Shenstone of the Leasowes in Herefordshire and Philip Southcote of Wooburn in Surrey. The idea was to integrate farming activity with the life of a gentleman: his house, his garden, his artistic endeavours and the wider landscape.

Shenstone started work on the Leasowes in about 1743 and continued until his death in 1763. He was a man of very limited means but quite unlimited pretensions to being a poet. He developed his farm – a real working farm – by laying out a walk around its outer hedgerows and plantations. There was little of art to what he created, so this sort of endeavour works only if there is a meeting of minds, an interaction between the owner's ideas and the visitor's perceptions. Shenstone therefore placed seats at strategic intervals for visitors to enjoy the various views and helpful thoughts were posted along the way – some thirty-five inscriptions, some from Virgil's *Eclogues* and others of his own composition. His admirers believed that Shenstone had displayed the topography of his pastoral farm so that it could be laden with dignifying images and associations. From reading his archly crafted letters, however, Shenstone comes across as a dull, impecunious bore, desperate to keep up appearances on a tiny income and using his garden as a means to do so. He craved fame and the chance to meet a better class of person; he was pathetically pleased and grateful when someone important, like a nobleman, called on him.

Philip Southcote's *ferme ornée* at Wooburn was less of a farm and more of a garden. He bought it in 1734, following his marriage to the Dowager Duchess of Cleveland, which brought him greater wealth than he had hitherto enjoyed. Wooburn had 116 acres near the confluence of the Wey and the Thames. The Burlington set – Lord Burlington and William Kent – advised on the landscaping.

Dr Richard Pococke's account of his visit in 1759 seems to sum it up with little enthusiasm:

> Mr Southcote's [garden] consists of walks to the left, first round two meadows on rather high ground, and then round another on low ground, on the right side of them, through the further side of which a canal is made from the poultry house, which is in the form of a temple, and extends towards the Thames. These walks are adorned not only with plantations of wood but with spots and beds of flowering shrubs to diversifie the scene; from the end next the house and behind it is a piece of water formed like a river, over which there is a bridge that leads to severall small fields mostly of corn and some meadows with walks and plantations around them.[9]

But the circular path was an original idea, and may have been influential in the development of more truly natural landscape garden design. Southcote also planted lots of flowers along the way. The results were pretty, much visited, much

A View of Wooburn Farm, Surrey, *painting attributed to Luke Sullivan, c. 1759. Philip Southcote sought to integrate his farm and garden at Wooburn so that agriculture and amenity were completely in harmony. The garden was, however, expensive to maintain.*

The English Garden: A Social History

talked about and fashionable, but Wooburn was far too expensively maintained for it to be considered a proper working farm. Horace Walpole was right – for once – when he commented that 'the profusion of flowers and the delicacy of keeping betray more wealthy expense than is consistent with the economy of a Farmer, or the rusticity of labour'. Years later, Humphry Repton was rather more scathing:

> If the yeoman destroys his farm by making what is called a *Ferme ornée*, he will absurdly sacrifice his income to his pleasure; but the country gentleman can only ornament his place by separating the features of farm and park; they are so totally incongruous as not to admit of any union but at the expense either of beauty or profit.[10]

The truth is that the *ferme ornée* could never be a viable economic proposition. It needed too much input in the way of labour and ornament for it to be sustainable by the supporting farm. When the true landscape garden was eventually developed by Capability Brown and his followers, it was so designed not only to give aesthetic satisfaction but also to provide for sport and recreation and to produce a net income.[11]

It is customary to see Capability Brown's landscapes as the culmination of a steady movement towards greater naturalness which began with Addison and Pope and worked through Bridgeman and Kent until Brown and his genius appeared. Some historians account for the rise of the landscape garden in terms of the growth of English empiricism and a national turning away from Cartesian constrictions, but the trouble with this argument is that there appears to be no connection between these somewhat abstract preoccupations and the garden-making motives of the people who actually set the trends. There is another problem, which is the usual one that arises when one looks back on developments and traces their origins. What may seem to us a natural sequence of changes leading from the fashionable formal gardens of the 1700s to the sweeping open landscapes of the 1760s may not have seemed such a natural progression to people at the time. There are always many experimental developments at any one time and most of them will be unrepresentative of the general direction in which gardens were then moving. Pope, Addison, Vanbrugh, Bridgeman, Burlington, Kent, Southcote and Shenstone were all concerned to influence tastes and be seen as leaders of fashion, but the landscapes of Capability Brown represented a complete break with what had gone before. When one looks at the career of a designer as instantly popular and successful as Brown, one needs to discover exactly why his styles were immediately recognized as fulfilling an unmet need.

Lancelot 'Capability' Brown

Capability Brown is probably the most celebrated name in the history of English gardening. There are two theories about him – two schools of thought. One maintains that he was an inspired genius, a creative artist who neatly assessed the capabilities of every site and developed its hidden potential to produce a landscape that was balanced, harmonious and fluent. The other sees him as a destroyer of all that was good – a one-idea man who churned out the same formula for far too many clients and, in so doing, defaced the landscape of all England. Certainly, Brown so dominates the history of eighteenth-century gardening that every development in the years leading up to his career is portrayed as a step towards the crowning glory of his work, and every new fashion in the years after he reached the peak of his activity is related in terms of how it developed or diverged from Brown's own methods.

Capability Brown was born in Northumberland in 1716. His family were prosperous yeoman-farmers. It is usual to relate that he started work as a gardener on the estate of the local landowner Sir William Loraine, but the truth is that Capability Brown had a good education – he did not leave school until he was sixteen – and his family was respectable enough for one of his elder brothers to marry Sir William's daughter.

Brown had already begun to do some garden-design work and landscaping when, like all Northumbrians in search of fame and fortune, he moved south in 1739. He is thought to have worked at first for a relation of the Loraines in Buckinghamshire. Then, in late 1740 or early 1741 – but we do not know how it happened – he was appointed head gardener at Stowe, where William Kent was the consultant garden architect. From this point forward, Brown's life is fairly well documented. We know, for example, that he soon had his responsibilities at Stowe extended to include a large measure of estate management. In this we see an early instance of two of Capability Brown's outstanding characteristics: a remarkable facility for profound understanding and quick learning; and his ability to attract work and responsibility. It was while working at Stowe that Capability Brown developed his skill in simplifying formal gardens and creating the distinctive curves and contours which we now recognize as an essential feature of the English landscape garden.

As head gardener attached to one of the most visited gardens in England, Capability Brown was much sought after for advice and inspiration; and Lord Cobham was happy to allow him to advise others how best to improve their own grounds. After Cobham died in 1749, Brown found himself in ever greater demand. Warwick Castle and Packington Hall, both in Warwickshire, Croome

Court in Worcestershire and Petworth in Sussex were four gardens with which he was to be associated for many years and for whose owners he first worked in 1749 or 1750. He then decided to move on and two years later set himself up at Hammersmith, from where he worked as an architect, landscaper and contractor. He was now launched on a busy career which would occupy him for the next thirty years.

Capability Brown was clearly a man of great charm. At least two of his clients, the Earl of Coventry at Croome and the Marchioness Grey at Wrest, erected memorials to him to commemorate his contribution to the design of their estates. To this day, many of England's finest landscapes are the work of Capability Brown: Longleat, Bowood, Harewood, Burton Constable, Corsham, Castle Ashby, Chatsworth, Tottenham, Blenheim, Wimpole, Euston, Claremont, Highclere, Grimsthorpe and Sheffield in Sussex. The roll call is deservedly famous.

By 1758 Capability Brown was such an establishment figure that his powerful friends made a move to obtain an official post for him in the royal gardens. A petition was circulated and sent to the Duke of Newcastle, then Prime Minister, signed by fourteen men of power and influence who,

Capability Brown (right) dominates Richard Cosway's sketch of the landscaper carousing with Lord Craven (left), 'Mr Shafto' and Cosway himself. Brown's fame and fortune were founded on good business sense and enormous personal charm.

being well-wishers of Mr. Browne, whose Abilities and Merit we are acquainted with, do most earnestly request the Duke of Newcastle to promote his speedy appointment to the care of Kensington Garden agreeable to his Grace's very obliging promises in that respect, the delay having already occasion'd great loss to Mr. Browne in his Business and great inconvenience to many Persons for whom he is Employ'd.

The fourteen signatories were Lord Anson, of Moor Park in Hertfordshire; the Earl of Temple, of Stowe in Buckinghamshire; the Earl of Ashburnham, of Ashburnham in Sussex; the Earl of Egremont, of Petworth in Sussex; the Earl of Holdernesse, of Syon Hill in Middlesex; Viscount Midleton, of Peper Harow in Surrey; the Earl of Stamford, of Enville in Staffordshire; the Duke of Ancaster, of Grimsthorpe in Lincolnshire; the Earl of Exeter, of Burghley in Lincolnshire; the Earl of Coventry, of Croome in Worcestershire; Lord Brooke of Warwick Castle, in Warwickshire; the Rt. Hon. George Grenville of Wotton, in Buckinghamshire; the Earl of Hertford, of Ragley in Warwickshire; and the Earl of Northumberland, of Syon in Middlesex and Alnwick in Northumberland.

In fact, Brown had to wait until 1764 before he was appointed as Surveyor to one of the royal gardens, Hampton Court, where he is chiefly remembered for refusing to entertain George III's suggestion that he should cut down London and Wise's avenues, and for planting the famous Black Hamburgh grape vine.

In 1767 he was rich enough to buy an estate, Fenstanton Manor in Hunting-donshire, from the Earl of Northampton for £13,000. Three years later he was appointed High Sheriff of the county of Huntingdonshire. He died a rich man in 1783. One of his sons became a Member of Parliament and another was an Admiral of the Blue.

So much for Capability Brown's career. Now we need to consider the reasons for his success and why his legacy proved so enduringly popular. Christopher Thacker sums up the typical Brownian landscape:

> Brown's landscaping is characterized by its simplicity – broad sweetly contoured expanses of grass, stretching between the uncluttered garden front of the house and an adjacent lake or stream; the lake or stream, winding in the valley, made to appear of some size, often majestic; and gently curving plantations or belts of trees enclosing the boundaries, providing a continually changing setting for a walk or drive round the grounds. A bridge, a temple or a monument might give a focus to the scene but, unlike the gardens of Charles Bridgeman or William Kent, Brown's landscapes, as he designed them, had few of the objects, and far fewer of the classical 'hints' which were so common in gardens until the mid-eighteenth century.[12]

Brown's way of doing business was to make a personal visit to a new client's estate, for which he charged ten guineas a day. This was when he assessed the opportunities for improvement which it offered. Then he sent an assistant to survey the site and draw up a detailed plan as a prelude to showing the develop-ments he proposed. Contrary to popular belief, Brown made individual designs for his clients. He *had* to customize his designs, because each situation was defined by a unique landscape, setting, house, topography – and capabilities. Nor is it true, as often suggested, that Brown and his imitators banished the kitchen garden to a remote corner of the estate. Most remained fairly close to the house, though well hidden behind shrubberies and belts of trees.

Brown is uniquely interesting for several reasons. First, because he also worked as an architect; it was his experiences at Stowe which convinced him that the arts of architecture and landscape were inseparable and complementary. Years later,

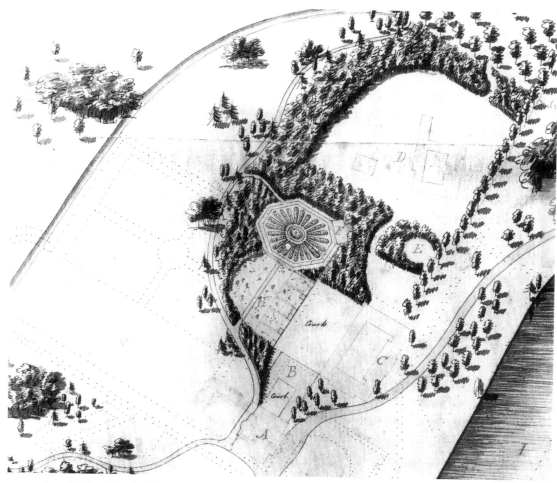

Brocklesby, Lincolnshire: a detail of Capability Brown's improvement plan, 1772.
The outline of the old formal garden is shown by dotted lines. Note the new formal flower
garden within Brown's new landscape.

Repton commented that, though Brown had lacked any formal training as an architect, through 'intercourse with men of genius and science, natural quickness of perception [and] his habitual correctness of observation, he became acquainted with ... the higher requisites of the art relating to *form*, to *proportion*, to *character*, and above all, to *arrangement*'.[13] In short, he learned quickly and understood everything. The second significant attribute of Brown's approach was that he also operated as a contractor. He made his money not just by giving advice but by undertaking the works he recommended: he offered an all-in service. He proved an exceptionally able manager, and should perhaps be compared to the founder and chief executive of an extremely prestigious young business with a high turnover. The third way in which Brown was quite unique was that he attracted a very large number of top clients within a very short time. There was a positive scramble among aristocratic society to employ him. No garden designer had been so popular and successful since London and Wise, and there has been none since Brown. Moreover – and here he differed from London and Wise – Brown's clients were well established. There was scarcely a *nouveau riche* among them, indeed nothing but the real top crust.

But Brown's most important legacy was the economic and social potential bound up in his landscape designs. The essential elements of his compositions were sweeping turf, enhanced by groups of well-grown indigenous trees, and contours which fell away in the middle distance to reveal a long curving lake and then rose up to a wooded skyline beyond. Belts of woodland were placed along all the visual and legal boundaries, to exclude any agricultural operation or any land not under the control of the landowner. Within that broadly defined landscape were lesser belts and clumps of trees to screen such features as home farm buildings and the walled kitchen garden. These plantings also served to enhance the movement and direction of the design – but that has no social or economic relevance. The house was protected from grazing animals by a ha-ha which separated (without seeming to do so) the sweeping lawns from the parkland pastures beyond. Brown's preferred trees were oak, beech and elm, supplemented by ash and lime, and occasionally 'nursed' by Scots pine and larch. It was a formula which had many imitators – William Emes and Nathaniel Richmond are the best known – and which continued to be applied to country estates for at least 100 years. What was it that made the Capability Brown landscape of such enduring value? Art historians attribute it to something unique about the English countryside and national character. They relate it to Hogarth's *Analysis of Beauty* or Burke's *Philosophical Enquiry into the Origin of our Ideas of the Sublime and Beautiful.* They explain how it arose from the essays of Addison and the Palladian genius of Kent and Burlington. They compare it with landscape painting and the rise of William Turner. But the truth is that Brown's formula perfectly suited the social and economic exigencies of country life among the landed classes.

It is time to look at them in greater detail.

The Rise & Rise of the Landscaped Park

Landowners and farmers have always been interested in improving their land. Better farming means more income for landlord and tenant alike. There has never been a time when cash flows and capital values were not of major concern and interest. 'If you lay out your money in improving your seat, lands, gardens, etcetera, you beautify the country and do the work ordered by God himself.' So wrote the first Marquess of Rockingham shortly before his death in 1750 in a letter of advice to his son, the future prime minister. Arthur Young approved the results at Wentworth Woodhouse, calling its landscape 'more elegantly beautiful than the brightest paintings of Zuccarelli and more noble than the grandest of Poussin's ideas'. Landscaping the grounds of an estate was therefore closely linked to other forms of improvement – above all, better economic use of the land. It might seem at first that there is an obvious contradiction between improving the income of the estate and turning much of it into an extensive landscaped park. But, in fact, the opposite is true.

One important trend throughout the eighteenth century was a desire on the part of landowners to consolidate their landholdings into homogeneous blocks – that is, to build up a position in one or more parishes where there was no possibility of their dominance being challenged. There were good administrative and financial reasons for this sort of consolidation. The acquisition, preservation and improvement of land were most easily undertaken when holdings had been compacted. Larger estates became important centres of influence not only locally but within the county and even nationally. The landowners controlled local government, tax-raising, the administration of justice and the county militias. The consolidation of estates was matched by consolidation of political power. The big landowner would build up a portfolio of constituencies which he could control in the House of Commons while of course being principally active himself in the House of Lords. Political patronage was the basis of power until well into the nineteenth century and beyond. Gardens, like houses, might be symbols of political success, but they could also be used – as Stowe was – as a focus for political intrigue.

Once a landowner had built up a block of land around his house, he could set to reorganizing the farms so that there was space to create his landscaped park. This necessitated removing all signs of human endeavour, especially agriculture and traffic. Parliamentary enclosures were an important tool. An individual landowner would submit a bill to Parliament to enclose and grant him a freehold title to the old, open arable fields, common lands and various 'wastes'. This process accelerated after about 1760. It has been estimated that all the enclosures up to that date did not exceed 400,000 acres, while in the next forty years no fewer than 21 million acres of land were enclosed by statute. And they increased still further after 1800, when the high prices of the war years brought more and more marginal land into cultivation. These enclosures favoured the large and medium-sized landholders at the expense of the small. The expanding population of the poor no longer had access to the common lands as a last resort against economic and

J. M. W. Turner's watercolour, Harewood House from the South East, *1798, shows the lake that Capability Brown constructed for the super-rich Edwin Lascelles and the plantations which now enclose the park.*

financial disaster. The Hon. John Byng, later the fifth Lord Torrington, was one of many who criticized the changes: 'I hate enclosures, and as a citizen I look on them as the greedy tyrannies of the wealthy few to oppress the indigent many, and an iniquitous purchase of invaluable rights.'[14]

Roads and footpaths too were often diverted or closed, to allow the landowner greater privacy and the opportunity to develop his land and garden as he might wish. After changes in the law in 1773, all that was needed to close or divert a right of way was the agreement of two county magistrates – probably friends or social acquaintances of the person who wanted to make the changes. The landowner usually built an alternative road, while the old road survived as the principal drive to his house. Gate lodges would be built at the entrance and the junction altered so that the driveway leading to the house appeared more important than the new highway.

The alteration which most attracted the ire and opprobrium of social critics was the removal of villages as part of a landscaping or estate consolidation. Examples include the destruction of the village at Burton Constable in Yorkshire,

Wimpole in Cambridgeshire and Houghton in Norfolk. Tenants were usually rehoused in a new village, sometimes designed as a 'model' village, and most were pleased by the prospect of more modern cottages in which to live. The first Earl Manvers built a model village of Gothic cottages at Thoresby in Nottinghamshire. A better-known example is that of Milton Abbas in Dorset, where the first Earl of Dorchester decided to put his new house on the site of the pre-Reformation monastery and built a pretty model village about a mile away. Such wholesale death and resurrection were uncommon, but attracted much hostile criticism, above all in Goldsmith's 'The Deserted Village':

> Sweet smiling village, loveliest of the lawn,
> Thy sports are fled, and all thy charms withdrawn;
> Amidst thy bow'rs the tyrant's hand is seen,
> And desolation saddens all thy green:
> One only master grasps the whole domain,
> And half a tillage stints thy smiling plain.
>
> ... The man of wealth and pride
> Takes up a space that many poor supplied;
> Space for his lake, his park's extended bounds,
> Space for his horses, equipage and hounds;
> The robe that wraps his limbs in silken cloth
> Has robb'd the neighbouring fields of half their growth;
> His seat, where solitary sports are seen,
> Indignant spurns the cottage from the green;
> Around the world each needful product flies,
> For all the luxuries the world supplies:
> While thus the land, adorn'd for pleasure all,
> In barren splendour feebly waits the fall.

More usual were lesser acts of 'improvement': consolidating farms into larger, more economic units and rebuilding a few cottages on the visible edge of the park, for instance.

Parks could be expensive to build. It depended on how much earth-moving went into them and, more particularly, on whether they contained such extra entertainments as lakes and follies. They were, however, cheap to maintain – much cheaper than formal geometric gardens – and often required little more than grazing by deer, sheep or cattle. But the detailed examination of individual estate accounts over recent years has revealed an interesting pattern which few anticipated. First, most landowners let out their parks for mowing or grazing, or managed it as part of the home farm; and, second, it is clear that total garden expenditure actually increased during the last fifty years of the eighteenth century. So landscaped parks produced income which was then spent on ornamental gardens, glasshouses and – that indicator of eighteenth-century smart life in the country – the cultivation of pineapples. The next question to consider is how that came to happen.

What did the landscape consist of? Grass, for a start. The rents from pasture were higher than those from agriculture. In the closing years of the eighteenth century, arable rentals in Norfolk were 50s an acre and 'pasture upwards of £3'.[15] The differential was greater in other parts of England: the rents from grazing could be as much as 50 per cent more than from tillage. The larger the park, the more income it earned. An extensive, private, landscaped park was within the power of any medium-sized squire or landowner. It was the value of park-grazing that made the proliferation of landscaped parks possible. Parkland became not just a self-financing change of use but also a net earner of income, quite apart from its recreational value. Landscaping the park became the most potent eighteenth-century symbol of gentility – just as the deer park had been in the sixteenth and seventeenth centuries.

The usual way to lay out a park was to survey the estate – a useful exercise – and to start by making maps which showed the contours and some of the existing features, including the better trees. One of the catch-phrases which recurs time and again in eighteenth-century accounts of park-making is Pope's injunction to consult 'the genius of the place'. The theory was that all improvements should be based upon a thorough understanding of the unique qualities of the estate – in other words, the potential for improvement. In practice this meant designing a park which maximized the possible returns from farming while making it seem as if everything was laid out only for pleasure. The home farm would be screened by clumps and shelter belts; so would any farm buildings or arable land. Grazing land and grazing animals were allowed in the park – indeed they were essential to this rural idyll – but the movement of grazing animals had to be carefully regulated and controlled, so that fences and enclosures were disguised as belts, clumps and ditches.

It follows that the design of the park – its layout and its plantings – was often determined by the need to control animal movements and to protect the land from over-grazing. Later on (c. 1800), the sight of sheep or cattle grazing in the parkland came to be considered an essential part of the parkland's allure. It suggested an ancient and superior way of living and farming – superior, that is, to arable. Landowners took an interest in stock-breeding and improving the quality of their herds and flocks. Stock-keeping had an air of being leisured and natural and not too energetic – in contrast to the rigours and disciplines of arable farming.

From the 1750s onwards, stock-breeding became one of the great interests of country landowners. This champion Old Lincoln ram was painted by W. Adamson in 1835.

Landscaped parks were for recreation, too. They were usually laid out as a circuit, so that the views of the countryside and its features were constantly changing. Large estates like Stourhead and Blenheim might offer a choice of two circuits, one for walking and the other for driving around in a carriage. Ladies would drive; gentlemen would ride – close-cropped turf is good for riding. And they might stop at one of the garden temples on the way to take tea.

Parks were symbols of power and wealth. Landscaped parks recalled the ancient deer parks of Tudor times, but could be made and maintained at a fraction of the cost. Some, like Petworth in Sussex, were actually made out of old deer parks and continued to hold deer, which conferred an extra prestige upon the owner – deer were symbols of long ownership and ancient families. And their association with the élite was bolstered by legislation in the 1720s and 1730s which made it illegal to buy or sell venison or game on the open market. Deer and venison thus remained prestigious commodities to give and receive.

So the landscaped park was a development of the deer park. It was an inexpensive way of creating a swathe of genteel space around a gentry residence. It insulated the owners from the growing problem of the poor. It opened out the countryside and supplied sweeping views around a man's estate. But the meadows and grasslands of the park were not the only component which brought an economic return. Just as important were the clumps of trees and the protective shelter belts around the edges.

When a park was made, some of the existing woodland or hedgerow trees were usually incorporated into the design. Even now, more than 200 years on, one can sometimes discern an oak or, occasionally, a beech that started life as a pollard or hedgerow tree. They were preserved because they offered instant effects. Shelter belts, too, were sometimes formed by linking up and extending the existing woods, hedges and copses.

It is one of the anomalies of park-making that, although the owners and makers of parks invariably said that they were opening up the countryside to view the beauties of nature, those beauties were often man-made and invariably contained within shelter belts to blot out the sight of anything which did not belong to the owner. These shelter belts were planted not for their aesthetic contribution to the landscape but to make the world a private place; they were background plantings to screen the park from people and things beyond the owner's control.

But just as the grass was mown or let, so the woodland plantings all had an economic function, too. Shelter belts and clumps were regularly thinned and replanted for their timber and firewood. Valuable hardwoods like oak, ash and elm would be interplanted with fast-growing softwood 'nurses' – usually larches – to increase the height of their trunks and therefore the length of their timber. Thinnings were regularly sold for props, poles and hurdles. The volume of timber grown and sold grew steadily, reaching a pitch of planting towards the end of the Napoleonic Wars. Mature hardwoods would be sold when they were seventy to ninety years old.

Thomas Gainsborough's painting of Thomas William Coke of Norfolk, first Earl of Leicester (the second creation), 1778, shows him as a sportsman in his park. The landscape movement enabled landowners to redevelop their estates for hunting, shooting and fishing.

They were a crop for the landowner's descendants, and an affirmation of faith in the future.

But the copses and shelter belts promoted by Brown and his followers had a much more important function: they provided cover for game. Towards the end of the seventeenth century, shooting with guns took over from bows and arrows as the rich man's preferred way of hunting for sport. There were good reasons for this, including the development of lighter and more accurate shotguns. The consolidation of estates made it easier for a landowner to manage his estate for shooting. In much of England it became increasingly common to hand-rear pheasants. Unlike partridge, which need open country, pheasants are denizens of woodland. Nowhere is better for raising a large number of game birds than the shelter belts and clumps of a landscaped park. And a wider selection of trees and shrubs was increasingly planted in these woodland areas to provide food and cover for pheasants. There were only two problems: poachers and foxes. The poachers were dealt with by stringent game laws. By the time that the sale of game was legalized again, in 1831, one-sixth of all convictions in English courts were for offences against the game laws. And the foxes were dealt with by that other popular pastime of the country gentleman, hunting with hounds.

No wonder, therefore, that the landscaped estate swept everything before it in the years 1750–1800. It produced income from its grass and timber; it provided ideal country for hunting and shooting; and it created an enclosed and private world where the landowner was lord of all he surveyed. The landed estate with its landscaped park became the epitome of power, wealth and the lifestyle to which all aspired.

Until quite recently, it was common for landed gentlemen to list their three occupations or interests as hunting, shooting and fishing. By about 1700, many large estates had canals or formal enclosures of water as part of their layout. These were usually stocked with fish. Lakes with more natural contours then became one of the great passions of the eighteenth-century landscapers and, wherever possible, were constructed at a position in the middle distance as an essential part of the view from the big house. They were expensive to make and could be attempted only where the soil was suitable – impossible, for example, on the porous chalklands of southern England. But aesthetic imperatives and the fashion for lakes are only part of the explanation for their popularity. They could be planted in an ornamental manner and used to set off fine buildings – reflected temples, handsome bridges and rocky cascades to conceal the holding dam. But they were also used for boating and fishing, and all manner of entertainments on the water. They even provided opportunities for wildfowling and otter-hunting. So, as with parkland and tree-plantings, the popularity of lakes in the late partly on his family (birth, marriage and connections), partly on his property (land and chattels), partly on his income (including his profession or way of life) and partly on a new notion known as 'politeness'. The trappings of wealth – a fine house and garden – were certainly a help, but they had to be backed by education and a responsible role in the community. Politeness was a code of behaviour which anyone who wished to be accepted by persons of quality had to follow.

Visiting spas, visiting houses and gardens, and the endless social rounds of an increasing number of apparently idle people also form the background to the growth of the landscape movement. The great landowners saw their grand formal gardens as unacceptable statements of superiority and exclusivity. They were among the first to convert their estates to the landscape movement. Many employed the great professionals like Capability Brown, but even Brown very occasionally worked for a number of new men seeking to establish themselves in the traditional English way as country gentlemen.

The established classes always laugh at the newly rich. 'In places where wealth is procured, it is ignorantly spent, for the upstart man of riches knows no better,' declared the Hon. John Byng in 1792, and he described his visit to Tong Park, a Capability Brown landscape garden in Shropshire 'recently purchased by a Mr D— [Durant, a West Indian nabob], and hired by Mr Plowden':

> Every part of this magnificent house is covered by pictures from Christie's and other auctions, of dying saints, naked Venuses and drunken bacchanals. Now why all this offensive show, disgusting to every English eye that has not been hardened in Italy? Surely the intention of paintings was to cheer the mind and restore your pleasures, to survey your ancestry with conscious esteem, to view the beauties of Nature, to restore the memory of famous horses and of faithful dogs; but why produce savage and indecent exhibitions before your children's eyes?

But, more importantly, the house had been built without an estate to support it. Byng commented: 'How people can build these pompous edifices without a sufficiency of surrounding estate is wonderful! And yet how commonly it is done. Vanity easily triumphs over reason. It impoverishes the first and now ruins the succeeding generations ... with an encircling estate of £10,000 per annum, this would be a grand place.'[18]

Yet there were fundamental changes already under way which affected the manner in which society organized itself at the top end. Status was becoming more closely allied to wealth, and to income in particular. The symbol of status – as ever – was a large house in a handsome park. The money to support such a house could come from manufacturing or business, at least until the owners decided to cut their ties with the industry that made them rich and transfer their capital to land. This was a time of extensive rebuilding of old houses, and the start of a period lasting up to the end of the nineteenth century when newly moneyed people were keen to build large new houses for themselves, whether or not the house was backed by land. Merchants, industrialists and bankers sought admission to the society of the landed élite.

Garden-visiting

Garden-visiting was a highly fashionable activity in the late eighteenth century, and certain landscape parks became positively smart. Among the most visited were the Leasowes and Hagley in Herefordshire, Stowe in Buckinghamshire, Painshill in Surrey, Hawkstone in Shropshire and Stourhead in Wiltshire. Persons of quality and taste descended upon them in great numbers. In practice they did so as part of touring a particular area. Derbyshire was one popular destination – Chatsworth, Kedleston and Hardwick; south Wiltshire was another – Wilton, Wardour, Longford, Longleat and Stourhead.

View of the Garden at Stourhead, Wiltshire, *sepia pen and ink and watercolour by Coplestone Warre Bampfylde, c. 1775. Stourhead became one of the best-known gardens in England after 'polite society' made garden-visiting a fashionable activity.*

men because he had 'seen upstart wealth trampling over all I have been accustomed to look up to with respect'. He blamed the newly moneyed parvenus who bought their estates from older gentle families for some of the social changes which he disliked: a lack of social responsibility and the passing of easy relations between squire and tenants. He said that

> the sudden acquirement of Riches by individuals has diverted *Wealth* into new channels; men are solicitous to *increase* property rather than to *enjoy* it; they endeavour to increase the *Value* rather than the *Beauty* of their newly purchased estates. The Country Gentleman, in the last century, took more delight in the sports of the field, than in the profits of the Farm.[26]

Repton thought that there was too great a 'thirst for riches', not only by the new proprietors, 'whose habits have been connected with trade', but also among 'the ancient hereditary gentleman, who condescending to become his own tenant, grazier and butcher, can have little occasion for the landscape gardener'.[27]

Repton was acutely aware of social distinctions and the aspirations and pretensions which accompanied them. He came from a slightly better social background than Capability Brown had done and could fairly claim to be a gentleman. But he never had such a prestigious portfolio of clients as Brown enjoyed. The truth is, no matter how much he may have resented and despised them, many of Repton's clients were newly rich villa-owners, loan-mongers and industrialists. In fact, Repton was particularly clever, for small clients, at borrowing other people's landscapes and making a small property appear larger than it really was. And when he addressed them, he couched much of his advice to clients in terms of social respect. Flattery was one of the tools of his trade.

Repton was actually a bit of a toady for whom one of the rewards of his job was the week or so he might spend in the company of the rich and titled, sharing their table, their conversation and their home entertainments. Something of his character may be gained from the diary note which the Hon. John Byng made in 1792 when they met at a hostelry:

> Mr Repton came in and delayed me for half an hour. He is a gentleman I have long known, and of so many words that he is not easily shaken off; he asserts so much, and assumes so much, as to make me irritable, for he is one (of the many) who is never wrong and therefore why debate with him? Having much discourse (for Repton is an everlasting talker), we did not part till midnight.[28]

Being both opinionated and loquacious, Repton was also a prolific writer and his essays on gardening and landscaping helped considerably to make him

Fence near the House, *a lithograph from* Fragments on the theory and practice of Landscape Gardening, *1816, underlines Repton's reputation as the man who reinvented the formal garden by placing Italianate terraces between a house and its landscaped park.*

and his work well known.[29] Repton was something of a self-publicist and his writings, like his Red Books, were carefully constructed advertisements for his business.

The art historians describe Repton as the man who restored flowers to English gardens and, as a generalization, this is correct. He also tended to insert a formal structure, typically a balustraded terrace, between the house and its park. The consumer society was becoming more interested in horticulture and the possibilities for ornamenting the immediate surroundings of the house. A flowery terraced walk was an agreeable enhancement to life in a country house. Another link to the Victorian age was his recommendation that a conservatory should run off the library, then the most used living room of the house, so that it formed a natural transition between the house and the world of nature outside.

Repton's own career bridged the years between the eighteenth-century land-scape movement and the nineteenth-century rediscovery of the pleasures of horticulture.

Horticulture

Throughout the debate about the English landscape movement it is important to remember that it was no more than a fashion for a small wealthy aristocratic minority. The vast majority of garden-owners and gardeners continued to do what they had always done: grow herbs for their usefulness, fruit and vegetables for their tables and flowers for pleasure. The upper classes, too, continued to attribute great importance to growing fruit and vegetables, together with flowers and hot-house plants as ornamentals. Flowering shrubs moved from the pleasure gardens to shrubberies within the landscape, while flowers retreated to the protection of the walled kitchen gardens. Repton himself recommended kitchen gardens: 'there are many days in winter when a warm, dry, but secluded walk, under the shelter of a north or east wall, would be preferred to the most beautiful but exposed landscape'.

The fashionable landscapers might demand that the park should sweep uninterrupted up to the windows of the house itself, but many owners resisted this logic. Horace Walpole, for example, was in no doubt that the 'total banishment of all particular neatness immediately about a house, which is left gazing by itself in the middle of a park, is a defect'. And many new flower gardens were made even when the landscape movement was at the height of its irresistible progress. The nurseryman John Veitch was said to have laid out gardens in every county in England except Rutland between 1785 and 1808. Veitch was of course a nurseryman, which means that he was laying out plantsmen's gardens.

The measure of interest in horticulture and plants of all sorts during the eighteenth century is the success of Philip Miller's *The Gardeners Dictionary*. When first published in 1731, its merits were extolled by a leading member of the Royal Society, who summarized its contents as

directions for the kitchen garden, with vegetables through the seasons; the fruit garden, where some erroneous methods of pruning are corrected; the flower garden, where both exotic and domestic blooms might be raised and, finally, the wilderness, where the correct choice of shrubs and trees and particularly their size and shape is all-important ... As to the practical part, [Miller] has given us hardly anything but from his own knowledge and of the great number of plants mentioned in his book there are scarce any which he has not cultivated with his own hands.

Miller's *Dictionary* covered every aspect of botany, horticulture and cultivation, and was very widely read by people great and not so great. There was nothing to match it throughout the eighteenth century: it was the last word in horticultural

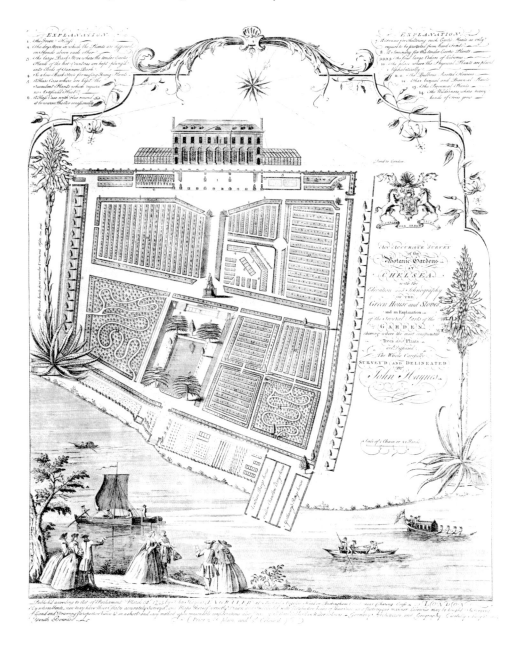

The Chelsea Physic Garden was the epicentre of English plantsmanship throughout Philip Miller's long tenure. This engraving is by John Haynes, 1753.

CHAPTER FOUR

From Waterloo to the Trenches 1820–1914

Taxation & Prosperity

The Napoleonic Wars were an extension of the war between Britain and France that began in 1793, long before the little corporal had started his rise to imperial power. Their effect was to impoverish the English both financially and culturally. Humphry Repton commented in 1816 that 'in the last ten years, the art of landscape gardening, in common with all other arts which depend on peace and patronage, has felt the influence of war and war taxes, which operate both on the means and the inclination to cultivate the arts of peace'. Looking back ten years later, John Loudon summed up the effect on gardens: landscape gardening, he wrote in 1826, gave way 'first to war and agriculture, and since the peace to horticulture'.[1]

It was during the course of the nineteenth century and up to the outbreak of a yet more devastating war in 1914 that English horticulture saw its greatest advances. Landscape parks continued to be made right through the nineteenth and into the twentieth century, remaining the ideal to which every landed estate-owner aspired. They were, however, supplemented by those specifically nineteenth-century horticultural innovations – shrubberies, woodland gardens, arboreta and collections of conifers. Plants of every sort were introduced to cultivation, and improved by systematic and scientific hybridization and selection. Nevertheless, it is the economic achievements and social changes of the time which underpin the triumphs of nineteenth-century horticulture. The period from the final defeat of Napoleon in 1815 to the outbreak of the South African war in 1899 was one of remarkable public financial stability, which gave rise to considerable wealth – wealth that was both national and personal, and from which every segment of English society benefited. Population doubled; inflation did not exist; the gold in a sovereign coin was worth its face value; the national debt, as a proportion of income from taxation, fell from 54 per cent to 11 per cent. Between

✤ *Detail of the illustration on page 175.*

'Araucaria imbricata' by William Richardson from Edward Ravencroft's The Pinetum Britannicum, *1884. Victorian landowners collected trees with competitive zest: a monkey puzzle was the ultimate fashion accessory.*

1850 and 1880 Britain's gross national product doubled and its population increased by a quarter. This growth was accompanied by low inflation, low taxation, expanding markets, rising wages, improved transportation and a growing service sector. It was unhindered by market regulations, organized labour or social legislation.

The nineteenth century was also the period in which the English were converted to the principles of free trade, a doctrine whose economic and social consequences were to have an immeasurable impact on every aspect of the Victorians' lives, including horticulture. Customs duties exist primarily to protect home producers from foreign competition. During the course of the 1830s and 1840s, they came to be seen as an unnecessary burden on the creation of wealth. As the doctrine of free trade grew in stature, it became responsible for the abolition of many forms of indirect taxation. Its culmination was the repeal of the Corn Laws in 1846. No one at the time could foresee the agricultural crisis which this would precipitate in the late 1870s, but the social and economic consequences for gardens, gardening and garden-owners were widespread. Of more immediate impact was the repeal of the taxes on bricks in 1850 and the final repeal of the window tax in 1851. Both had an immediate and measurable effect on the laying out of gardens, the building of garden walls and the proliferation of glasshouses and conservatories which the Crystal Palace inspired. Even more important was the abolition of paper tax in 1861. From about 1830 onwards, gardening and gardening design had been led by writers and journalists in a spate of new gardening periodicals which were accessible to persons of every class and education. It was through them that new ideas were transmitted, skills learned and fashions developed; aspirational lifestyle gardening was universally promoted.

The explosion of gardens and gardening in the course of the nineteenth century was underpinned by social and political changes which followed on the expansion of manufacturing and trade. The landed gentry and aristocracy saw their traditional income from rents supplemented by substantial mineral rights. They also benefited initially from the agricultural reforms which had been carried on in the latter part of the eighteenth century. As it happened, almost everyone was able to benefit from the great economic changes of the day, as more and more people sought and found a better life working in the fast-growing industrial towns. Rapid changes always create social problems. Victorians from the upper and middle classes had their solutions to contemporary woes: education was the answer, allied to religion, self-help and self-improvement. All this was reflected even in the garden, a microcosm of the whole world of Victorian England. The effect on professional gardeners was immeasurable. A modern commentator sums it up: 'in a world in which wealth, taste and acceptability were measured out in flower gardens and orchid houses, asparagus and grapes, the gardener's role gained new prestige'.[2] In the century leading to the outbreak of the Great War in 1914, the working gardener had never had it so good.

Old Money & New

Life was even better for his employer, of course. Eighteenth-century England had been governed by an aristocracy of land, birth and confidence; nineteenth-century England belonged to the mercantile classes. Economic power was the first to pass from one to the other, but political power soon followed. The Reform Act of 1832 started the process of opening up the franchise to property-owners, so that the middle and upper classes were bound to one another in the face of Chartist agitation and revolutions on the mainland of Europe. But it was the newly expanded and expanding towns which broke for ever the system of patronage operated by the old landed aristocracy. During the course of the nineteenth century the landowning electorate was converted into an urban property-owning democracy. Power passed from the agricultural labourer to the industrial worker, from the gentry to the bourgeoisie, from the aristocracy to the plutocracy. This had significant consequences for gardens and gardening.

At the beginning of the nineteenth century England's wealthiest men were all landowners. By 1914 the situation could not have been more different. It was during this period that a new aristocracy of wealth emerged, usually based on a fusion of old money and new, there being no better way of topping up the fortunes of an impoverished but ancient family than by marrying into new wealth. They had much to offer each other. The possession of land meant prestige and power. It also produced the rents which sustained a comfortable way of life. By the latter part of the nineteenth century both these assumptions were challenged.

After the economy began to recover from the Napoleonic Wars, it became apparent that those with money to spend were either the newly rich or those, like the Duke of Devonshire, who had greatly increased their income from such activities as mining. It is worth remembering that the Great Conservatory and all the bachelor duke's extravagances at Chatsworth were paid for by revenues from coal. The money to pay for the Duke of Sutherland's grand gardens at Trentham Park in Staffordshire came from investments in canal transport. Witley Park in Worcestershire was another garden which owed its magnificence to coal, while the Grosvenors rebuilt Eaton Hall in Cheshire three times in the nineteenth century, largely on the strength of earnings from their Belgravia estate.

Old families and new were equally happy to flaunt their money in building and rebuilding their houses and gardens. The aristocrats tended to commission one-off sculptures, buildings and designs from the likes of Paxton, Barry and Nesfield. The newly rich spent just as much money but would often buy from a catalogue. So far as the design of their houses was concerned, there was one distinct difference: *nouveaux riches* landowners preferred the classical style, while the Gothick or neo-Gothic style of architecture was patronized by the old aristocracy.[3] This distinction is not apparent in their gardens, where everyone agreed that size and variety were most desirable. Two nice examples are the first Earl of Dudley and the first Duke of Westminster.

No one epitomizes the enjoyment of wealth better than the nineteenth-century Rothschilds at their estates in Buckinghamshire. Hand-coloured postcard from 1912 of the formal gardens at Ascott House.

*The first Earl of Dudley built Witley Court in Worcestershire to display his enormous
wealth (derived from coal) and commissioned Nesfield to lay out the grandiose formal garden.
The Pegasus fountain (*right) *was said to be the largest in Europe.*

The first Earl of Dudley's wealth was remarkable. As a boy, he inherited vast estates and mineral riches from a distant cousin, but he also took an active interest in developing them, so that his income increased from £36,911 in 1833 to £157,900 in 1847. In the 1840s, his estates sold 1,400,000 tons of coal annually to iron works in Worcestershire alone, the county where most of his 25,000 acres lay. His trustees bought the Witley estate for him in 1837 for £900,000. Dudley's earldom was granted in recognition of his wealth in 1860; that was the year that he started to rebuild the house and gardens to display it. Nesfield was commissioned to lay out the pleasure grounds of thirteen acres around the house. The formal garden was dominated by a vast sculpted fountain representing Pegasus and Andromeda. It was said to be the largest in Europe: fifty yards in diameter, ten yards high and capable of blowing a fountain thirty yards high into the sky. To this day the sheer size of the roofless conservatory and the abandoned fountains is remarkable. Witley remains a place to fantasize about life among the Victorian super-rich.

It was the third Marquess of Westminster who was finally rewarded with a dukedom in 1874, thus providing the only instance of a family reaching the highest ranks of the peerage not through political or public services but in recognition of their sheer financial clout. The vast revenues from the Grosvenors' London estates were used to maintain an exceptionally large and impressive household and garden at Eaton. A visitor in 1884 reported that fifty-six gardeners were employed in the gardens, there were six miles of hot-water pipes to heat the greenhouses and conservatories, and so many glasshouses that the gardeners themselves were hard pressed to count them all. Many were attached to a glass corridor, 125 yards long, filled with allamandas, passion flowers and bougainvilleas; they included a water-

boundless enthusiasm for the beautiful and marvellous in nature, controlled by a judgement that is faultless in execution, and a taste that is as refined as it is enterprising and daring, are the cause of increased approbation in those who observe in his habits and character the most practical, the most zealous, and the least obtrusive of servants. Exciting the good will and the praise of the highest and the lowest, unspoiled and unaltered, he has risen to something like command over all persons who approach him, without one instance of a complaint, or a word said or insinuated against him by anybody. Beloved and blessed by the poor, considered and respected by all. To me a friend, if ever man had one.[11]

The Duke was fulsome, too, in his praise of Paxton's achievements as head gardener, manager, plantsman and engineer. Between 1828 and 1832 Paxton built twenty-two hothouses and forcing pits in the kitchen garden at Chatsworth, four for pineapples, several for peaches and cucumbers as well as vineries and a mushroom house. Then the Duke visited a horticultural show in London and was so affected by his first sight of a butterfly orchid, *Psychopsis papilio*, that he immediately began a collection of orchids, instructed Paxton to build three further hothouses to hold them and shortly amassed the largest private collection in England. By 1835 the Duke was sending a young gardener from Chatsworth called John Gibson to hunt for new orchids in India. In 1838, he organized a syndicate to sponsor two further plant-collectors and became president of the Royal Horticultural Society, a position he held until his death twenty years later. Paxton, meanwhile, took over more and more of the management of the Duke's affairs – not at the legal and financial end, which was handled by the Duke's long-suffering solicitor in London, but in making his employer's daily life in every way more agreeable and efficient.

At the same time Paxton showed his hand as an author and journalist. He founded two magazines: *The Horticultural Register* in 1831 and *The Magazine of Botany*, which he edited from 1834 to 1849. John Loudon was jealous of Paxton and attacked his work at Chatsworth – most unfairly – in his *Gardener's Magazine*. But a few years later they were reconciled and indeed after Loudon's death in reduced circumstances it was Paxton who was instrumental in raising funds for his widow and daughter.

Paxton first came to international fame as the designer of the new conservatory at Chatsworth, which was built to a distinctive ridge and furrow pattern: plate glass had yet to be perfected, so the individual panes of glass were no more than four feet long and six inches wide. When it was finished, in 1840, the Great Conservatory was 277 feet long, 123 wide and sixty-one high; it covered three-quarters of an acre. Its eight boilers were fuelled by 300 tons of coal a year, which arrived by underground trams. It had seven

This handcoloured lithograph of 1837 by Paul Gauci after a painting by Robert Schomburgk was rushed out to commemorate the first flowering of Victoria regia.
The cultural requirements of the giant water-lily offered a challenge to the hothouse gardener's skills – and considerable expense for his employer.

miles of six-inch hot-water pipes and forty miles of sash bars. It cost over £33,000.

Queen Victoria herself was impressed. The highlight of her visit to Chatsworth in December 1843 was a night-time visit to the Great Conservatory by carriage. 'Mr Paxton is a very clever man – quite a genius,' she wrote shortly afterwards. The Duke of Wellington, who was in the royal party, remarked to his host, 'I would have liked that man of yours for one of my generals.'[12]

Paxton continued to embellish and develop the Duke's gardens – Chatsworth in the 1840s was the most famous garden in England. In 1844 he finished the vast rock garden and began the Emperor Fountain, which necessitated digging out a nine-acre reservoir in less than six months. The jet of the fountain shot 264 feet into the air – seventy-four feet higher than the previous world record at Wilhelmshöhe in Kassel. But, despite his work as a designer, engineer and administrator, Paxton remained a skilled cultivator of plants: it was he who first flowered the giant Amazonian water-lily *Victoria amazonica* in Europe. He built a special glasshouse in the kitchen garden to plant the specimen which he received from Sir William Hooker at Kew; it had to be rebuilt twice within weeks to accommodate its fast-growing charge. Paxton's seven-year-old daughter Annie was pictured standing on one of its leaves.

Paxton's greatest public success was the Crystal Palace of 1851, whose design he took from the leaf-structure of *Victoria amazonica*. Though he remained at Chatsworth, he occupied himself towards the end of his life with his own enterprises. In partnership with Thomas Brassey, he became a director of several railway companies and left a fortune of £180,000 when he ended his days as Sir Joseph Paxton, the Liberal Member of Parliament for Coventry.

As for the Duke of Devonshire, he can certainly stand as one of the greatest patrons in the history of horticulture. But there was a price to pay for such munificence: the bachelor Duke was also a most profligate example of a nobleman living beyond his means. His tendency to overspend had already taken him some way down the road to ruin before Paxton's arrival. Wyatville had remodelled the house at Chatsworth at enormous expense over many years. In fact he designed the Orangery there in 1827, with Paxton advising on its construction. The Duke loved every form of display. He was a natural collector and an enthusiastic builder. It has been said that so strong were these passions, they amounted almost to a mania. The Duke was certainly extremely proud of his collection. In August 1836 he recorded in his diary that he was 'drunk with Chatsworth . . . I drove in *britchka* on two tired post horses to the kitchen garden . . . nobody can come up to me about plants'.[13] Undoubtedly the high point of his life was the visit in 1843 by Queen Victoria and Prince Albert, but it ate into the accumulated wealth of his family and, as the Duke was quite unable to live within his means, the cost had to be recouped by sales.

His heirs for many years regretted the financial irresponsibility which gave us the glories of Chatsworth's nineteenth-century gardens. The Duke's income in the 1830s was just short of £100,000, of which more than half went in interest payments on loans alone – and this was before the really big spending on the gardens at Chatsworth got under way. When his intimacy with the Duke brought home the true extent of his employer's overspending, Paxton took the lead in making arrangements which would relieve the debts. By 1844 the Duke's indebtedness was nearing £1 million and two of his Yorkshire estates had to be sold. They raised £575,000 towards reducing the borrowing – in addition to earlier sales, which had raised nearly £500,000 but had not brought the Duke's desire to spend under control. His heir, the Earl of Burlington – another lonely man, but a widower not a bachelor – wrote, 'I cannot disapprove of the large sales he proposes to make, though I cannot help regretting the extravagance which has rendered them necessary.' The Duke died in 1858 but, thirty years later, when the agricultural depression hit hard at the eighth Duke's income and the value of the assets with which he had secured his inherited debts, the Devonshire estate paid twice over for the extravagances of the man who had made the gardens at Chatsworth great.

Joseph Paxton's family, however, moved up quickly into the upper middle classes. Two of his grandchildren excelled in this world: Charles Markham was created a baronet and his sister Violet became a distinguished historian and a Companion of Honour. Nowadays Paxton's descendants are educated alongside the Duke's own heirs – at Eton.

The Loudons: John & Jane

John Loudon was a farmer's son from Lanarkshire, born in 1783, and so skilled as a boy at both writing and drawing that he was expected to become an author or a draughtsman. His abiding interest as a young man was botany, and by the time he was twenty he had been drawn into the circle of Sir Joseph Banks in London and published his first article. In 1808 he took to farming at Pinner in Middlesex and applied his scientific knowledge of how to improve the land to such effect that by 1812 he had acquired a fortune of more than £15,000. He then set off for a year and a half of travel on the Continent. Germany was where he spent most of his time – England being at war with France made it difficult to travel overland to Italy. On his return, Loudon discovered that much of his fortune had been lost in speculative investment and he decided in future to earn his living as a writer. After a further trip in 1819 – this time to southern Europe – his first great work appeared as *The Encyclopaedia of Gardening* in 1822. It was a monumental achievement and one that made his name as a gardening writer, as well as his fortune. The book was by far the most important practical work on the horticulture of its day and took over from Philip Miller's *Gardeners Dictionary* as the most consulted English gardening reference book. It went through several editions very quickly, reaching its fifth by 1835 and its eighth in the 1870s, long after Loudon's death. Loudon also did some work as a landscape designer in the picturesque school of Uvedale Price and Richard Payne Knight, but left most of his design work behind him when he started to live by his pen.

John Loudon was the first horticultural journalist. In 1826 he established *The Gardener's Magazine* as a monthly publication to 'disseminate new and important information on all topics connected with horticulture, and to raise the intellect and the character of those engaged in this art'. In the first edition, he set out his claims on behalf of horticulture with uncharacteristic gentleness: 'The love of gardening is so natural to man, as to be common to children, and the enjoyment of a garden so congenial to our ideas of happiness, as to be desired by men of all ranks and professions, who toil hard in cities, hoping, with [Abraham] Cowley, one day to retire to "a small house and a large garden".' The aim of *The Gardener's Magazine* was to 'put Gardens in distant parts of the country on a footing with those about the metropolis' and to improve the knowledge and skills of gardeners. In fact Loudon did much to raise the respect with which good gardeners came to be regarded throughout the nineteenth century. He insisted that gardeners should be remunerated in proportion to their education, skills and experience – after all, they worked in an open market. *The Gardener's Magazine* offered, for the first time, a regular bulletin of news and events in which gardeners could exchange opinions, record their experiences and articulate the concerns of their profession.

Loudon was a man of encyclopedic knowledge and inexhaustible energy, determined to leave the gardening world a better place than he found it. His interests were immensely far-reaching, which meant that his influence was equally extensive. His preference was for formal design and a wide choice of plants. He encouraged technical excellence and was interested in innovation. He directed his writings mainly towards the growing middle classes; one of his most popular books was called *The Suburban Gardener and Villa Companion*. He also emphasized the importance of public parks for the recreation, education and enjoyment of the working classes.

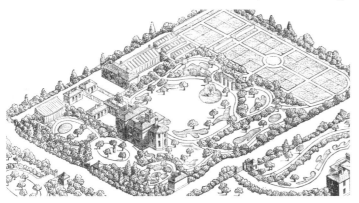

John Loudon's design for a suburban villa was typical of his work. The horticultural polymath wrote mainly for the new suburban classes.

Loudon coined the word 'gardenesque' to describe his way of planting every tree and shrub so that it could grow and be appreciated as an individual specimen. In due course 'gardenesque' also came to represent a style which involved irregular designs and specimen plantings in lawns. It was used to contrast with the wild and picturesque landscapes of the past. Finally 'gardenesque' came to stand for a ragbag of principles and practicalities which included a preference for formal design, a passion for collecting exotic plants and a willingness to employ science as the handmaid of horticulture.

Loudon always gave an explanation for the reasons behind the practices of gardening. By listing the wealth of good things that might be enjoyed, he made owners realize what was possible – what they might aspire to and how it might be achieved. He fed and created the middle-class market. He also encouraged middle-class garden-owners to become hands-on gardeners themselves. 'It has often struck us with surprise,' he admitted, 'that the proprietors of the finest residences in England, noblemen and gentlemen of high education and refinement in other things ... should commit the laying out of their gardens to their gardeners.' Gardening was no longer an activity merely for employees. It gave all men the opportunity to show something for their labours – Loudon was a Scottish Presbyterian.

Loudon recognized that 'the impulse which the London Horticultural Society has given to horticultural improvement in Britain is truly astonishing', reporting regularly and fully on its activities.[14] He also thought that there were areas relating to 'design and taste' which were not part of its remit but where his magazine had a part to play. The real discovery of the nineteenth century was horticulture. Improved cultivation and much greater use of hothouses and conservatories were among its achievements. Loudon's *Gardener's Magazine* became the forum for horticultural discussion. Garden-visiting became associated not with landscape and statues but with plants. Queen Victoria herself was always interested to see a new plant in flower.

Loudon himself was particularly interested in growing better fruit cultivars. 'There are few things relating to kitchen-gardening in which there is not greater room for improvement than in the selection of fruit-trees,' he declared. 'A number of the fruits grown in almost every garden are of very inferior flavour, arising from the sorts originally selected either not having been good, or from the plants sup-

plied not having proved true to their names. A great many excellent sorts of hardy fruits have been originated or imported within the last twenty years.' By 1834, when he embarked on his greatest publication, the *Arboretum et Fruticetum Botanicum*, Loudon was successful enough as a writer and publisher to employ seven men as draughtsmen to prepare the illustrations of trees and shrubs. He felt that the cultivation of fruit was an appropriate interest for men rather than for women. In fact almost all the articles about fruit in *The Gardener's Magazine* – and about trees and shrubs too – were written by John Loudon. Flowers were more a woman's province, so his wife wrote about them for a predominantly female readership. It is largely to Mrs Loudon that we owe the deeply ingrained belief of every Englishwoman that having a garden is all about growing flowers.

Jane Loudon started her adult life as J. Webb the novelist. Her futuristic novel *The Mummy* (1827) was favourably reviewed by John Loudon, who expressed a wish to meet the author, whom he imagined to be a man. She presented herself to him, and married him within months. Jane said it was her marriage to Loudon

Frontispiece to Mrs Loudon's Practical Instructions in Gardening for Ladies, *1843. Mrs Loudon was the first writer to target her gardening books at female readers – a market that still grows and grows.*

Jane Loudon was by far the most successful gardening writer of the 1840s and 1850s, producing a torrent of books for a new market – middle-class, young and female. Her major titles were influential for much of the nineteenth century. Her gardening books were highly practical and based on an informed and scientific approach to horticultural practice. For example, she had no interest whatsoever in the old herbal tradition. When a reader asked her about herbal remedies for medical ills, she replied, 'When I am ill I always apply to a doctor, and advise my correspondents to do the same.'

Jane Loudon also wrote for children. Her last book, *My Own Garden: The Young Gardener's Year Book* (London, 1855), sets the tone. 'Almost all young people are fond of a garden', it begins, 'and, as gardening is a fine healthy exercise, it is desirable to encourage a taste for it as much as possible.' It seems incredible to us that she should recommend gardening for children not because of the pleasure it gives, or because it might be useful or instructive, but because it is 'a fine healthy exercise'. But it is as well to remember that Victorians wanted their children to be better in every way than they were themselves, and believed that it was possible to bring about fundamental improvements in humankind through industry, piety and health in mind and body. It was a mistaken belief, but one that they shared with their Puritan ancestors.

New Gardening Magazines

Loudon's *The Gardener's Magazine* set a trend and provided the model for many other gardening periodicals, most of them short-lived and unsuccessful, in the 1830s and 1840s. They included *The Gardener's Gazette*, *The Horticultural Magazine*, *The Cottage Gardener*, *The Floral World and Garden Guide*, *The Gardener*, *The Garden*, *Gardening Illustrated* and *Amateur Gardening*. The *Gardener's Magazine* ceased publication on Loudon's death in 1843, which left the field clear for the *Gardener's Chronicle*, founded by Joseph Paxton in 1841 and edited by John Lindley, to become the leading periodical of record and quality for the next 100 years. Its main rival throughout the nineteenth century was *The Cottage Gardener*, which began in 1848 and changed its name in 1861 to *The Journal of Horticulture*, because by then its market focus was thought to be closer to an establishment with a double coach-house than a cottage.

The new magazines were a forum for information, reportage, comment and debate. Every conceivable aspect of gardening was covered, among them the latest plant introductions, new developments at fashionable gardens, book reviews, show reports (always very detailed), the weather, latest scientific reports, gardeners' wages, prices for produce and book reviews (the books often in French, German or Italian). All were well put together, with line drawings and a riveting section of advertisements showing the latest developments in mowing machines, glasshouses, secateurs, patent insecticides and plants. Nurseries advertised their new lines and hoped for a favourable 'editorial' comment too.

The appearance of gardening catalogues was a significant development: almost everything could now be bought by mail order. This advertisement for seeds dates from the 1880s.

The top magazines, *The Gardener's Chronicle* and *The Journal of Horticulture*, were avidly read by everyone, from the head gardener to the boys in the bothy, but they were also seen in the drawing rooms of their employers and indeed many of the leading amateur plantsmen wrote for them. Sir Thomas Hanbury of La Mortola and Dean Reynolds Hole of Rochester were fairly regular correspondents and the reputation of these gentleman-amateurs was considerably enhanced by their contribution. The gardens and gardeners of reputation and influence were those whose activities were reported in the working gardeners' press – above all in the *Gardener's Chronicle*. Nowadays the owners of a good garden will consider themselves to have 'arrived' if they are the subject of an article in today's most influential gardening publication, *The Garden*. So it was in the nineteenth century, save that the publication which conferred the greatest recognition and respectability was the *Gardener's Chronicle*.

The circulation battle between *The Gardener's Chronicle* and *The Journal of Horticulture* was fought in the quality of their reportage. What the vast majority of garden-owners and head gardeners wanted was technical advice on how to grow more plants of every kind and how to grow them better. But the arrival of William Robinson's new magazine, *The Garden*, in 1871 heralded a new style of journalism. Robinson used his magazine to propagate his own opinions. His articles were as informative as ever, but increasingly he used them to argue on matters of taste and fashion. Above all, *The Garden* became the vehicle for Robinson's ideas on wild and woodland gardening – and a platform from which to sneer at such formalists as Sir Reginald Blomfield.

Railways

The expansion of the railways in the 1840s and 1850s had an enormous effect upon gardens and gardening. Commercial growers were able to send flowers, fruit and

The National Apple Congress in 1883 had over 10,000 exhibits of apples from all over the country. Entirely organized in less than five weeks, the congress would not have been possible without three great Victorian inventions – gardening magazines, the penny post and railways.

vegetables to London from all over the country, which helped to consolidate the national market at Covent Garden. And, since the railways were an international phenomenon, flowers, oranges, lemons, grapes and peaches were by the 1880s being delivered in London less than thirty-six hours after they had been cut on the

Riviera shores. For the same reason, London also ceased to be the centre of the nursery trade, which was diffused throughout the country and served by the railways. In Bristol the number of nurseries increased from seven in 1821 to fifteen in 1870. Most of them answered the increased local demand for plants, but some established themselves with a national or international reputation and clientele, using the railways for their supplies and deliveries.

The coming of the railways made it possible for plants and materials to be moved quickly around the country. Before then, many plants were sent long distances by sea and canal. For example, as late as 1843 James Veitch delivered rhododendrons by sea from Topsham in Devon to London's St Katherine's Dock. But the railways could guarantee much quicker delivery. Nurserymen and manufacturers of garden equipment sold their wares through catalogues and delivered them by train. Railways were not used only for small deliveries. Gardens and nurseries consumed vast volumes of coal to heat their glasshouses and the great coal-owners were among the leading builders of railways. Their private tracks ran right to the coal face, connecting the mines to the public railway system. It was only natural that they should also build branch lines to bring coal to their country estates. From the 1850s onwards, free coal began to replace free wood as one of the perks of garden boys living in the bothy.

The penny post, introduced in 1840, succeeded because it was cheap, quick and reliable, and satisfied a need. To gardeners it brought plant catalogues, correspondence and magazines – the printed papers being much more readily produced as a result of cheaper and more efficient methods of printing. Gardening magazines were not the only ones to spawn energetically in the 1840s; specialist publications of every kind multiplied. The postal system by which such periodicals reached their destinations relied for its distribution upon the railway network.

The postal system and the railways brought about a revolution in transport and communications. The National Apple Congress of 1883 owed its success entirely to this revolution. The congress took place at short notice, when it became clear that this was going to be a bumper year for fruiting. On 1 September, an *ad hoc* committee declared that 'it was decided to hold a conference on Apples, in the Great Conservatory of the Society at Chiswick, from the 4th to 18th October'. The response was enormous: it 'far exceeded the most sanguine anticipations, promises of support and consignments of fruit being received from all parts of the country, completely filling the Conservatory as well as several others of the houses in the Gardens'. Some 230 exhibitors came from all over Britain, and they contributed 10,140 separate exhibits of apples. Organizing an event so quickly and on such a scale would not have been possible fifty years earlier.

The railways made it easier to travel to shows, to visit gardens and to make personal visits to distant nurseries. It gave rise to the travelling salesman. The representatives of the leading nurseries and seed houses were men of substance in the world of horticulture and remained so well into the twentieth century. Percy Thrower remembered the salesman from Suttons Seeds as late as the 1920s: he 'wore a black coat, pinstripe trousers and a bowler hat, and would stroll into the gardens of the big houses as if he owned them. He was always insistent that he was not a commercial traveller, but "a representative of the House of Sutton".' He would be given an order perhaps in the nature of £150–£200 for seeds and sundries, graciously accept a midday dinner from the head gardener's wife and depart to make his leisurely way to the next aristocratic garden, arriving, if he had planned it properly, just in time for tea.

In the latter half of the nineteenth century, the railways gave rise to the tradition of supplying a London house from the family's country estate. Fresh fruit, vegetables and flowers would be sent daily to London while the family was in residence there. A rich man with several houses often charged one of his establishments with supplying all of them. The brewing millionaire Michael Bass (1799–1884) had fruit sent from Rangemore Hall near Burton-on-Trent to his Scottish estate in Inverness, 'it not being unusual to send to Scotland 7 or 8 cwt. twice a week during the autumn months'. It was reported in 1876 that grapes would be 'packed in stout glazed brown paper, each bunch forming a perfect cone; the bunches are packed with base and apex interfitting, and frequently arrive with little or no loss of bloom'.[17] The fruit gardens at Windsor supplied the royal household wherever the royal family might be in residence, sending fresh produce even to Balmoral.

As the railway system grew in extent and services became quicker, so country life became more popular. Living in the country did not mean permanent exile from the flesh-pots of London. As early as 1850 we find a garden-writer lauding 'the benefit of country air and rural pleasures' made possible by the railways. The great Loder family gardens of Leonardslee, High Beeches and Wakehurst would not have been developed without easy access to a railway system which carried their owners to their desks in the City, and the same is true of other Sussex garden-owners – Ludwig Messel at Nymans and Frederick Stern at Highdown. Lionel de Rothschild became a familiar figure, racing to catch the train on a Monday morning after a weekend at Exbury.

Lawn Mowers

Technological changes have often had a direct effect upon gardening. Sometimes they free up gardeners for other work; sometimes the consequences are so far-reaching as to create temporary unemployment. On some occasions horticultural innovations may create a fashion – and hence a demand – and generate an entire new market: conservatories became highly desirable after the Crystal Palace showed the middle classes what could be done with sheet glass, wood and cast iron. Likewise the machinery invented by William Barron in the 1840s for moving large trees with their root-balls intact to minimize losses. The instant effects sought by garden-owners in a hurry like the Rothschilds in Buckinghamshire would not have been possible without it.

Few inventions have had such far-reaching consequences as the lawn mower. It certainly meant changes in working habits for gardeners, but it also created the fashion for English lawns that we now take for granted but was by no means assured in 1830, when Edwin Budding patented his lawn mower. Grass was at that time associated with landscape gardening, that manifestation of beautiful nature which the followers of Loudon and Paxton were busy reacting against. Lawn mowers made grass respectable again and, in due course, even desirable.

Before 1830, grass was always cut with a scythe. It was hard and tiring work, which was best done very early in the morning when the grass was wet with dew. In large establishments, teams of scythers worked together, keeping the lawns and grasses short. They were not well paid, being treated as semi-skilled labourers and ranking below the gardeners, who knew about difficult things like plants and were therefore more highly esteemed. But one of the reasons why lawn mowers were successful – and recommended by such writers as Loudon, who cared for the working gardener – was that they worked best when the grass was dry. In short, the lawn mower meant more civilized working hours for garden labourers. Grass also suffered from a period of unpopularity during the 1830s and 1840s. The lawn mower was so easy and cheap to use that it made grass popular again. Lawn mowers also proved to be easier to use than the scythe – and quicker – and, after some early improvements, better for the surface of the lawn, too. By 1850 their success was assured. In that year, the garden-writer Edward Kemp discussed the relative costs and values of lawns and flower-beds:

> To maintain a lawn in good order is, by some, deemed more troublesome than keeping beds and masses of plants clean. But, if the whole of the labour has to be paid for (none of it being done by members of the family) and beds have a variety of flowers in them, and are required to be kept very neat and duly raked, they will be much more exacting in point of labour than grass, especially when the constant trouble of keeping their edgings cut with the shears is computed. Lawn is ... less expensive to keep up than flower-beds and borders, and should therefore abound where economy of keeping is sought.[18]

Further improvements to lawn mowers in the 1850s and 1860s made such financial savings even greater, so that grass began to be regarded as a most suitable setting for plants and plantings. William Robinson's ideas on wild gardening and woodland gardening on a large scale would not have been possible without the lawn mower.

Edwin Budding's invention of the lawn mower offered gentlemen the opportunity to be actively involved in the garden. An illustration from The Gardener's Magazine, *1832.*

When Budding applied for his patent, he declared that 'country gentlemen may find, that in using my machine themselves, an amusing, useful and healthy exercise'. Lawn mowers provide an example of how, during the nineteenth century, it might be possible for rich men to get their hands dirty in the garden. But Budding's invention was as popular for small gardens as for large estates. Loudon pointed out that a lawn mower enabled the owner of a modest garden – the villa gardener – to cut his grass himself. And so it proved. The middle-class garden-owner's obsession with grass-cutting may be dated back to the 1830s. The size and beauty of a lawn became one of the status symbols by which such men might hope to be judged by their peers.

Glasshouses

Technical innovations also explain the development of modern glasshouses during the course of the nineteenth century. In 1800, the preferred method of heating glasshouses was coal-fired flues. A new system of steam heating was tried in the 1810s, but the boilers proved liable to explode. The technology was, however, revolutionized by the invention of hot-water pipes through which heat circulated – still the basis of all modern domestic central-heating systems. Without it, there would have been no satisfactory and reliable method of heating such huge glasshouses as the Great Conservatory at Chatsworth and the Palm House at Kew.

These hot-water pipes were backed by coal-fired boilers which were much easier to operate and could be maintained at variable or consistent temperatures. Thereafter throughout the century both boilers and piping improved by leaps and bounds. Boilers stayed alight for much longer and were much more responsive to manipulation. The sudden oncoming of cold weather was countered by complicated systems of stopcocks and valves which gave greater control in each of a series of greenhouses operating at different temperatures. Humidity was maintained by placing trays of water over the pipes and glasshouse design allowed for free ventilation. In short, the head gardener had complete mastery of the glasshouse environment and the technical means to grow anything. When the Palm House at Kew was first built in the 1840s it was heated by a battery of furnaces whose chimneys were disguised as an Italian campanile more than 100 feet tall. These

were fed by a two-track railway, running through a tunnel to bring coal and remove the ashes.

There were other technical inventions which brought the price of glasshouses within reach of the many. Most important was the invention of sheet glass in 1833. Chance Bros. of Birmingham were the first to produce sheets as long as thirty-six inches – at least fourteen inches longer than was possible using crown glass. Further improvements by James Hartley in 1847 led to panes that were yet larger, flat and free from the bubbles and bulges of older glass. Even such simple inventions as pliable putty using linseed oil made an enormous difference to the durability and safety of glass and indeed of domestic windows. It meant that panes were much less likely to crack as a result of expansion and contraction.

In 1816 John Loudon patented a wrought-iron glazing bar and sold the

The Palm House at the Royal Botanic Gardens, Kew, would not have been possible without new glass-making and heating systems – and a fashion for collecting tropical plants.

patent to W. and D. Bailey of Holborn, who flourished on the glasshouses they then sold to such eminent plantsmen as Loddiges Nursery in London and Lord Rolle at Bicton in Devon. It was the first indication that iron, whether wrought or cast, was to be the material of the future. Iron was strong and light; without it there would have been no great Victorian conservatories. It was possible for the first time to ensure that enough light reached plants from the roof of a glasshouse for a very much wider selection of plants to prosper in cultivation than previously. Loudon also designed a glazed dome which would allow a substantial tree like the Norfolk Island pine (*Araucaria heterophylla*) to grow to its natural height and spread. Loudon was a shrewd thinker who habitually anticipated fashion and sometimes created it. As early as 1817, for example, he observed, 'Modern taste has in some instances judiciously disposed the whole in one magnificent range *en suite* with the principal apartments of the house, and this is perhaps one of the greatest luxuries of a modern country residence.'[19] Unfortunately, however, he then went on to make an over-inventive suggestion as to how a rich man might divide his glasshouses into several different climatic zones and fill them all in an appropriate manner: 'Perhaps the time may arrive when such artificial climates will not only be stocked with appropriate birds, fishes, and harmless animals, but with examples of the human species from the different countries imitated, habited in their particular costumes, and who may serve as gardeners or curators of the different productions.'[20]

This was not the strangest idea about glasshouses and how to make them work for an owner. In 1831 Loudon's *Gardener's Magazine* commended

> a Mr M'Diarmid, *the very intelligent editor of the Dumfries and Galloway Courier*, who was persuaded that the best way of heating 'forcing houses' was by the breath of cattle, a method he insisted was common in Russia and had a further advantage that, since the breath also provided carbonic acid gas (CO_2 enrichment) and moisture, 'it completely supersedes the necessity of watering'.[21]

As so often, taxation was one of the great bars to social and technical progress. Glass was taxed by weight, so manufacturers strove to make their glass as light as possible; this affected its strength and durability. Then in 1845 the tax on glass was abolished, followed by the tax on bricks in 1850 and a relaxation of duty on timber in 1851. All these changes in taxation made it possible for many more people to own glasshouses and conservatories. These became more affordable for the middle classes, and indeed for large landowners, who would now have dozens of greenhouses and glasshouses on their estates, each devoted to a particular form of cultivation or activity, while even the most modest gardener could afford at least a little glass. Dean Reynolds Hole recalled going with several exhibitors after a show in the late 1840s to see where they grew their roses in tiny glasshouses on their workers' allotments just outside the city of Nottingham.[22]

The outstanding glasshouse of the nineteenth century (and indeed of all time) was Paxton's Crystal Palace of 1851. It was finished ahead of schedule as a result of being prefabricated and brought to the site for assembly. Everything about it encouraged superlatives. It covered an area of nineteen acres and was over 150 feet high at the centre. The main building was 1,848 feet long, which made it more than six times longer than the Great Conservatory at Chatsworth, and 408 feet wide, three times wider than Chatsworth. It was also four times the size of St Peter's in Rome. It used 3,800 tons of cast iron, 700 tons of wrought iron, 600,000 cubic feet of timber, twenty-four miles of guttering and 205 miles of glazing bars, plus a staggering 900,000 square feet of sheet glass, about a third of the country's annual glass output.[23] The success of the Crystal Palace stimulated thousands of visitors to build their own conservatories. But the Crystal Palace, and the vast glasshouses built in botanic gardens at this time, should also be seen as statements of national pride and civic dignity, ambition and progress.

After the abolition of glass taxes in 1845, and the success of the Crystal Palace in 1851, the market for practical glasshouses and ornamental conservatories boomed. Magazines like The Gardener's Chronicle *promoted both.*

Conservatories were ornamental rooms leading off a house and planted with tender exotics. The plants they contained were not rare, but adapted to the sorts of temperature and humidity which suited humans, too. Among the middle classes, a conservatory had a dual purpose. In winter, it was used to conserve tender plants, especially orange trees and other exotics grown in pots, which were then put outside for the summer. Then the conservatory was spring-cleaned, furnished with chairs and tables and became a room in which to eat, entertain and enjoy life between the house and garden during the summer months. Grand houses would have a conservatory designed by an architect as an extension to the house, but an integral part of it. Most people, however, bought them off the peg from one of a dozen manufacturers who advertised in the gardening press. They were special places not just for family relaxation and entertainment, nor even for the display of plants, but also for quiet moments during a dance or even for a proposal of marriage.

The glass conservatories did, though, raise questions of taste and aesthetics. Could they ever be considered compatible with domestic architecture? Did they look better on Georgian houses or Gothic Revival? Would it not be better to set up a conservatory as a freestanding garden building at some distance from the house and to landscape it with the grounds as a whole? The owners of small properties and town houses did not have the options. In the event, a distinction was made between 'architect conservatories', which harmonized with the house but were no good for plants, and 'gardener conservatories', where the plants were happy but the building contrasted incongruously with the house.

Plants would be wheeled in from a distant greenhouse in the walled garden to fill a conservatory. Among the rich, it became customary on a large scale to bring potted plants into the house too. They would be kept there for display until they had finished flowering or needed to be returned to the glasshouses to recover and then replaced by other specimens. Palms, ferns and dracaenas were popular in entrances and halls; orchids graced the drawing room and often the dining room. Tea roses were produced all year round in rich houses; they were symbols of wealth. The similar but hardy China rose was the preserve of the poor. Their hybrids were known as 'China teas'.

Glasshouses during the nineteenth and early twentieth centuries were classified according to their purpose – orchid houses and peach houses, for example. There were three pineapple houses, pine houses, at Sandringham, each 100 feet long. At Rangemore Hall near Burton-on-Trent, the brewery millionaire Michael Bass had forty glasshouses ('beside pit and frames') containing three and a half miles of hot-water pipes fed by three boilers which cost £700 a year in coal to run. Tending the fires was a full-time occupation for one of the garden boys. The walled garden extended to six acres and contained 'glass structures of such size and number as are seldom seen in a private establishment'. There £70 worth of asparagus crowns were forced every year, 'the best being prepared in France and supplied by Messrs. Veitch & Sons'. The gardeners were expected to supply French beans, mushrooms and saladings all through the year, and green peas at Christmas.[24] It was said that you could measure the importance of a host by the sheer variety of flowers and fruit on his dining-room table. When service *à la russe* arrived in the 1860s, it made space on dining-room tables for gardeners to display their expertise and owners their wealth.

As the nineteenth century wore on, however, the import of exotic fruit made it possible for oranges, grapes and pineapples to be widely available in shops. The rich continued to raise such luxuries but for many people it was no longer an economic proposition, nor socially advantageous, to maintain vast palaces of glass for the cultivation of exotic fruit. By 1900 commercial horticulture was near to technical perfection: cheap coal, ready labour, large glasshouses and sophisticated controls for advancing or retarding crop seasons made anything possible.[25]

Fruit

When William Taylor went to Longleat as head gardener to the Marquess of Bath in the 1870s, his brief was to 'improve the quality of the dessert'.[26] For much of the nineteenth century it was essential for a head gardener to be a good grower of fruit – grapes and pineapples in particular. Pineapples represented the greatest challenge to the cultivation skills of a head gardener. As late as 1872 the *Journal of Horticulture* described the pineapple as 'the king of fruits'. Quality counted for more than size and nurseries offered a very large choice of cultivars. Not until cheap imports from the Azores began to flood the market from the 1870s onwards did their prestige diminish. Names such as 'Charlotte Rothschild', 'Smooth-leaved Cayenne', 'White Providence' and 'Black Jamaica' were known to every Victorian head gardener. The measure of the pineapple's decline may be seen from the fact that not a single cultivar is listed today in the *Royal Horticultural Society Plant Finder*.

Throughout the nineteenth century, substantial advances in the breeding of fruit and vegetables were made. Between 1860 and 1890, Thomas Laxton produced potatoes, roses, strawberries and pelargoniums that were

Many new grape cultivars, bred for English conditions, circulated among head gardeners throughout the nineteenth century. They included the Cannon Hall Muscat Grape, delicately painted by Mrs Augusta Withers, c. 1825.

considered the best of his day. His sons Edward and William, in the early years of the twentieth century, continued his work and occupied themselves with strawberries ('Royal Sovereign'), apples ('Laxton's Superb', 'Laxton's Fortune', 'Lord Lambourne'), pears ('Laxton's Superb', 'Laxton's Satisfaction', 'Beurré Bedford') and plums ('Laxton's Gage', 'Early Laxton'). Thomas Rivers introduced the 'Manettii' stock for roses and was a successful rose breeder and more especially a raiser of peach trees in the middle of the nineteenth century. His son P. Francis Rivers bred apples ('Francis Rivers', 'Rivers' Early Peach') and pears ('Conference').

More than any other fruit during the nineteenth century, apples were bred on a wide scale. They were selected for sweetness and flavour as dessert apples, so that by 1900 it was not unusual for a connoisseur pomologist to grow as many as fifty different eating apples specifically selected for their long season and variety of flavours. By the 1850s it was possible to have apples for eating in every month of the year, from the earliest 'Irish Peach' right through to 'Sturmer Pippin', which could be stored until the new crop took over in late summer of the following year. The English also selected cooking apples for the kitchen. This is a uniquely English phenomenon, the development of a particular group of apples, typically larger and sharper in flavour (less sweet) than the eating apples, for their use in the kitchen.

Throughout the nineteenth century, English-raised apples replaced cultivars of French origin. The Blenheim Orange, which became one of the most popular dual-purpose cooker-eaters, is illustrated here in a chromolith by G. Severeyns after a drawing by Alice B. Ellis.

The Royal Horticultural Society was deeply involved in selecting the best cultivars and growing them to perfection. Typical of its commitment was the National Apple Congress of 1883. Its main aims were to correct names and dubious synonyms from as many districts as possible. The Royal Horticultural Society's own collection of apples would be the basis of the exhibition. Just in case any head gardeners thought otherwise, the committee added that 'this Conference will not take the form of an ordinary exhibition, as there will be no competition and no prizes; the sole object being to seize so favourable an opportunity of gaining information, and making the meeting instructive and educational'. Exhibitors were asked to comment on the situation where each cultivar was grown ('sheltered, or otherwise'), the soil type, the stocks on which they were grafted and the shape of the trees. They were also asked to re-commend their best twelve culinary and dessert apples. A large Conference Committee examined all the exhibits, over several days, and concluded that there had been 1,545 distinct cultivars, known by 2,020 different names – that is, 475 names were synonyms. They also announced – and this is very typical of the Victorian passion for categorizing – that apples could be classified or readily grouped into twenty-four primary classes. Their findings were published as a *Descriptive Catalogue of the Apples exhibited at the Congress*, as were the results of the poll, county by county, region by region, and finally for the whole of Great Britain. Modern pomologists will not be surprised to learn that the best dessert apple was adjudged to be 'King of the Pippins' and the best cooker 'Lord Suffield'.[27]

The Horticultural Society of London

The Horticultural Society of London emerged during the first half of the nineteenth century as the leading English society for the advancement of horticulture and horticultural science. It was not the only one. The Royal Botanic Society in Regent's Park, where both Robert Marnock and William Robinson worked, was a fair rival and seemed at times to have a better chance of success. The Horticultural Society differed in one particular way: it insisted that the plants grown in its gardens – acquired from the 1820s onwards – should be either useful or beautiful. Plants of botanic interest only were not accepted. In 1823 it leased land from the Duke of Devonshire at Chiswick and three years later the society published a catalogue of the fruits grown in its new garden, totalling 3,825 cultivars. The society's garden came to be seen as a national school for the propagation of horticultural knowledge and a magnet for the best brains among ambitious young men interested in pursuing a career in horticulture. Chiswick was the place for professional gardeners to learn their trade. Here were the most modern methods of cultivation, the most splendid glasshouses, the largest collections of fruits, trials of vegetables and ornamental plants – in short, the hub of horticultural activity. Trainee gardeners had to be between the ages of eighteen and twenty-six, unmarried, educated as gardeners and capable of reading and writing moderately well. Up to twenty-six young men at a time were taken on for a two-year stint of training, for which they were paid 14s a week. One of the earlier entrants was Joseph Paxton, who added a couple of years to his declared age to secure his position.

For many years the Horticultural Society regarded the distribution of plants as one of its principal objectives. It purchased vegetable seeds from foreign seedsmen like Vilmorin of Paris and in due course distributed them among its members. In the 1830s it distributed over 350,000 packets of seed, 90,000 plants and nearly 50,000 parcels of cuttings among members alone. From the start, it employed its own collectors to introduce exotic plants from foreign countries. John Reeves sent a number of important new plants from China after 1817, including the common *Wisteria sinensis*. Chrysanthemums were another interest. The society asked Reeves to collect and send back as many cultivars as possible, so that by the late 1820s there were already more than fifty in cultivation in this country and hybridization continued apace. The introduction of Japanese cultivars by Robert Fortune in 1860 gave a new fillip to their breeding and popularity. These cultivars, instead of showing the perfect incurved petals of the Chinese forms, had florets which curled and twisted in all directions, as well as strange and exciting colour combinations.

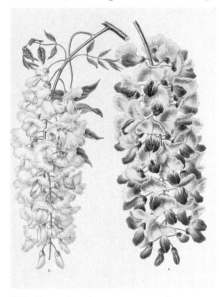

The first wisteria was not seen in England until 1817, the direct result of plant collectors being sent to China by the Horticultural Society of London. An example is shown here in a chromolith by G. Severeyns after a drawing by A. J. Wendel.

The collectors that the Horticultural Society sent out were, in effect, collecting for the members' benefit. Most of those expeditions were to countries whose plants would not grow outside in England. Not until the 1860s did it dawn upon the society that this was somewhat inequitable. Tender plants were of interest only to its richest Fellows who could afford to cultivate them. By the time the society put a greater emphasis on collecting and distributing hardy plants, much collection was being undertaken by nurseries and syndicates of garden-owners; the society had primed the pump and the engine of horticultural introduction was now running. Nevertheless, the society remained the preserve of the aristocracy and gentry until Sir Trevor Lawrence undertook a systematic extension of its franchise in the 1880s. It did, however, offer lower rates of membership to working gardeners and in the 1830s it began to run shows at its Chiswick gardens which were so popular with professional gardeners that they were expanded in number and repeated regularly until Chiswick became the leading forum for plant shows.

The Royal Horticultural Society (as it became in 1861) had a fairly rackety history through much of the nineteenth century and triumphed as a national organization, well run and universally respected, only in the twentieth century. In 1859 the society's offices in Lower Regent Street had to be quickly sold at a substantial undervalue and the magnificent collection of books and original drawings which composed the society's library was likewise disposed of for a pittance. Forced sales are a bad way of recovering from financial extravagance. In the same year, the Prince Consort, then president of the society, suggested leasing twenty acres at Kensington Gore for a new garden. The society – at that time an extra-

The RHS garden at Kensington (1861), an extravagant Italianate design, was plagued by financial problems throughout its short life and was finally sold for development.

vagant borrower – raised a large sum on debentures to lay out the gardens.

When Prince Albert obtained the grant of a new, royal charter to the Royal Horticultural Society, new members (always called 'Fellows') joined in great numbers. The membership doubled in the course of 1861 alone and about one-third of them were women. The Kensington garden was formally opened by the Prince Consort and widely reported in the press. The society was suddenly fashionable. In 1879 it even allowed the new game of lawn tennis to be played at Kensington.

One of the responsibilities of the Horticultural Society was to apply the correct nomenclature to cultivated varieties of plants. In 1835, it was able to declare that although it grew more than seventy apricots with different names within its gardens, they amounted to no more than seventeen distinct cultivars. Likewise the forty-three distinct varieties of peas enjoyed 130 synonyms. During the 1880s and 1890s the Royal Horticultural Society organized and initiated a series of conferences devoted to sorting out the nomenclature of particular plants. Thus it organized the National Apple Congress in 1883, a Daffodil Conference in 1884, an Orchid Conference in 1885 (followed by a second one entirely devoted to orchid nomenclature during the following year) and a Primula Conference in April 1886 which was dominated by auriculas. There followed a Vegetable Conference in 1889, a Dahlia Conference in 1890, a Conifer Conference in 1891 and a Begonia Conference in 1892.

The Kensington garden did not fare well, largely because the society's finances continued to be badly organized. In 1882 the Court of Appeal gave the landlords permission to repossess the garden and the society defaulted on its debenture holders, most of them private individuals and benefactors. In 1903, the society moved its experimental garden from Chiswick to Wisley. This was possible only as a result of the munificence of one wealthy Fellow of the society, Sir Thomas Hanbury, who bought the original fifty-nine acres and put them into a separate trust for the society's benefit. Wisley was in a remote part of Surrey with no public transport to serve it. The move would not have been possible without the invention of the motor car; 6,000 Fellows visited it during its first twelve months.

As at Chiswick, much of the labour for maintaining the new garden at Wisley came from running a school for gardeners: a two-year course for which the students had to pay an admission fee of five guineas. Wisley was unashamedly a gardener's garden, where the society practised the perfect cultivation of every type of plant that could be grown in England, from alpines to hothouse orchids to conifers, whether in the open ground or in artificial conditions. This was backed up by an important system of trials, both permanent and periodic, which grew, tested, examined and made awards to flowers, fruit and vegetables. In 1906–7, 271 stocks of *Canna*, representing 220 distinct cultivars, were the subject of a trial. At the same time, in conjunction with the National Dahlia Society, a trial of 197 stocks of cactus dahlias representing 170 distinct cultivars was judged by the joint committee of the society and the National Dahlia Society. Wisley was, above all, conceived as a scientific garden. To this day, the main building which dominates the formal garden near the entrance is known as the laboratory. By 1914 its staff included a gardens superintendent, a mycologist, a chemist, an entomologist, a trials officer and an assistant director responsible for educating the students. The Royal Horticultural Society was on its way at last to becoming a responsible, well-run charity.

In Search of Style

Right through the nineteenth century, the landscaped park continued to be the proper setting for a large country house. Between the park and the house, formal gardens flourished once again. There were two popular styles among the very rich:

the Italianate and the neo-Tudor. After 1870 they were joined by the Arts and Crafts style, which appealed to a more middle-class owner, and by the wild or woodland style of gardening which William Robinson preached.

The apostle of the Italian revival was Sir Charles Barry (1795–1860). Barry was very much an establishment architect and garden designer. His first major com-

The Parterre, Trentham Hall Gardens, *lithograph by E. Adveno Brooke (fl. 1844–64). Italian – or Italianate – was the only style for the super-rich for most of the nineteenth century.*

mission was at Trentham Park in Staffordshire, where he helped to remodel the house for the Duke of Sutherland in 1833 and began work on the gardens in 1840. He excavated two extensive terraces between the house and the lake, and edged them with balustrades and statues which included a cast of Cellini's *Perseus*. A gondola plied the lake. The Italianate gardens and the spectacular display of bedding plants put out by the gardening staff were instrumental in popularizing the system of using bedding plants. Barry's other commissions included Bowood for the Marquess of Lansdowne, Cliveden for the Duke of Sutherland (again), Edgbaston Hall for Lord Calthorpe, Harewood House for the Earl of Harewood, Highclere Park for the Earl of Carnarvon and Sandon Park for the Earl of Harrowby. All these landowners were 'old money', even if richly supplemented by income from property, minerals and manufacturing.

William Andrews Nesfield (1793–1881) worked with Barry on certain projects and eventually took over from him as the leading exponent of the neo-Italian formal style. Nesfield started life as an army officer and then gained some fame in his thirties as a watercolourist. His brother-in-law was Anthony Salvin, who employed Nesfield's pictorial eye on some of the landscapes and gardens associated with his buildings. Some enthusiastic publicity in Loudon's *Gardener's Magazine* in 1840 catapulted Nesfield into becoming a favoured designer for well-established, titled society – he was himself socially well connected. Nesfield worked for the Earl of Carlisle at Castle Howard, laying out formal parterres and rearranging the Atlas fountain from the Great Exhibition, which remains the centrepiece of the formal gardens. Other clients included the Duke of Northumberland at Alnwick and the Marquess of Westminster at Eaton. In the 1860s Nesfield worked on his masterpiece, Witley Court in Herefordshire, for the coal-rich Earl of Dudley. Practically the only work he did for a *nouveau-riche* client was to redesign some parterres at Basildon Park in Berkshire for the millionaire draper James Morrison. He also worked for the Royal Botanic Gardens at Kew (1844–8) and for the Royal Horticultural Society in Kensington (1856–61).

William Robinson's onslaught on the formal garden began quietly in the 1870s and got louder and louder as the years passed. 'The Italian influence has been wholly evil ... heaps of money wasted in a theatrical show!' he declared.[28] His principal opponent in the 1890s and thereafter was an architectural historian,

Gardens in the old-fashioned style – whether truly ancient or modern – were admired as the embodiment of old English virtues and distinct national character. This is Joseph Nash's romantic view of Levens Hall, Westmorland, in The Mansions of England in the Olden Times, *1849.*

Reginald Blomfield (1856–1942). Blomfield wrote a fairly influential book (with F. Inigo Thomas) called *The Formal Garden in England*. It was a civilized architect's riposte to the back-to-nature tendencies of subversive self-educated William Robinson. 'We protest entirely against the view that there is one art of the house and another of the garden,' they declared; 'they rest on the same principles and aim at a common end.' But by the 1890s, the whole social structure among the rich and very rich had changed, and Blomfield's clients as a garden designer were all upper middle class or newly moneyed, with scarcely a great landowner or a minor title among them.

Victorian England was keen to establish its roots and to identify the essential parts of English history which made the English the greatest power in the world. The turning points were seen to be Henry VIII's Reformation and Elizabeth I's long reign, during which the Spanish Armada was beaten. Sir Francis Drake was seen as the archetypal Englishman, finishing his game of bowls as the Spanish Armada sailed towards the shores of Devon. Sir Philip Sidney and Sir Walter Raleigh, too, had their part to play. These great heroes were icons within a wider movement towards the glorification of old English virtues and a distinct national character – the sea-borne empire of a Protestant parliamentary democracy. They were also associated with a type of neo-Elizabethan garden which became very popular during the 1850s.

Overgrown late-seventeenth-century gardens like Levens Hall in Westmorland were among the first to be admired as examples of the true, old-fashioned style. The historian Lord Stanhope commented:

> through the whole of England, there remains scarcely more than one private garden presenting in all its parts an entire and true example of the old designs; this is the fine old seat at Levens … There along a wide extent of terraced walks and walls, eagles of holly and peacocks of yew still find each returning summer their wings clipped and their talons pared.[29]

Little remained of the original garden at Levens; most was added in the early nineteenth century – silent witness to the speed with which yew topiary acquires critical mass. The topiary at Hardwick Hall in Derbyshire was commended by Blomfield as a rare survival: it was substantially replanted by Lady Louisa Egerton in the 1860s. Another nineteenth-century garden which was commonly thought to be much older, and was praised for its old-fashioned air, was Castle Bromwich. Packwood House in Warwickshire is a substantially nineteenth-century garden. Likewise, the north garden at Montacute dates back no further than the middle of the nineteenth century and the splendid old maze at Hatfield was planted in 1841 with new money the Cecils inherited from the Gasgoynes. It was a small step from describing such gardens as old-fashioned to believing that they dated back to the sixteenth century. And they were widely copied. After all, neo-Elizabethan gardens gave their owners an image of old-established squires dispensing genial hospitality as in the days of Good Queen Bess.

The Arts and Crafts movement appealed to quite a different sort of person – modern, artistic, upper middle class and comfortably off, but by no means rich. William Morris himself was not interested in gardens and wrote practically nothing about them. His ideas were said to be derived from medieval illuminated manuscripts and his ideal medieval garden was expressed in the *Story of an Unknown Church*, published in 1856:

> At the edge of the lawn, near the round arches, were a great many sunflowers that were all in blossom on that autumn day; and up many of the pillars of the cloister crept passion-flowers and roses ... in the garden were trellises covered over with roses, and convolvulus, and the great-leaved fiery nasturtium; and specially all along by the poplar tree were there trellises, but on those grew nothing but deep crimson roses; the hollyhocks too were all out in blossom at that time, great spires of pink, and orange, and red, and white, with their soft, downy leaves.

Morris's vision of beauty was no more than a fantasy: passion flowers, nasturtiums and deep crimson roses were unknown in medieval times.

It is best to regard Gertrude Jekyll (1843–1932) as a child of the Arts and Crafts movement. Her interests were legion: music, painting (she enrolled at the School of Art in South Kensington), furniture, metalwork, embroidery and photography. Horticulture came comparatively late in life and she brought all her skills and experience in the other decorative arts to bear upon the art form with which her name is now most associated. Like her friend Edwin Lutyens, Jekyll worked for the comfortable upper middle classes. So did Harold Peto (1854–1933), though his commissions were few. He was much influenced by his travels in Italy and the period in which he lived and worked on the Riviera. Jekyll, Peto and Lutyens reconciled the architectural formalism of Blomfield with the naturalistic plantsmanship of Robinson.

The 1890s saw the start of yet another short-lived fashion: Japanese gardens. They were largely inspired by two sumptuous books by Josiah Conder, *The Flowers of Japan and the Art of Floral Arrangement* (1891) and *Landscape Garden-ing in Japan* (1893). These were the first studies to show just how great was the gulf between Western and oriental ideas on gardening: the difference in the flowers available, the way plants were pruned and trained, and the features that were peculiar to Japanese gardens – temple stones, tea houses, herons. The first Japanese garden was made at Cliveden in 1893. In 1901 Louis Greville brought

Japanese gardeners to Heale House in Wiltshire to create a Japanese garden. The Japanese garden at Gunnersbury was designed from photographs taken by Lionel de Rothschild from Villa Melzi on Lake Como. After it was opened in 1901, the Japanese Ambassador said to Lionel's father, Leopold de Rothschild, 'We have nothing like it in Japan.'

Gardens & Parks

Throughout the nineteenth century, horticulture was seen as a practical skill, not a proper subject for academic study. Agriculture was taught to degree level, but nothing was available for would-be horticulturists. When it was seen that the agricultural revolution had brought measurable results, progressive thinkers turned their attention to creating the conditions for a scientific improvement of horticulture. The Worshipful Company of Gardeners planned a school for gardeners, to be called the British School of Gardening and Small Husbandry. It was over-ambitious and came to nothing. In fact, it was way beyond the company's resources. The lead in horticultural education came from Kew, where by 1848 there was a dedicated reading room for students who wanted to study in the evenings. Training was formalized in 1859 and in 1870 Kew began to issue diplomas in horticulture. Kew always took in older apprentices, a tradition which still continues today. They had to show at least five years' good experience, including time spent under glass. By 1898 the French journal *L'Eclair* referred to Kew as '*une université de jardinage*'. Meanwhile, the Royal Horticultural Society had been spurred into action in 1865 to set examinations in horticulture. By the turn of the century, the society could fairly claim that

> young men nowadays have advantages quite out of the reach of men who started twenty or thirty years ago. There are books and illustrated papers, lectures, classes, and technical schools or institutes in all large towns and in many of the villages throughout the country. Knowledge is in these days obtainable by all, and knowledge is not only power, but profit and pleasure as well.[30]

The principal purpose of a botanic garden during the nineteenth century was to make living collections of plants so that they were available for research and for public benefit. Gardens were places where God's handiwork might be displayed for the edification and education of the public at large. There was an explosion in the number of botanic gardens and arboreta, usually founded by universities or learned societies and supported by amateurs: Liverpool in 1802, the Horticultural

Society at Chiswick in 1804, Hull in 1812, Bury St Edmunds in 1819, York in 1822 and the University of Birmingham (designed by Loudon) in 1832. Arboreta received a great fillip from the introduction of conifers from North America. Probably the most significant new arboreta were Westonbirt in 1829, Bicton in 1839, the Derby Arboretum (designed by Loudon) in 1840, the Bowood Pinetum in Wiltshire in 1848 and the Nottingham Arboretum in 1850. Loudon was the first to recommend planting arboreta as collections of both foreign and native trees – never more than one specimen of each kind. Quite a new concept at the time, this represents the final unmaking of the landscape movement and the triumph of the gardenesque. Both botanic gardens and arboreta were places for the acclimatization, growth and study of exotic trees.

Kew became the giant of all botanic gardens, but this was not obvious in the years following Sir Joseph Banks's death in 1820. The report on the management of Kew drawn up by John Lindley and Joseph Paxton in 1838 led to the royal gardens becoming 'a garden of science and instruction' – a national Royal Botanic Garden. Kew's prestige quickly reached great heights under the directorship of Sir William Hooker, especially after the Palm House was completed in 1848. The power of Kew was based on its research, its worldwide network of correspondents, its scientific publications and its acquisition and distribution of plants. By 1900, there were botanic gardens in every part of the Empire. Four were designated Royal Botanic Gardens – Calcutta, Pamplemousses, Peradeniya and Trinidad – and such gardens were an integral part of British imperial culture. Linked to Kew, as the colonies were to the great white queen, these gardens were centres of botanical research where living collections were made, taxonomy studied, seeds and plants exchanged, economic experiments practised and information dissem- inated worldwide. Their directors were Kew-trained and saw themselves as part of a great imperial network of scientific excellence continuing the work which Sir Joseph Banks had begun 100 years before. The gardens were, of course, laid out in the English style, as gardenesque landscaped parks tricked out with palms, cycads, ferns and orchids, and pools where tropical water-lilies grew. Plants from such gardens were often introduced into cultivation in private gardens at home and abroad, and into the nursery trade. Kew was enormously influential, too, among garden journalists in a way that is difficult to comprehend today. Kew-trained journalists worked for *The Gardener's Chronicle* and *The Gardener's Magazine*.

Municipal parks were publicly owned and urban. England has always had places of public recreation, many of them publicly owned, but throughout the nineteenth century it was increasingly recognized that people who lived in towns had a special need for open parks. Some were laid out by local authorities, others belonged to semi-learned societies or to adjoining owners (such as the gardens in London squares). Three elements, all horticultural, are common to such parks:

large areas of grass on which people may sit and children play; a framework of ornamental trees to give pleasure and instruction at all seasons; beds and bedding, often of colourful and complex design, intended to give pleasure for as much of the year as possible and, most particularly, during the summer and early autumn.

Carpet bedding developed after about 1840 and was very popular in public parks: it was the principal benchmark of their excellence. This photograph shows Castle Ashby, Northamptonshire.

The first public park had been Regent's Park in London, opened as a subscription park in about 1810 and then made public in 1835. It was followed by the Victoria Park in Bath, whose acquisition and development were entirely financed by public subscription. It was opened by the eleven-year-old Princess Victoria of Kent in 1830. When she acceded to the throne as Queen Victoria in 1837, she renamed it the *Royal* Victoria Park. Its collection of plants was a fair match for the more famous Derby Arboretum and incorporated the Bath botanic gardens. When Veitch's nursery introduced the wellingtonia *Sequoiadendron giganteum* in 1853, Bath's subscribers were among the first in the country to buy and plant a specimen. Such gardens were often associated with horticultural shows and exhibitions, and with learned lectures. Bath continued to be managed by wealthy subscribers until 1921.

These early public gardens made a charge to any member of the public who wished to enjoy them. The first park designed by a local authority which guaranteed free entry was Birkenhead in Liverpool, designed by Paxton in 1843. One of the great spurs to the public parks movement was the need to defuse social unrest, itself the result of uncontrolled industrialization. Another was the shortage of available space. By 1840, it was clear that, if local authorities did not act quickly, all the available inner-city sites would soon be covered in houses and factories. And a third reason for making genuinely public parks was the sheer speed of the population explosion – 9 million in 1801 and 14 million by 1831. By the end of the nineteenth century every town and city up and down England had its public park.

Some parks were donated by philanthropic landowners and endowed by the wealthy middle classes. It was part of the Victorian concern for public utilities, prisons, hospitals, sanatoriums and cemeteries: all were laid out in accordance with horticultural principles. Carpet-bedding began to be widely copied in the 1840s. It was popular with visitors; indeed, all floral displays have always been popular – the brighter, larger and more colourful the better. Towards the end of the nineteenth century, more working-class people – and certainly all the middle classes – could afford travel and holidays, which gave rise to the winter gardens, parades and extensive public plantings designed as tourist attractions in seaside towns from Blackpool to Weston-super-Mare. To this day, some municipal parks are the guardians of standards of horticultural excellence and display which date back to the middle of the nineteenth century.

Garden Style

The formal gardens which staged a comeback in the 1830s were decorated with large numbers of plants chosen for their colour, effect or shape; the system of bedding out was under way. Such plants offered every garden-owner and his gardener the chance to show off the heights of the gardener's skills and the depth of the owner's pocket. Some 100,000 plants a year were used at Shrubland and Trentham Park. The use of bedding plants on a large scale, often within Italianate parterres, involved considerable expense in both plants and labour – planting and maintaining. It therefore made an ideal vehicle for the display of wealth and fashion.

In the 1820s the smart plants were geraniums, dahlias and clematis. The old florists' flowers – pinks, auriculas, roses and polyanthus – were plebeian, as were such cottage favourites as honeysuckle. At first, the mainstays of the bedding system in the 1830s were pelargoniums, quickly followed by calceolarias, lobelias and alyssum. By 1840 the most popular plants – each being a genus that was undergoing rapid evolution through hybridization – were chrysanthemums, roses and dahlias. By 1839 there were more than 500 cultivars of dahlia and their popularity soon slipped down the social ladder.

A generation later, fashions had changed completely. Robert Louis Stevenson's cousin Mrs Loftie wrote in 1875, 'We rejoice heartily at the turn of the wheel which has given us back those dear old flowers. Queen Anne has come into her own again . . . turkscap lillies and stately hollyhocks . . . lavender and lupin . . . passion-flowers and musk roses . . .'[31] Yet another generation on and the Royal Horticultural Society was recording the following recent trends: fewer ericas, pelargoniums, ferns; less bedding; fewer florists' flowers, especially anemones, ranunculus, pansies and exhibition tulips; fewer 'show' roses; more garden roses; more irises, peonies and violas, taking the place of auriculas, phlox, hollyhocks and anemones. Sweet peas had moved up in the world. And there was a dahlia revival.[32]

Orchids were at all times held in high regard; they were expensive to acquire and difficult to cultivate well. In the 1830s Paxton cultivated eighty species in the glasshouses at Chatsworth. Fifty years later there were estimated to be 2,000 species in cultivation. John Seden bred orchids for the world's wealthy at Veitch.

His first hybrid, *Cypripedium sedenii*, flowered in 1873. Thereafter he raised 150 cypripediums, 140 laelio-cattleyas, sixty-five cattleyas, forty dendrobiums, twenty-five laelias, sixteen phalenopsis, twenty epidendrums, twelve masdevallias, nine calanthes, six disas, four zygopetalums and many others, including the first bigeneric hybrid, *Zygocolax veitchii*.

Rhododendrons also became so fashionable towards the end of the nineteenth century that they were a mark of social respectability. It was said that *nouveaux riches* in search of a country residence would first make sure that the soil was suitable for growing rhododendrons before buying an estate.

Plants were – and always have been – unpopular only because of the fashions or styles that are associated with them. Gertrude Jekyll made this point when she discussed bedding, which she regarded as tedious and stupid:

> It was not the fault of the Geranium or of the Calceolaria that they had been grievously misused and made to usurp too large a share of our garden spaces. Not once but many a time my visitors have expressed unbounded surprise when they saw these plants in my garden, saying, 'I should have thought that you would have despised Geraniums.' On the contrary, I love Geraniums ... for massing in sheltered places in hottest sunshine; and I love their strangely pleasant smell, and their beautiful modern colourings of soft scarlet and salmon-pink.

She concludes, 'even the better ways of gardening do not wholly escape the debasing influence of fashion'.[33]

During the nineteenth century, flower shows and horticultural societies began to multiply. 'In 1805,' Ray Desmond pointed out, 'only one horticultural society existed; by 1842 there were more than 200.' The same was true of shows, which increased throughout the nineteenth century, from the Royal Horticultural Society's Temple Show to local shows in every county and village. Flowers competed for prizes. The plant mattered not at all, what really counted was the size and regularity of the flowers. It was through visiting shows that many people got to know their plants, so breeders bred for show. Competitions and prizes provided the ultimate validation.

Perhaps the most competitive partnership in the history of English gardening was the alliance between the Hon. Vicary Gibbs and his head gardener, Edwin Beckett. Gibbs was a rich bachelor banker who also served as Conservative MP for St Albans from 1892 to 1904. His father, Lord Aldenham, had inherited Aldenham House as a young man, and lived there from 1869 until his death in 1907. At first Gibbs worked closely with his father, but increasingly he took over from Lord Aldenham as his own interest in gardening grew. He extended his father's avenues and planted new ones across the 200-acre park. He filled unsatisfactory lakes and made two new ones.

Beckett was a seeker after glory and he saw his opportunity in the garden of a rich, plant-loving banker who was prepared to employ up to 100 gardeners. By 1887, three years after his arrival at Aldenham, he was able to secure a laudatory article in *The Gardener's Chronicle* detailing the plantings in his subtropical beddings. By 1889 there were reports of greenhouses 'full of eucharis, croton, peaches, nectarines, grapes, figs and melons'. By 1891 they contained figs, fruiting bananas and dracaenas, with underplantings of a fine strain of celosia worked up by Beckett, and anthurium growing beneath the melons. There were also pineapple pits.

Meanwhile, Beckett had carried out all Gibbs's plans for landscaping and planting with such efficiency that he was in effect given the freedom to do what he enjoyed doing most, which was growing giant vegetables and winning as many prizes as possible at the Royal Horticultural Society shows. Gibbs, too, came to share this interest, so that master and servant for nearly fifty years worked to secure Aldenham's reputation, and their own fame as horticulturists. Winning prizes took such priority that Beckett was said to keep the dining room short of fruit and vegetables. Gibbs backed him. Beckett also bred Michaelmas daisies, phlox, penstemon and delphiniums. He was awarded the Royal Horticultural Society's Victoria Medal of Honour in 1906, ten years before his employer earned his.

Beckett was also an industrious horticultural writer and journalist. His most successful title was *Vegetables for Exhibition and Home Consumption*, which went through several editions between 1899 and 1927, but he also wrote books on roses, potatoes and strawberries. When he died in 1935, his estate was worth over £20,000, partly the result of building up a property portfolio for himself. Towards the end of his life, Gibbs also wrote a few articles about his collection of trees and shrubs. He was an enthusiastic collector of plants, and he demanded very high standards of order and cleanliness in the garden. In Beckett he found the perfect complement. Between them, they won over 100 gold medals from the Royal Horticultural Society. Beckett did not retire until Gibbs died in January 1932. His garden died with him. His collection of plants was auctioned off – there were over 2,000 lots – and by the 1950s there was little or no trace of his garden at Aldenham.

Working Gardeners

The profession of gardening took on a modern structure during the course of the nineteenth century. At the top of the profession was the head gardener of a large country estate, running a substantial enterprise like the managing director of a modern business. Below him were foremen, under-gardeners, journeymen, apprentices, boys and labourers.

An experienced gardener at the end of the Napoleonic Wars earned about 10s a week. A head gardener in a large household could expect about £40 a year, compared with the butler's £50. Self-employed men were worse off, since they did not have the advantage of free board and lodging. The lowest rank of all – then, as now – was the jobbing gardener. One such unfortunate wrote that this condition was 'greater slavery than being a common labourer' and expected to end his days in the workhouse.[34] And even a retained gardener on a large estate at all stages of his training and service was paid less than the butler.

But wages rose steadily. Average earnings for all workers in England in 1868 were 13s 9d. Forty years later they had risen to 17s 11d and the cost of most necessities – notably food and clothing – had dropped not only in real terms but also in absolute terms. There was more money for everyone, and gardeners and their families were among the millions who lived more comfortable lives, and consumed more imported food, than ever before. This was the time, too, when the number of people employed as domestic servants, including gardeners, reached its

The parade of gardeners outside the Great Conservatory at Chatsworth, c. 1900, gives a good indication of the scale of private service in the nineteenth century. The foremen wore bowler hats.

peak. The agricultural depression of the 1880s onwards led to severe cutbacks. Shrublands Park in Suffolk had had fifty-two gardeners in 1848; by 1900 the number was under thirty and in the decades after the Second World War it was down to fewer than five.

Most professionals learned their craft from the experience of older gardeners. A gardener's boy started full-time work in a large establishment at about fourteen, though it was possible for twelve-year-olds to spend only part of the day at school and the rest at work. His jobs would be the most basic and least agreeable: washing pots, sweeping paths and humping coal for the boilers. After a year or so, he might start work in one of the departments like the kitchen garden or the glasshouses. But by the time he was seventeen or eighteen, a young man would be encouraged to move on, gaining new experience and skills as an 'improver'.

Improvers were upwardly mobile young gardeners. They learned their profession at the same time as practising it and they backed up their work by studying everything from botany and physiology to trigonometry (useful for laying out beds). Often their jobs would still be fairly menial, but experience at this stage in a garden of major reputation – Chatsworth under Paxton, for example, or Regent's Park under Robert Marnock – would be of considerable help in getting a further step or two up the ladder. Meanwhile, gardeners of all ages had to abide by the head gardener's rules and regulations, which would be matched by sanctions, usually fines. Misdemeanours included anything dangerous (like leaving flammable liquids near the boilers), negligent (forgetting to water or ventilate the glasshouses) or antisocial (swearing was invariably punished with a fine).

After another three or four years, when he was in his early twenties, an improver would seek a job as a skilled journeyman and begin to specialize in a particular section of the garden, like fruit-growing. Earnings would vary between regions but were increasingly related to national rates established in the gardening press. Improvers and journeymen lived in the bothy, which was bachelor accommodation usually set into the walls of the walled garden, with dormitories, a kitchen and scullery. They were expected to continue to study at the same time as gaining useful experience. Usually a woman would be employed to clean, wash, make the beds and cook for them, but sometimes the men were expected to perform some of these tasks for themselves. They were also expected to remain single. Any attempt to make the acquaintance of the housemaids was discouraged and a young man who married would have to leave immediately and find a job with a cottage – usually as a gardener in a smaller establishment. In 1824, a student gardener at the Horticultural Society's garden at Chiswick was summoned by the magistrates to provide for an illegitimate child. His statement of means was not believed by the magistrates, which left him with the 'alternative of paying [an allowance to the mother of his child], going to prison, or marrying the girl . . . in the simplicity and goodness of his heart he chose the latter'.[35]

But the world of nineteenth-century horticulture was a many-layered pyramid and few twelve-year-olds would end up as head gardeners. What happened to the other garden boys in later life? Some took jobs as gardeners in small households, but most left altogether. A surprisingly large number sought better-paid work in public service – the army, the police, the post office or the railways. It gave them better working hours, more freedom, the social status which comes with wearing a uniform, and sometimes a house while working and a pension on retirement.

By the time he was thirty, a top-flier would be looking for a job as head gardener on a fair-sized estate, advertising his availability in *The Gardener's Chronicle*. The head gardener in a large establishment was principally an adminis-

This illustration from The Child's Book of Trades, *1867, depicts a typical Victorian gardener engaged in the typical activity of potting.*

trator, but when in charge of a smaller staff was described as a 'working head gardener'. His deputy would be known as a second gardener in a large establishment and an under-gardener in a small one.

On small properties, the working head gardener would be directly responsible to the owner. The requirements of a typical small estate were described in 1875 as follows:

> For the kitchen and fruit gardens two men will be required, one for the lawn and flower garden, one for the drive and shrubberies, and a journeyman gardener and apprentice or youth of sixteen to eighteen for the houses, with a youth or two or women for leaf-clearing etc. We have made an allowance for a man for the extra labour and odd jobs ... the calculation does not include the head gardener, who can always be profitably employed in the higher branches of the art without participating in higher labour.[36]

The head gardener on a large estate was usually appointed by the owner's agent, bailiff or steward. Head gardeners, for gardens of whatever size, might also be recommended by nurserymen, the Horticultural Society or other garden-owners. Personal recommendation was central to the system. Estates were generally on very good terms with each other at all levels: thus owners spoke to owners, agents

From Waterloo to the Trenches 1820–1914

to agents and head gardeners to head gardeners. The appointment of a head gardener was an important one, and the expectation was that the man would stay for many years. *The Gardener's Chronicle* began to advertise for gardeners at all levels from 1863. Towards the end of the nineteenth century employment agencies started to take gardeners on to their books, and other agencies grew up which specialized in gardeners. There was a certain amount of poaching good gardeners from other employers – just as there was a wry grain of truth in Saki's jest that his cook 'was a good cook as cooks go, and as cooks go she went'. But this was unusual. It was more common for the head gardener who sought a move – perhaps for family reasons – to approach a potential employer and let it be known that he would be available when the present incumbent retired.

Head gardeners were employers, too. People came to work for them, learned and advanced themselves, and then moved on to other head gardeners' enterprises. They were responsible for the maintenance and development of the parkland landscape and pleasure grounds. This gave them artistic fulfilment and an opportunity to display their learning – especially when planting exotic trees – as well as the wealth of their employers. Generally speaking, the policy for developing and embellishing the grounds would be discussed and agreed by the head gardener with the lady of the house or perhaps an unmarried daughter who had responsibility within the household. Then it became the head gardener's task to implement the agreed policy.

Throughout the nineteenth century an important part of the job of the head gardener was to produce the widest possible selection of top-quality fruit and vegetables for the kitchen every day of the year. This gave rise to a constant search for novelty and a striving after technical perfection in the science and art of cultivation. It also meant that the head gardener and the housekeeper had to work closely together to ensure that their master's expectations were fulfilled. The demand for substantial flower decorations on dining-room tables grew after about 1860. This, and the arrangement of flowers in bedrooms, tended to be the preserve of the ladies of the house. The head gardener's responsibility was to arrange flowers, whether as cut flowers or in pots, in the principal reception rooms – that is, the hall, drawing room and other living rooms. Here, too, the head gardener's main aim was variety, and diversity probably reached its highest point at around 1900. Only in the late twentieth century did garden-owners begin to rediscover the sheer variety of what had been available to their Victorian ancestors, for whom such plants as globe artichokes, salsify and scorzonera were by no means unusual.

On the whole, gardeners in private service were well looked after. They had free accommodation, free fuel and access to free produce from the garden. It was always possible that the free cottage would be damp, insanitary and in need of repair, but gardeners' working conditions at all levels improved throughout the nineteenth century – and not just their wages and conditions of service, but their accommodation, education and indeed their social standing. Gardening became regarded as a respectable vocation – even, perhaps, a learned profession. It was a means to get an education, obtain a management job and acquire social status. The most able might eventually leave to set up as nurserymen or hybridists on their own account, but most were content to enjoy the success and status they had achieved.

Head gardeners on large estates in the middle of the nineteenth century wielded enormous power and influence. They were highly respected and could be treated, as Paxton was, as persons of national importance in a way that is hard to imagine today. This importance was founded on several social and economic changes which took place in the 1820s and 1830s: a greater influx of new plants from abroad for which there was a demand among garden-owners, bigger budgets to spend, changes in taste which tested their skills as cultivators (particularly the requirement for tender bedding and large-specimen exotic plants and orchids) and a constant demand for variety and opulence on the tables of the rich. A head gardener might become a confidential friend of his employer, as Paxton was, entrusted with more power and consulted more frequently than his job title might suggest. On the other hand, head gardeners might also be accused, on occasions, of keeping their distance too much from their employer as they sought glory and success in prizes won at exhibitions and publicity in trade magazines. The life of a head gardener could be very competitive. And even the most supportive of employers could make the head gardener's job difficult by having unrealistic expectations and not making allowances for occasional disasters, like a complete crop failure caused by freak weather or a new disease of plants. Likewise their wives and daughters could create mayhem not by interfering but just by allowing their crinolines to knock pots over in the glasshouses and decapitate flowers as they walked along the edge of a border.

Most head gardeners were greedy for recognition and thirsty for reward, which was usually calculated by prizes at shows and reports in such publications as *The Gardener's Chronicle*. But such events and the prizes they brought home conferred renown on the gardens and their owners, too. These employers might even bring their friends and visitors to the walled garden to meet the head gardener and see the certificates and prizes displayed on the walls of the garden office.

Not all employers were supportive or appreciative. Henry Bright commented in 1881:

> nothing can be more spoiling to the gardener than these flower-shows. In the first place, the prize-ticket generally asserts that the prize is adjudged to 'Mr. —, gardener to —.' The owner of the garden is nobody, and the gardener is everything.

The prize is in almost every case regarded as the unchallenged property of the gardener, who has, nevertheless, won the prize by his master's plant, reared at his master's expense.[37]

To which an employer might reply, 'I for one trust that no employer [has] the least wish to claim any prize won by his gardener. There would soon be an end of horticultural shows if the employer took the prize.'[38] There was always a suspicion that the gardener would be growing for exhibition rather than for beauty or taste and that he would neglect his other duties in search of growing a prize-winner. The essayist Mrs Loftie expressed this forcefully in an essay on 'Modern Gardens' written in 1879:

> The ordinary modern gardener ... must appear to a real lover of flowers the most insufferable mixture of conceit and ignorance. He makes no attempt to learn how to keep the pleasure-ground in beauty all the year round, and the kitchen-garden well stocked with necessary crops. On the contrary, his only ambition is to see his name appear on prize-tickets at neighbouring flower-shows, and to sell in Covent Garden the fruit he cultivates at his master's expense. To gratify these noble aspirations he does not scruple to appropriate the hours which legally belong to his employers, nor will he hesitate to sacrifice all the flowers of a plant which should be covered with blossoms in order to perfect a single bloom for exhibition.[39]

The truth is that there were good and bad gardeners at every level. Much depended upon how well they were managed by their employer, but even the best and most knowledgeable of owners was sometimes badly let down. John Wedgwood, a leading light of the Horticultural Society, described in his garden book how he returned home after a few weeks in 1831 to find his garden 'in great confusion, having been entirely neglected. No onions, no carrots, no parsnips, no red beets. All my early peas gone, the seed beds in many cases evidently not dug, only raked over. The broccoli in holes all gone ... I immediately discharged Hooper for his entire neglect during my absence.'

On the whole, employers got the employees they deserved – and sometimes very much better. Often badly managed, without clear instructions or consultation, head gardeners ran a large and efficient operation in return for neither recognition nor understanding. In one famous instance – still quoted as an authority in cases of defamation – an employer said something about her gardener which she knew to be false and ended up in court. The background to this case, called *Barnes* v. *Rolle*, was James Barnes's tenure of nearly thirty years as head gardener at Bicton in Devon, during which time he developed Lord and Lady Rolle's gardens into a mid-Victorian cynosure. William Robinson attested in court that they were second to none in England. Then Barnes was obliged by illness to retire, at fairly short notice. The widowed Lady Rolle was understandably piqued and, rather foolishly, made derogative remarks about him in a couple of letters she wrote shortly afterwards. In one she told a member of the public who had written to ask if he could visit the gardens that she did not want to take up the time of her new gardener with such visits because 'everything in her garden and hothouses and greenhouses and arboretum are left in such a neglected state'. A keen attorney took up the case on Barnes's behalf, but Lady Rolle did not take the matter seriously enough to reply to his letters and, as a result, Barnes's barrister obtained judgement in default of her entering a defence. A hearing was called to assess the quantum of damages which, in those days, was always decided by a jury. Lady Rolle's counsel invited the members of the jury to show their disapproval of the action by dismissing the claim with token damages of one farthing. Barnes's lawyer replied that 'persons in high stations were to be respected, but when they forgot what was due to those who had faithfully served them they became contemptible'. Barnes was awarded £100.[40]

The real trouble, more often than not, was that owners did not know what to expect, did not understand what was possible and did not estimate what it would cost. Mrs Loftie put it across forcefully:

> Ignorance and want of taste in those who have money to spend must always have a fatal effect upon everything produced. Rich people ... know nothing about flowers, and can only judge of the merits of their pleasure-ground by the length of the bills and the number of men they keep employed. It never occurs to them that ... no garden can be at all satisfactory without the nameless charm that only can be given by the superintendence of a person of taste and cultivation.[41]

Henry Bright agreed. Owners needed to take the management of their garden into their own hands and be masters not in name but in reality. It was not necessary to understand every matter of detail, but they did need to decide what should be done and then take care that the gardener carried out their orders.[42]

Gertrude Jekyll identified another problem: that many new garden-owners have difficulties arising from 'the ignorance and obstructiveness of gardeners'. The problem arises because the new owner wants the old gardener to stay on and do new things for him and with him, and the old gardener has neither the inclination nor the knowledge, training and experience to do so. The trouble with this sort of gardener is that 'He forgets what is the main pleasure of a garden, namely to give its owner the best and highest kind of earthly pleasure.' But Jekyll does point out that frequent causes of irritation arise from the master's ignorance and unreasonable demands. Most of Jekyll's clients were people who had made a lot of money quite recently, often in the City of London, and had little previous experience of country life. So she shrewdly flattered her readers by emphasizing that the sort of man who comes to gardening in middle age with a fine fortune behind him was in every way a superior being, 'always widening his ideas and experience, cultivating his tastes, searching for the noblest and most divinely inspired examples of human work and seeing with an eye that daily grows more keenly searching, and receiving and holding with the brain ever gains a firmer grasp, and so acquires some measure of the higher critical faculty'. And she clinched the argument by adding that so far as composing beautiful borders was concerned, 'the servant may set up the canvas and grind the colours, but the master alone can paint the picture'.[43]

Visiting other gardens was an important part of a head gardener's job, exchanging plants, discussing problems and seeing at first hand how others managed. Head gardeners needed to attend national shows and conferences to continue their own education as gardeners. Such were the knowledge and skills of these professionals that they were held in high regard not just by their own employers but by other landowners, professionals, nurserymen and expert amateurs. At this level, gardening became one of those activities, like racing, where people of every class, age and sex could mix, if not on equal terms, at least without many of the restrictive taboos of contemporary society. Keen and knowledgeable amateurs also visited large gardens to see and learn from the achievements of these heavyweight head gardeners. One such expert was the rosarian Dean Reynolds Hole, who described the impression he made on the head gardener to the Duke of Rutland at Belvoir Castle:

> I once asked the head gardener whether I could walk through the grounds, and added that my name was Hole. And when he inquired 'Mr *Reynolds* Hole?' and I replied in the affirmative, I was first of all astonished by the abrupt manner in which he turned his back upon me and then elated by the words which he spoke to one of his subordinates, 'John, set the fountains playing!'[44]

William Robinson

William Robinson (1838–1935) was an opinionated and irascible Ulsterman who, like so many of his countrymen, found fame and fortune in England. He was born to middle-class Protestant parents. His father was a land agent who deserted his family and eloped to America with the wife of his employer, a Lady St George. William's uncle and aunt stepped in to help the family and suggested that he, the eldest, should start upon a career in horticulture. His first job was as a gardener at the Marquess of Waterford's estate at Curraghmore, after which he trained at the National Botanic Gardens in Dublin and went to work for the Reverend Sir Hunt Johnson-Walsh, Bt, at Ballykilcavan in Queen's County. There is a story that Robinson quarrelled with Johnson-Walsh, drew the fires which warmed the glasshouses in midwinter and ran away to England. This cannot be true, because after he left Ballykilcavan Robinson went to see Dr David Moore at Glasnevin, who gave him an introduction to Robert Marnock, the curator of the Royal Botanic Society gardens at Regent's Park in London – which Moore would most certainly not have done if there were a shadow over Robinson's employment history.

His move to England was the making of William Robinson. Robert Marnock was a man of power and influence, and gave his Irish charge considerable freedom and responsibility. Robinson began writing articles and travelling. He made influential friends and was elected, while still in his twenties, a Fellow of the Linnean Society of London. His first book was called *Gleanings from French Gardens* (by William Robinson, FLS – Robinson was proud of his membership of the Linnean Society) and came out in 1868. It was reprinted in the following year, at the same time as his second book, *The Parks, Promenades and Gardens of Paris*, was published, and his third, a revised edition of Jane Loudon's *The Amateur Gardener's Calendar*.

Robinson was a most prolific writer, though his writings are full of contradictions and *volte-faces*. In 1870, he visited his father, who had prospered in San Francisco, and returned with enough money in 1871 to found his first weekly magazine, *The Garden*, which he edited for twenty-five years. This was followed by several further gardening periodicals, some aimed at the owners of smaller gardens and others at the top end of the market. Most made a lot of money for him.

Robinson was the leading proponent of natural gardening. He was horrified by the scale of carpet-bedding in England, which was uncommon in his native Ireland, writing that 'the flower-gardener was trying to rival the wall-paper man'. His beliefs were first articulated in *The Wild Garden* in 1870 and then at much greater length in his compendium of articles put together in book form as *The English Flower Garden* in 1883. After a slow start, *The English Flower Garden* became extremely popular. It was reprinted frequently in the 1890s and 1900s and went through a total of fifteen editions during his long lifetime. For fifty years and for at least two generations of gardeners, *The English Flower Garden* was the book of books – the gardener's bible.

The formal style of gardening which Loudon and Paxton had advocated was expensive and labour-intensive. Robinson's attack on formal bedding and plea for a more wild approach to planting found an echo in the thoughts of the Arts and Crafts movement. William Morris himself criticized 'over-artificiality in flowers'.

Alfred Parsons engraved the frontispiece to William Robinson's Wild Garden *in 1880. Robinson's wild gardening, like Capability Brown's landscaping, was an inexpensive way of turning large areas to amenity.*

It was in part a reaction against the institutionalized improvement of human life by confident Victorians. But Robinson's success was undoubtedly aided by the cost which bedding out involved – costs incurred not only in the acquisition of plants but also in the expense of heating glasshouses and employing gardeners. Fashion, too, had a hand in the change towards William Robinson's style of gardening. It was thought wrong to breed flowers so much that they became grossly artificial. Indeed, some of Robinson's allies urged their readers to stick to species and to shun hybrids and freak forms. Wild flowers were God's purest creation; artificial breeding could not improve upon His handiwork. At first Robinson confined his ideas about wild gardening to the remoter parts of the garden, to complement the more formal areas near the house and the utilitarian aspects of gardening. His views were therefore fairly acceptable to those who wished to extend their gardening and the domain of their control over a wider area. Then, as more and more suitable plants came into England from the plant collectors, Robinson declared that wild gardening should be practised not merely with native English plants but also with any plant which will survive under English conditions. It should be said that Robinson modified his views time and again in response to people's changing needs, constantly re-creating himself as the arbiter of horticultural fashion. In this he was very successful.

One effect of William Robinson's espousal of wild gardening with hardy shrubs was that plant collectors eschewed the import of tender and tropical plants for rich men to grow in glasshouses and turned instead to plants that could survive outside in the English climate. Hence the demand for hardy trees, shrubs, herbaceous plants and alpines which was satisfied by such collectors as Forrest, Henry and Wilson. Wild gardens were especially popular with plantsmen, for whom they gave an intellectual justification for making a collection. It enabled them to distribute the plants around their garden as was convenient for them, with minimal regard for their effect upon the composition, and maximum regard for how they would grow, flourish and be enjoyed as specimen plants. William Robinson's natural gardening was assisted by the opening up of China. The

CHAPTER FIVE

Riches to Rags to Riches
1915–2000

War & Peace, Death & Taxation

When Edward VII rebuilt the glasshouses at Windsor in 1901–5, he laid them out on an imperial scale. The contractors used 1,900,000 bricks, 1,800 tons of lime, 1,000 tons of Portland cement, 160 tons of Rangoon teak wood and 156,500 square feet of glass. The finishing touches required eleven miles of piping, eighteen tons of putty and ten tons of paint. The builders were Mackenzie and Moncur Ltd, who proudly described it as 'probably the largest private range in the world', and listed its component parts for many years afterwards in their catalogue:

> fourteen Vineries, eight Peach Houses, three Fig Houses, two Palm Houses, six Orchid Houses, two Show Malmaison Houses, two Carnation Houses, two Flowering Show Houses, Tropical House, Laelia House, two Propagating Houses, Stove Houses, two Cypripedium Houses, two Dendrobium Houses, Begonia House, two Cyclamen Houses, two Geranium Houses, three Azalea Houses, Fernery, two Amaryllis Houses, four Cucumber Houses, four Melon Houses, two Tomato Houses, two Eucharis Houses, two Imantophyllum Houses, two Pelargonium Houses, Rose House, two Connecting Plant Corridors, also Gardeners' Quarters Cottages, Back Offices, Stables, Cart-sheds, Workshops etc.

The 'Gardeners' Quarters' was a bothy for twenty-two men and an annexe for the caretaker. Each man had a separate bedroom and there were bath-rooms, recreation and dining rooms and central heating throughout. The fruit ranges, each a quarter of a mile long, were divided into four, one to serve each season of the year. The plant corridors were also planted with fruit – figs, apricots and plums. By the early 1930s, when the young Percy Thrower worked there,

❧ *Detail of the illustration on page 239.*

Edward VII rebuilt the glasshouses at Windsor in 1901–5. The builders described them as 'probably the largest private range in the world'.

the early range held peaches and nectarines growing in pots, early grapes ('Black Hamburgh' and 'Foster's Seedling'), two more strawberry houses, more peaches and nectarines on the walls and another vinery where the grapes ripened later. This early range had to provide ripe strawberries for when the Court came to Windsor Castle from Buckingham Palace at Eastertime and those in charge were also responsible for ensuring that grapes, both black and white, peaches and nectarines were ready and at their best by May 26th, Queen Mary's birthday. The other range produced the later fruit: peaches ('Peregrine', 'Duke of York', 'Hale's Early'); nectarines ('Humboldt', 'Pine Apple', 'Lord Napier') and grapes ('Muscat of Alexandria', 'Alicante', 'Madresfield Court' and 'Mrs Pince').[1]

The King's kitchen garden at Sandringham was likewise enormous – sixteen acres in all, with hothouses for codiaeums, dracaenas and anthuriums. Cool-house plants were substituted after the First World War: in the 1920s and 1930s, Sandringham had three houses for orchids, three for winter-flowering carnations and three crammed full with nothing but *Begonia* 'Gloire de Lorraine'.[2]

The first half of the twentieth century was a period of enormous social, economic and political upheaval, perhaps the most extensive of any in this book. A man who started work as a gardener in 1900 and retired in 1950 would have witnessed the complete extinction of the traditions of Victorian garden excellence, and the reduction of gardening to near-subsistence levels. The trend was already visible at the start of the century, at the same time as Edward VII was building his empire of glass in Windsor's royal gardens. One truism was central to the entire system of private gardening: the head gardener and his staff existed only to provide their employer with the prestige on which his social credibility depended. Fruit, vegetables and fruit of the highest quality and greatest rarity were consistently produced in sufficient quantities and at every time of the year – especially out of season.

The trouble was that the luxuries which bolstered the privileged lifestyle of the landed classes were constantly turning into staples. Grapes were successfully grown by market gardeners. Pears, peaches and apricots came by train from southern Europe. Like the flowers that grew in commercial forcing houses and nurseries along the Riviera, they arrived in London in perfect condition. They graced the tables of both landed gentry and rich townspeople alike. Pineapples and bananas came from the Canary Islands, apples from North America, out-of-season vegetables from France and Italy. Roses in large numbers were forced by commercial growers in the Lea valley; carnations and orchids were imported from Holland and Belgium. It is scarcely surprising, therefore, that towards the end of the nineteenth century the owners of large country houses began to downsize their kitchen gardens. One-time luxuries were available to anyone who was willing to buy them, and now more readily available in London and provincial cities than in the country. The social advantages of a large, private kitchen garden were proportionately diminished. At a time of reduced rentals and agricultural depression, money might more usefully be spent than in maintaining expensive glasshouses. Even the eating habits of the rich were changing: puddings and sweets assumed the same status as fruit and the word 'dessert' began to be used – at least by some people – to describe all three.

Covent Garden grew in importance as improved transport brought produce to London from all over the world. The demand for exotic fruit and vegetables, grown in the glasshouses of the rich, declined accordingly.

By the 1900s the landowners were also under attack from the redistributive policies of the Liberal government. Lloyd George was the first prime minister to use taxation to achieve social reform. It was part of a deliberate campaign to diminish the power and wealth of the established classes. His 1909 budget raised income tax from 1s to 1s 2d in the pound (i.e. from 5 per cent to 5.8 per cent) and introduced a new 'super-tax' on incomes over £3,000. The rates and applicability of death duties were restructured with the specific intention of raising more revenue from these capital taxes than from income tax. A new land value duty was proposed, to take effect as a levy of 20 per cent on the unearned increment of land value and payable whenever land changed hands, together with a duty of ½d in the pound (0.2 per cent) on the capital value of undeveloped land and minerals. The budget was thrown out by the House of Lords and led to two general elections, followed by a once-for-all curbing of the political power of the peers. The old order, based on hereditary political power and the security of landed wealth, was finally broken. Soon the First World War would change the world for ever.

The immediate effect of the First World War on gardens and gardening was undramatic. The government was keen to increase home food production and the exhortation to 'Grow More Food' was heard for the first time, but food continued to be imported from the Empire and from North America, so that there was comparatively little need to increase home production. Gardens were still staffed and maintained, not by women (who tended to work in factories) but rather by men too old and boys too young to fight. During the first two years of the war, the Royal Horticultural Society continued to conduct its meetings and shows with every semblance of peaceful normality, but in 1917 the Old Hall in Westminster was requisitioned by the War Office and the society had to transfer its fortnightly meetings and shows to temporary accommodation in Buckingham Gate. Membership dropped during the war, but only by about 10 per cent, and it regained its pre-war strength by 1920, continuing to grow thereafter. Throughout the war, the society was actively involved in the government's food production campaign; it also sent bulbs and seeds to British prisoners of war in German camps.

Demobilization led to massive unemployment – returning ex-servicemen flooded the employment market – but the most significant result of the First World War was that the national debt increased very substantially, from £650 million to £6,850 million, a factor of more than ten. In order to finance this borrowing, taxation remained at a high level for several years into the peace. Rich men were encouraged to employ as many people as possible but lacked the means to do so. The slump of 1921–2 saw unemployment rise to its highest level for 100 years – it was never less than 1 million between the wars and remained by far the biggest social problem in the 1920s and 1930s. New wage regulations were an added disincentive. The average minimum for men rose from 30s 6d in 1918–19 to 46s 10d in 1920–21, as compared with an average of 16s 9d per week in 1914. In real terms, however, the minimum wage represented a deterioration in living standards, because the cost of living was also much increased.

The extra revenue the government needed to meet its payments of interest on public borrowing could only come from yet higher taxation – which fell hardest upon the rich. Income tax rose to 4s in the pound – 20 per cent. This created a vicious circle for the owners of large gardens: high unemployment meant that labour was readily available but high taxation meant that people could not afford to employ gardeners on anything like their pre-war scale. When a visitor to the gardens in 1938 asked the Duchess of Devonshire how many gardeners she had at Chatsworth, she replied, 'We used to have seventy, but now we manage with fifty. We have to be economical.'[3] Middle-class people were encouraged to live modestly on their unearned incomes and even to live abroad, so as to free up their jobs for others. Households were run with greatly reduced domestic staff. Women who had spent their war years working in factories and in the public utilities were unwilling thereafter to return to domestic service. The rise in the cost of living meant that 60 per cent of landed income was now expended on maintenance, management and making improvements, as opposed to 35 per cent before the war. Little wonder, therefore, that many of the larger estate-owners concluded that their traditional way of life was dead for ever. Houses and gardens designed to be serviced by cheap and plentiful labour could not be run on a skeleton staff. In 1920 the ninth Duke of Devonshire ordered the Great Conservatory at Chatsworth to be blown up. Such an extravagance, he believed, had no place in the post-war years of austerity.

'Land gives one position, and prevents one from keeping it up', said the hero of Oscar Wilde's *The Importance of Being Earnest*. It was a witticism whose underlying truth too many landowners now appreciated. The power and the glory of owning large estates had faded beyond measure. Death duties were increased in 1919 to 40 per cent on estates valued at over £2 million. Families where one or more heirs had died in the war were faced with a sequence of capital tax bills. The sales of land which began with the great agricultural depression of the 1880s now turned to a flood. One-quarter of England changed hands in the years 1918–21; it was a 'revolution in landowning'. But the most important factor – and perhaps the most unexpected – was the emergence of willing buyers. These new owners made a very different sort of garden from those of the traditional landowning classes.

The 1920s & 1930s: New Money & New Gardens

The market for land remained strong. Most of the buyers were tenant farmers whose purchase marked the first step in a process of social advance and gentrification. But some were men and women whose money came from commerce or good fortune – among them were Sir Philip Sassoon at Port Lympne, the first Lord Fairhaven at Anglesey Abbey, Lionel de Rothschild at Exbury, and the Hon. Vita Sackville-West and her husband, Sir Harold Nicolson, at Sissinghurst Castle. All had a genuine interest in some aspect of gardening. All were newly monied, and regarded their gardens as symbols of their wealth or taste. The houses and gardens at Port Lympne, Anglesey, Exbury and Sissinghurst were not dependent upon agricultural rentals for their well-being. Acreage was no longer an issue: a hundred acres or so was enough to ensure privacy. Nevertheless, such gardens kept alive the idyll of country life and its association with peace and tradition, old values and old money. When 'Chips' Channon visited Polesden Lacey in August 1939 he noted in his diary, 'the gardens are glorious, the grounds magnificently green and well-kept. Everywhere there is the silence, and spaciousness that comes from long-established wealth.'[4] The irony of Channon's observation is that 'Chips' was himself a complete *arriviste*, perhaps even a bounder, while his host at Polesden Lacey was Mrs Ronnie Greville, the rich but illegitimate daughter of a self-made Scottish millionaire.

Nevertheless, the distinctions which separated the classes had not entirely disappeared. Aristocratic haughtiness and bourgeois self-confidence were still present in abundance, and the gulf between the employer and the employee, the educated man and the professional gardener, was as great as ever. Fred Streeter –

The gardens at Aldenham were famous in the early twentieth century. Both their owner, the Hon. Vicary Gibbs, and his head gardener, Edwin Beckett, were seekers after horticultural glory.

later well known as one of the first garden broadcasters – was head gardener to Lord Leconfield at Petworth in Sussex during the late 1920s and, like most head gardeners, travelled around the country to learn from other gardens and gardeners.

One of the best-known gardens of the day belonged to a London banker called Vicary Gibbs at Aldenham in Hertfordshire. Gibbs had no hesitation in correcting Streeter's Latin pronunci-ation. 'Of course,' he said on one occasion, 'it's only a gentleman who can pronounce some of these names; even Beckett [Gibbs's own head gardener – a distinguished exhibitor and writer] makes an awful muddle of them – nearly as bad as you.' When Beckett came down for a visit to Petworth, Streeter introduced him to Lord Leconfield. Keen to make a good impression, Beckett said to Lord Leconfield, 'You have some-thing to get on with here, my Lord; a lot of these trees want coming out; they're over crowded. Look at that one.' To which Lord Leconfield replied, 'Yes, I am looking. Who do you think has to live here – you or me? I don't want an Aldenham with its toy trees and curves. I like to think of these trees as friends, and as they are mine they are welcome. Good day.'[5]

Philip Sassoon built the garden at Port Lympne in the 1920s as a setting for political entertaining. It was planted entirely for August and September.

Philip Sassoon inherited a banking fortune when his father died young in 1912 and, despite a remarkably lavish lifestyle, was still worth nearly £2 million when he himself died aged fifty in 1939. His mother was a Rothschild, which meant that Philip and his sister united the two most prominent, though very different, Jewish families who had made good in nineteenth-century London banking. Philip Sassoon was a politician, socialite, art-collector and passionate gardener. Though possessed of considerable charm and ability, he was also fussy, precious and rather flashy – a show-off who developed his house and garden on the Kent coast at Port Lympne as a way of displaying his wealth and impressing his political friends. Starting shortly after the Great War, Sassoon employed Philip Tilden to rebuild Port Lympne in a mixture of exotic and neo-classical styles. The finest feature was a broad flight of 100 brilliantly white marble steps leading to the house from one of the terraces, but Sassoon decided that they were too steep for some of his more elderly friends and had them replaced by 130 rather more gentle steps of the same brilliant white marble. A Moorish courtyard sported six vigorous fountains, and the heated swimming pool, also of marble, was designed on Roman models. There were separate gardens dedicated to begonias, dahlias and roses, and a rock garden thickly planted with lots of late-summer alpines to interest the keen amateur horticulturist Austen Chamberlain when he came to stay. When a guest commented on the almost miraculous perfection of the flowers, Sassoon explained, 'At twelve noon on the first of August each year, I give a nod to the head gardener who rings his bell and all the flowers pop up.'[6]

Lionel de Rothschild described himself as 'a banker by hobby, but a gardener by profession'. It was the money he made from banking which made the garden possible. Starting in 1919, he set out 'to beautify nature with colour' at Exbury. Rothschild had grown up in the grand style at Ascott and Gunnersbury, and had inherited the Rothschild passion for collecting things and for doing everything on an enormous scale. It was Lionel de Rothschild who said, 'No garden, however small, should contain less than two acres of rough woodland.' Rothschild was one of the few garden-owners who was able to garden and operate after the First World War on a significant scale and although his garden contained some interesting elements of design, it was as a collector of plants that he became best known. Rhododendrons are synonymous with Exbury, but he was also a successful and distinguished breeder of new orchids and nerines. As preparation for the garden, 150 men double-dug the ground two spits deep for ten years. Then a team of sixty gardeners did the planting; an additional fifteen worked in the greenhouses. Lionel had two acres of greenhouses. His collection extended beyond nerines to include hippeastrums, clivias and amaryllis. Rothschild's aim as a rhododendron breeder was to prolong the season with earlier- and later-flowering cultivars, to have something flowering in every month of the year if possible, and to breed rhododendrons with purer colour – above all, with less magenta. The garden, though planned, grew organically, filled with the plants that streamed out of his hybridizing houses. But, unlike his cousin Philip Sassoon, Rothschild had no interest in public recognition except among fellow horticulturists.

Sir Harold Nicolson and his wife began to create the garden for which Sissinghurst became famous in 1930. It would not have been possible without the substantial gifts of money which the Nicolsons received from Vita Sackville-West's mother. Old Lady Sackville was the illegitimate daughter of a Spanish gypsy, but had been left a fortune by an admirer called Sir John Murray Scott. Vita was her only daughter. Harold Nicolson was a career politician and journalist of modest means. Scott's money was the foundation of Sissinghurst's greatness. Nevertheless, Vita Sackville-West had impeccable aristocratic antecedents – her father owned Knole in Kent and her ancestors were the Dukes of Dorset. She had an intensely romantic view of her family and its history; she disliked the vulgarity of modern life and longed for 'another and different world'. In the garden at

Sissinghurst, she accommodated her 'love of the graces of life and retirement'. Sackville-West was also something of a snob, who mocked the 'shillingses' who paid to visit her garden and described the lower orders as 'bedint'. She would not have azaleas in her garden because they were 'Ascot, Sunningdale sort of plants', while rhododendrons were like 'fat stockbrokers, whom we do not want to have to dinner'. There was no place for bedint flowers at Sissinghurst.[7]

Often, it was American connections which made such gardens possible. Lawrence Johnston's Hidcote was the creature of Winthrop old money. 'Sunny' Marlborough used Consuelo Vanderbilt's fortune to restore much of the gardens at Blenheim both before and after the Great War. He called in Achille Duchêne, a French architect and designer, to make the beautiful water gardens which now set the massive house so exquisitely in Capability Brown's landscape. The Duke's second wife, Gladys, was also American, and she used her more modest resources to make herself a rock garden as a respite from boredom.[8]

Achille Duchêne (seen here on the left) created the formal water garden at Blenheim in the 1920s. This would not have been possible without Vanderbilt money.

But perhaps the best example of an inter-war garden founded on American wealth is Anglesey Abbey, which Urban Broughton bought in 1926 with funds from the fortune of his wife, Cara, an oil heiress. The garden we see today was really the achievement of their son, Huttleston, first Lord Fairhaven, a fussy bachelor who entertained a passion for the royal house of Windsor and longed to be accepted as a true Englishman. His garden is enormous: 100 flat acres of lush grass laid out with stately avenues of horse chestnut, beech, hornbeam and lime. Underneath are millions of snowdrops and daffodils. Within the structure are separate gardens entirely devoted to hyacinths, dahlias and Hybrid Tea roses – thousands of them massed in brilliant and colourful displays – and a collection of homoerotic sculptures.[9]

Such gardens are essentially an essay in self-indulgence, unlikely to survive their makers. In fact, Port Lympne, Anglesey, Exbury and Sissinghurst are all among the lucky ones which have either survived under the auspices of the National Trust or continued to develop as well-managed, privately owned tourist attractions. Many that were well known in the 1920s and 1930s have since passed into oblivion – not least, Vicary Gibbs's Aldenham and Ellen Willmott's Warley Place. The same fate could have overtaken Nymans in Sussex. When Ludwig Messel died in 1915, his son Leonard moved into the house, knowing nothing about gardening. Much of the Messels' fortune was invested in Germany and Russia, which meant that they suffered relative impoverishment during and after the Great War. But Leonard Messel was by nature a collector – a connoisseur and lover of art – and his instinct was to increase the collections of plants in the garden at Nymans. During the 1920s, Nymans was at the heart of the Sussex gardens mafia – which means that it was also right at the centre of English horticulture. Fellow plantsmen came from afar to stay at Nymans and see the gardens: the Williams cousins from Cornwall, Arthur Dorrien Smith from the Scilly Islands, Henry Elwes from Gloucestershire and Anglo-Jewish gardening friends like Lionel de Rothschild from Exbury. But when the house burned down in 1947, there was not enough left of the Messel fortune to rebuild it.

Tree-moving on a grand scale was developed throughout the nineteenth and twentieth centuries to satisfy rich but impatient garden-owners.

Fashionable Plants: Rhododendrons & Roses

William Robinson's ideas on wild and woodland gardening were perfectly suited to the stream of new plants that were introduced from the 1900s onwards. 'Chinese' Wilson was sent to China by Veitch in 1899 to discover the dove tree, *Davidia involucrata*. In 1903 he was engaged again, specifically to introduce *Meconopsis integrifolia*. George Forrest undertook seven expeditions between 1904 and 1932: the first was sponsored almost single-handedly by A. K. Bulley of Ness in Cheshire. Forrest's other plant-hunting trips were financed by private syndicates, usually headed by J. C. Williams of Caerhays Castle in Cornwall. The other members were the great and good horticulturists of the day, active in the affairs of the Royal Horticultural Society and, for the most part, possessed of large gardens of their own. Bulley – a rich amateur – also sponsored Frank Kingdon Ward in 1911 and Ward became a regular plant-collector in the Himalayas and in China until his death in 1958. Bulley also engaged R. E. Cooper as his personal collector, travelling from 1913 to 1916 in Sikkim and Bhutan.

The riches such expeditions to south-east Asia and the Himalayas produced for English gardens cannot be understated. The subscribers who benefited from them built up substantial woodland gardens richly planted with great numbers of rhododendrons, magnolias, stewartias, enkianthus, maples, sorbus and euonymus, and underplanted with meconopsis, primulas and lilies. Many went on to try their hand at hybridization, as did specialist nurserymen. The William Robinson style of woodland garden, colourfully planted with exotic shrubs and herbaceous plants, dominated English horticulture from 1910 to 1960. The greatest collections were built up by J. C. Williams at Caerhays, Colonel Stephenson Clarke at Borde Hill, Sir John Ramsden at Muncaster Castle, Lionel de Rothschild at Exbury, Charles Ely at East Bergholt and Gerald Loder (later Lord Wakehurst) at Wakehurst. These garden-owners tended also to distribute their bounty among others. Cornwall, for example, still has some twenty large woodland gardens lushly underplanted with rhododendrons introduced from the great plant collections of the early twentieth century, the result of gifts and exchanges between owners. As a result, Cornwall developed a sort of horticultural apartheid, sustained by its own garden society and flower shows well into the latter half of the twentieth century.

These woodland gardens were usually made in and around the clumps and shelter belts of traditional eighteenth-century landscaped parks. Visiting a garden like Sheffield Park in Sussex, now so full of exotic trees and shrubs, it is difficult to realize that, less than 100 years ago, this was a classical landscaped park on which both Capability Brown and Humphry Repton had worked. Woodland gardens became statements of wealth and power, because they could easily extend over 100 acres or more while needing fewer gardeners to maintain them than a five-acre kitchen garden. But they were also the sign of a serious garden-lover or plantsman, a fact which thus conferred intellectual credibility upon their owners. And woodland gardens were – above all – fashionable. The principles governing their layout and planting could be applied to a two-acre patch in suburban Surrey as easily as to a grand estate in Cornwall or on the Sussex hills. This universal popularity in turn gave rise to a strong demand for woodland plants from middle-class and yet more modest garden-owners which the nursery trade was quick to accommodate.

The demand for colourful and exotic woodland plants was met by a concentra-

Leopold de Rothschild, seen here by the lily pond at Gunnersbury in 1912, was a great collector and breeder of plants; so was his son Lionel de Rothschild at Exbury.

tion of nurseries in north-west Surrey – the area roughly bounded by Chertsey, Godalming and Farnham. The sandy soil known as 'Bagshot sand' was unsuitable for farming, but inexpensive, easily worked and ideal for growing American plants and calcifuges. The individual nurseries often had complicated histories, but collectively this was the world centre for the hybridization and popularization of the rhododendron in the first half of the twentieth century. After 'Chinese' Wilson introduced (first into the USA and then into England) fifty Japanese hybrid azaleas from Kurume in 1918, azaleas too were widely bred and selected in the Surrey nurseries.

Knap Hill Nursery, run by the Waterer family, introduced over 200 hybrid rhododendrons (including azaleas), mainly in the first half of the twentieth century. Bagshot Nursery also raised about 200 new rhododendron hybrids over the years. It, too, was a Waterer fiefdom, but amalgamated with the Wargave Plant Farm of Twyford in 1914 to become John Waterer, Son and Crisp (Bernard Crisp was the son of Sir Frank Crisp, the alpine gardener). In 1968 the company took over Sunningdale Nurseries, but in 1982 the Bagshot Nursery was sold to Notcutts of Woodbridge. Goldsworth Nursery at Woking was owned throughout the twentieth century by the Slocock family; Martin Slocock is the Treasurer of the Royal Horticultural Society. Goldsworth Nursery introduced about 100 rhododendron hybrids in the course of the twentieth century. Standish and Noble at Sunningdale were the most substantial of the Surrey nurseries in the nineteenth century. They were acquired by Major Herbert Russell in 1939 and managed by his Old Etonian son James after 1944. Graham Stuart Thomas worked for them in the 1950s. In 1968 the nursery was sold to John Waterer, Son and Crisp. Sunningdale bred a number of rhododendron hybrids but also introduced other plants, including *Astrantia major* 'Sunningdale Variegated' and *Buddleja* 'Lochinch'.

Rhododendrons were not the only plants to be widely bred and grown in the twentieth century. Daffodils and orchids were bred in their thousands. Pinks and carnations continued to be popular: the Allwood pinks developed from the 1920s onwards. New genera were hybridized: the Russell lupins, bred in 1911, were eventually released in 1937. The popularity of sweet peas was given a great boost by the development of the Spencer sweet pea in 1900. And specialist nurserymen satisfied the demand for such popular genera as camellias, peonies, irises and clematis. But the most popular flower of all, and the most widely hybridized by far, was the rose.

No plant has been such a creature of capricious fashion as the garden rose. The type which dominated in English gardens from 1900 to 1960 was the Hybrid Tea, first bred in the 1870s and 1880s by a Wiltshire cattle farmer called Henry Bennett. The success of the Hybrid Teas was part of a move away from the cultivation of roses principally for exhibition, where the size of individual flowers counted for more than their number, scent, carriage or colour. The new Hybrid Teas were garden roses, to be grown in beds and borders, enjoyed as plants and picked for their flowers. By 1900, their fortune was firmly in the ascendant and it was true to say that the rose was the 'queen of flowers'. This growth in popularity can be measured. Membership of the National Rose Society of Great Britain had hovered for many years at around 500. Then it suddenly took off in about 1900. In 1903 membership topped 1,000; by 1908 it was more than three times this figure and by 1913 had grown to 6,000. This was almost entirely the result of the emergence of the Hybrid Teas.

Queen Mary's Rose Garden in Regent's Park (seen here in 1938) was planted in 1932. It is evidence of the remarkable popularity of Hybrid Tea roses for much of the twentieth century.

The popularity of the rose was boosted by the widespread planting of dedicated rose gardens, where roses were massed in special beds of their own. By the 1920s and 1930s, it was usual to plant fifty or 100 plants of one cultivar in a single bed, packed in to create a solid mass of a single colour which repeated on and off throughout the summer and autumn. The market in roses has always been fuelled by novelty, but the Hybrid Tea is close to the limits of its natural adaptability in the British Isles – all roses fare better in climates with hotter summers than ours. The English require lightly petalled flowers to cope with their cool, wet climate. Breeders like McGredy and Dickson in Northern Ireland developed strains that were perfectly adapted to meet this need. The English – or Irish –

Hybrid Tea was a large-flowered rose of supreme elegance and floriferousness, and proved historically to be by far the most successful and enduring of all roses.

The arrival of a remarkable French rose called 'Peace', in 1945, gave a further boost to the popularity of roses in England. 'Peace' had the ability to shine and perform in all climates and in all weather conditions. Its vigour and health gave everyone an entirely new benchmark by which to judge their roses. Soon its progeny were available in every colour, shade, tone, tint and combination except blue and, when crossed with the old polyantha shrub roses, gave rise to a yet more floriferous and gaudy range of roses known as Floribundas. In the mid-1950s, the membership of the Royal National Rose Society was nearly twice that of the Royal Horticultural Society itself. Harry Wheatcroft and Ena Harkness were household names.

Fashions come and go. The downfall of the Hybrid Tea rose as England's most popular plant began within the ranks of the rosarians themselves. In 1955 Graham Stuart Thomas published a book called *The Old Shrub Roses*, in which he extolled the merits of the roses like Gallicas and Damasks, which had held sway during the early part of the nineteenth century. It was a successful and influential book, and was followed in due course by *Shrub Roses of Today* in 1962 and *Climbing Roses Old and New* in 1965. These three books, and the aesthetic they articulated, brought about a complete change of perception among garden-owners. The upper classes and upper middle classes, whose tastes and activities determine the fashions in gardening, abandoned their partiality for the bright colours of Hybrid Teas and Floribundas. Suddenly these popular and successful beauties were vulgar, blatant, unscented, shapeless and sickly. Old-fashioned shrub roses, by contrast, were the embodiment of good taste and sensibility. No matter if they suffered badly from mildew or rust and flowered only once, they were utterly redeemed by an exquisite array of button-eyed, picotee, imbricated or quartered shapes and sometimes a scent which set them apart from other roses. Hybrid Teas were common and ugly; no one with even a modicum of good sense or good taste would choose to grow them. They were 'startlingly vulgar', 'brash as a Cambridge Union debater' and of 'positively apoplectic appearance'.[10]

It was during the 1970s that a new type of shrub rose started to emerge in quantity, bred by a Shropshire farmer called David Austin, mainly by crossing Floribundas with old-fashioned Gallica roses. They combined the best features of the old roses – their floral shape and scent – with the main attractions of the Hybrid Teas – vigour and remontancy. Fashion being the creature it is, these new 'English' roses swept away first the Hybrid Teas and then the older roses themselves. Austin's roses remain at the cutting edge of popularity today – though nothing stays fashionable for ever, and doubtless we shall yet see further shifts of taste among garden roses in years to come. Alternative forms have already emerged, but have found little favour so far with the horticultural establishment. Miniature and patio roses, for example, have failed to attract today's wealthier gardeners because they are associated with small and modest gardens. The bigger your garden, the bigger the plants should be.

Dig for Victory:
The Second World War & Its Aftermath

When the Second World War broke out in 1939, the need to increase home production of vegetables and fruit was immediately understood. The government's food production campaign began with the slogan 'Grow More Food', but this was replaced in 1940 by the far more memorable 'Dig for Victory'. There was an enormous demand for information. People anticipated correctly that, unless they grew their own, they might have little in the way of fruit and vegetables to eat. The Ministry of Information issued helpful pamphlets with such uplifting titles as *The Garden Goes to War* and *Cloches versus Hitler*. The press, too, was full of advice on how to grow your own food. County horticultural advisers gave information locally, aided by professional horticulturists who volunteered to give talks and lectures in villages and towns. In the larger towns, production was increased by increasing the number of allotments. Playing fields, common land and public parks were all turned over to vegetable production. Women were encouraged to learn horticulture at a high academic level. Graduates of such colleges as Swanley in Kent or Studley in Warwickshire were appointed to positions as head gardeners in schools and hospitals. Untrained enthusiasts signed up for the Women's Land Army, which eventually had 90,000 members. Some estate gardens where all the gardeners had been called up were entirely taken over by Land Army girls, who moved into the bothy and turned the gardens to food production. In large gardens, with greatly reduced staff, the head gardeners would be encouraged to sell the surplus produce in the national effort.

This Ministry of Information poster encouraged people to grow more food. During the Second World War, playing fields, common land and public parks were all turned over to allotments.

Right from the early years of the Second World War – this picture was taken in August 1940 – most people realized that they might have little in the way of fruit and vegetables to eat unless they grew their own.

Right from the start, the Royal Horticultural Society cooperated with the Ministry of Agriculture in producing pamphlets and broadcasting advice on how to grow more fruit and vegetables in private gardens and allotments. The society ran courses for the Women's Land Army, sent its employees to lecture all over the country and published a series in its monthly *Journal* on how to increase the supplies of home-grown food. The Royal Horticultural Society did, however, have differences with the Ministry on how the increased production should be achieved. The official advice was that people should dig up their lawns and grow vegetables in place of annuals in the front of their borders. The Royal Horticultural Society, by contrast, advised people to practise more intensive cultivation of their vegetable gardens rather than digging up lawns and borders: 'the mental refreshment and recreation which flowers can give us all will be a notable contribution to the national spirit', it insisted. The society's own catch-phrase was 'Economy in the Garden'. It meant abandoning bedding out, reducing labour spent on mowing lawns and deferring structural repairs – for example, to gravel paths. In short, everyone should spend less time and money on maintenance. The society advised garden-owners to clip their hedges only once a year, to minimize watering, to abandon the dead-heading of rhododendrons and roses, and, of course, to abandon such extravagant practices as the early forcing of fruit and vegetables. Everyone should choose vegetables which were nutritious (especially peas and beans for their protein, and 'greens' for their vitamins), sow high-yield cultivars, bottle and preserve as much as possible and save seed from year to year, provided the seed maintained the vigour and high yield for which it was originally bred. But the Royal Horticultural Society also had an eye to the long-term needs of the country when the war was finally won. Garden-owners should economize on fuel for glasshouses, but do whatever they could to save and preserve valuable collections of plants and individual specimens.

Commercial horticulturists and market gardeners were in the forefront of the push to produce more fruit and vegetables. Growers of cut flowers and potted plants, whether they worked under glass or in the open, were required to turn 90 per cent of their nurseries to food production. Only the remaining 10 per cent could be used to preserve stocks of permanent flower crops. Seedsmen sent surplus seeds to British prisoners of war: vegetable seeds were especially valued. The scheme was organized by the Royal Horticultural Society in conjunction with the International Red Cross. In 1943, for example, 979 parcels of seeds were dispatched to seventy-two camps containing about 141,000 prisoners and internees. Work at the Royal Horticultural Society continued as best it could – a semblance of normality was maintained. In 1944, for example, Wisley conducted trials of dahlias, narcissi, border carnations and early-flowering chrysanthemums. The society's *Journal* published an article in June 1945 on the Exotic Gardens in Monaco, with no mention of the ferocious and destructive war which had been fought during the previous year inch by inch along the Riviera coast, between the advancing French army and the retreating Germans.

But many great and important gardens suffered terrible damage in England, too. Exbury was singled out for German attack, because the owners were Jewish. A bomb destroyed the house where Lionel de Rothschild raised his remarkable rhododendron hybrids. The Rothschilds dispersed their collections of orchids and nerines to anyone who could care for them and grew vegetables in the glasshouses. Typical of the changes was the reduction of the garden staff at Nymans from eleven to three and at Petworth from sixteen to three. And in contrast to the Great War, all Royal Horticultural Society shows including the Chelsea Flower Show were cancelled for the duration.

In national terms, the borrowing needed to finance the Second World War was relatively less than for the Great War. Nevertheless, the national debt expanded in absolute terms from £7,784 million to £56,310 million. This was an enormous and potentially crippling increase – and it had to be serviced. During the war, income tax (when combined with super tax) rose to a maximum of 19s 6d in the pound (97.5 per cent) and this rate remained in force for reasons of social policy long after the war had ended. Indeed, as late as 1979, the top rate for income tax stood at 83 per cent. The effect upon the better-off was lethal – as it was intended to be – and not until the first budget of the Conservative reformer Margaret Thatcher did the emphasis begin to shift from direct to indirect taxation and give the taxpayer more control over his income and expenditure. The renaissance in good gardening, and in many other fields of endeavour, can be accurately dated to the Thatcher reforms which began in 1979.

The post-war years were difficult for all England – perhaps more difficult than the war years themselves. Petrol, electricity and fuel of every kind were rationed or restricted. Chief among the problems for horticulturists was the shortage of materials, building materials in particular. Glass for glasshouses was hard to come by and precedence was given to commercial glasshouses, which produced food for the nation. Such glasshouses as were sold in the 1950s and 1960s were functional buildings mainly designed for raising such crops as tomatoes and cucumbers.

For big houses, the aftermath of compulsory billeting took many years to repair. Houses were often left in a condition which rendered them unfit for the return of the owners. Grounds were destroyed by military activity. Even the super-rich Duke of Westminster felt that the house his ancestors had so confidently built less than 100 years before was no longer habitable, and moved into a smaller house in the grounds of Eaton Hall. But the main problem was the shortage of servants – the absence of skilled labour at affordable prices. As with the Great War, people who had been in domestic service before the war did not return to it. Houses and gardens whose way of life was supported by staff were unsustainable in the 1940s and 1950s. The bitter winter of 1946–7 increased the national sense of woe. Edmund de Rothschild sold his father's arboretum at Exbury and returned the land to agriculture.

R. T. Cowern's wartime painting of a cottage garden masks the reality: even medium-sized country gardens, during and after the Second World War, were badly hit by high taxation and a dearth of skilled gardeners.

After 1945, social legislation, including the introduction of National Insurance, meant that the costs of employment rose substantially. Many nurseries failed to get re-established after the war. In the 1950s and 1960s, people who tried to run their kitchen gardens at a profit almost invariably failed. The cost of labour, fuel and materials was prohibitive.

Already hit by high taxation, both of capital and of income, the owners of large gardens had to alter their way of life to survive. Flowering shrubs became more highly esteemed because they offered all the harmonies and contrasts of colour, form and variety without the intensive maintenance work required of herbaceous plants. Labour-saving ground cover became an integral part of the strategy. Writing her weekly column in the *Observer* on 10 October 1954, Vita Sackville-West summed up the need to be cheerful in the face of extinction:

We have reached the era of simplification in gardening and, so far as one can ever feel sure about any question of taste, always a dangerous venture, I feel almost sure that we are now travelling along the right lines. We are gradually abolishing the messy little bedding-out system, and are replacing it by generous lawns of our good green turf. We are replacing our bad herbaceous borders, hitherto stuffed with poor specimens of lupins and Golden Rod and what-have-you, by flowering shrubs which entail far less work and are far more interesting to grow and to observe.

When Nymans burnt down in 1947, the Messels had neither the will nor the funds to rebuild it.

The world of the traditional head gardener in private service had long since passed away. Most had seen the writing on the wall and turned to commercial horticulture or concluded, like Percy Thrower, that their future lay in the public parks. Neither change of career carried the personal status or security that an old head gardener enjoyed, but working for local authorities enabled them to plan the same large-scale colourful bedding schemes which they had learned to do well in private service. Then their municipal employers also began to scale down their budgets and cut back on public amenities. Finally, under the same Thatcher government which put more money into the pockets of them in the future. The maintenance and development of these gardens – each very distinct in its history, design and planting – would require extra skills and extra staff. Soon the remit of the National Trust's Gardens Committee was extended to include the important gardens attached to houses that were already owned and managed by the Trust. Thus were many of the historic gardens which are among the Trust's greatest visitor attractions restored and remade in the post-war years: Stourhead, Blickling, Cliveden, Hardwick Hall, Montacute, Packwood, Polesden Lacey, Powis Castle, Tintinhull and Upton House.

One man was central to this renaissance of English gardening. Graham Stuart Thomas began his working life as a plantsman and working gardener in the Cambridge University Botanic Garden, but his intellect, creativity and ability to get on with people took him in the 1950s to the position of Gardens Adviser to the National Trust. Thomas had all the talents needed to turn the Trust's gardens into its crowning glory – vision, persistence, persuasiveness and an ability to work within budget. Each garden had its own management plan, with day-to-day power devolved to the individual head gardeners. When the garden attached to a National Trust property had been lost or proved untraceable, Thomas was there to create a suitable historic and artistic setting for the house. He designed over 100 gardens. Much of what we see today at Benthall, Little Moreton, Lyme Park, Montacute, Mottisfont, Powis Castle, Shugborough and Wallington is Thomas's own work.

The National Trust pioneered garden restoration from the 1950s onwards. Compare Graham Thomas's own pictures of Mrs Winthrop's garden at Hidcote: overgrown in 1957 and renewed in 1967.

The National Trust and its expansion had one effect which was not confined to its gardens: it opened the eyes of visitors to things they had never seen before – it led to the popularization of aristocratic culture. The National Trust was seen to do things properly; it set the standards for lesser folk to follow. The Graham Thomas style of gardening had its roots in the firm designs of the Arts and Crafts movement and the romantic Edwardian plantings of Gertrude

Jekyll. It became the style that dominated the period from 1960 to 2000. A series of useful books secured Thomas's reputation and propagated his style of gardening yet further: *Plants for Ground-cover* (1970), *Perennial Garden Plants* or *The Modern Florilegium* (1976), *The Art of Planting* (1984) and *Recreating the Period Garden* (1984). In his books and in his gardens, Thomas's combination of plantsmanship, conservation and charm captured the spirit of the age. His creative appreciation of lost Edwardian glories was supremely influential and set the standard for private gardens, too. Thomas's vision may have started at the top of the social pyramid but its effects trickled down into every level.

'Graham Thomas' was one of the new-style 'English' roses bred by David Austin from about 1960 onwards.

The National Trust's timely concern for the conservation of England's gardening heritage was the first of many such initiatives in the latter half of the twentieth century. The Garden History Society was founded in 1965 to study garden history and to preserve parks and gardens. By the 1990s it was one of the statutory authorities to which all planning applications with implications for a historic garden or landscape had to be referred. Meanwhile its twice-yearly journal, *Garden History*, has published a conscious stream of new research, usually individual articles which examine a particular garden or designer. These have built up over the years into an immense corpus of valuable historical material and amount to a detailed overview of garden history.

Then, in 1978, the Royal Horticultural Society founded the National Council for the Conservation of Plants and Gardens to encourage the conservation of plants and gardens – principally plants. The need for this sort of conservation work had long been appreciated, but only by a few keen and knowledgeable plantsmen. At Petworth in the 1940s and 1950s, some forty different cultivars of potato were grown – not because they were necessarily the best available, but because 'if private gardens gave up these old varieties of fruit and vegetables they would be lost for ever – and some are worth a permanent place in our English gardens'.[11] The National Council was the first national organization to coordinate the new interest in plant conservation and took to heart its commitment to finding, identifying, propagating and distributing rare plants by establishing a national network of plant reference collections. These were grown in both private and public gardens and usually consisted of as many species and cultivars as could be found of a given genus or part of a genus. In effect, individual plantsmen were encouraged to become experts on a particular

Plant conservation – this is the National Collection of old roses at Mottisfont Abbey – got under way in the 1980s, when people first had the necessary funds and the information.

type of garden plant – growing as many as possible, researching their history and advising on their merits. By the late 1990s there were nearly 700 such collections.

Some statutory system of assessing the importance of old gardens was still needed. The problem was that no one had surveyed gardens in every part of the country or devised a way of comparing their merits. How could an important plantsman's garden like Sissinghurst be compared with a major landscaped park by Capability Brown? The National Heritage Act in 1983 gave authority to establish registers of some 1,100 parks and gardens in England which were to be considered of special historic interest. Those registers – one for each of the forty-six counties which then were the unit of local government – were compiled between 1984 and 1988 by Dr Christopher Thacker, an academic who was a core member of the Garden History Society. In the event, the different types of garden were compared only with each other when assessing their relative merits. Thus plantsmen's gardens would be compared with other plantsmen's gardens in every part of England, landscape gardens with landscape gardens and so on. All were graded according to their importance and quality; little account was taken of their present condition. Thacker was at pains to emphasize that his registers 'list and describe what is here now ... a statement that these gardens exist, and that they are, in many and glorious ways, places of interest, beauty and incalculable value'.[12]

During the 1970s and 1980s, conservation became not only the prevailing orthodoxy in the world of English gardening, but also the justification by which most major historic gardens were judged. One aspect of this rise of conservation was a change of emphasis in botanic gardens. Instead of building up and maintaining 'living collections' of plants introduced from the wild, they initiated ways of conserving them in their natural habitats and turned their own collections to supporting seriously threatened plant populations. But perhaps the most remarkable change in the course of the 1980s was the result of much greater individual prosperity: there was enough money around to undertake large restoration projects in English gardens. It was inconceivable in the 1950s and 1960s that the walled kitchen gardens of our Victorian ancestors would ever be used again for their original purposes.

The vinery at Dinton, a National Trust property in Wiltshire, in 1987. Until very recently, the Trust could seldom afford to restore a kitchen garden to its Victorian prime.

But this sort of restoration, on a substantial scale, became a reality. It was the top end of a general trend towards more leisure, greater spending power and better information. It was backed by a new generation of well-educated working gardeners with university degrees in ornamental horticulture who chose gardening as a satisfying way of life and were intellectually equipped to manage such projects.

Kitchen gardens made a comeback in the 1980s and 1990s, though it was more fashionable to refer to them as *potagers*. Their popularity can in part be explained by a desire for greater variety and a reaction against the limited choice available in

Kitchen gardens made a comeback in the 1980s and 1990s as potagers. *Rosemary Verey's at Barnsley in Gloucestershire was among the first – and was very influential.*

supermarkets. There was also a realization that *potagers* which copied the formal gardens of the sixteenth and seventeenth centuries made for great aesthetic possibilities. Another reason, not to be underestimated, is that kitchen gardens are expensive to run and have therefore become a status symbol again. A large, immaculate and productive kitchen garden where quantities of every imaginable variety of fruit and vegetable are raised is a potent statement of wealth. Its ornamental attraction plays a part here: how rich a person must be who grows his vegetables principally for visual enjoyment. Such gardens are the antithesis of the allotment where vegetables grow large to feed many.

There was, however, one garden initiative in the 1980s which did not find favour: the Garden Festival. These were based upon the German Bundesgarten-schau, which dates back to the 1920s and takes place every two years in a different German town. Five were mounted in Britain before the idea fizzled out: at Liverpool in 1984, Stoke-on-Trent in 1986, Glasgow in 1988, Gateshead in 1990 and South Wales in 1992. The publicity which surrounded them – and they all had excellent coverage in the horticultural press – encouraged people to suppose that they would be horticultural bonanzas. In fact, all were built on newly reclaimed sites with urban regeneration as one of their prime aims. The local authorities were more interested in the direct and indirect environmental benefits which would follow: landscaping, inward investment, image building, tourism and such economic spin-offs as new employment. Alongside these municipal concerns they promoted the idea of creating a showcase and stimulus for the landscape and horticultural sectors. The landscaping industry saw the Garden Festivals in general terms as a showcase for its skills. The horticultural industry, by contrast, regarded them principally as an opportunity to sell plants. The official report on the Garden Festivals commented that the horticultural sector 'appears to have had too high expectations of what can be achieved for their sector'.[13] It was true that the horticultural industry benefited from selling plants to the organizers to clothe the site and from sales to visitors, but the sales were infinitesimal as a proportion of the whole industry's turnover, and its total sales to the public throughout the summer-long Liverpool festival were valued at less than £360,000.

Ground cover and labour-saving practices were one aspect of post-war gardening. A fondness for pesticides was another. The English love affair with DDT was one of its stranger manifestations. DDT was an artificial compound, first used against clothes moths and Colorado beetles in Switzerland in 1938. During the war it was issued to troops to free them from such infestations as body lice. Later it proved crucial in winning another war – the centuries-old struggle against mosquito larvae in malarial regions of the Mediterranean. It was said that DDT was so effective that it 'should be considered among the most far-reaching developments in pest control methods of recent years'.[14]

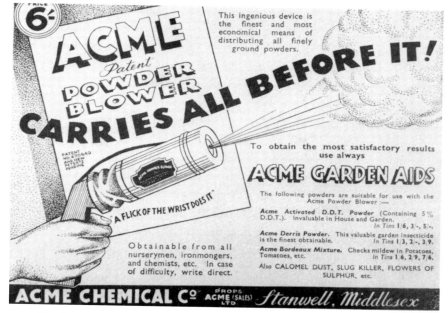

Gardeners were always keen to avail themselves of new products. The Royal Horticultural Society warned against the speedy introduction of DDT, but was powerless in the face of public demand for this new weapon of war.

Newspaper publicity led to a widespread demand for it to be made available to farmers and gardeners. The Royal Horticultural Society's voice was one of the few to counsel caution:

DDT is a powerful insecticide, but its limitations ... should be recognized ... the impatience shown by the community in obtaining supplies is due to the wide but premature publicity given to this compound, which fact is strongly deprecated both by biologists and chemists before investigations are completed on its effect upon warm-blooded animals, beneficial insects (predators, parasites and pollinating insects) and upon the widest range of plant pests generally.[15]

It was to no avail. DDT was widely used all through the 1950s and 1960s. The availability of pesticides of every sort was a political issue. They were thought to be an essential weapon in every gardener's armoury. Since the 1920s, gardening had increasingly been portrayed as a constant struggle against malevolent foes. Clover and moss were no longer acceptable in lawns; roses should be free from mildew and black spot; it was far better for fruit and vegetables to be sprayed with insecticide than fall prey to worm, caterpillar, scab and other pathogens. To some extent the use of pesticides was a substitute for the labour and manpower which had been lost, but the willingness to use chemicals to prevent invasions by pathogens was also part of people's desire to control their environment after the experience of the war. Keeping the greenfly off your roses was good practice for keeping the Germans away from British shores.

And the popularity of DDT was driven by commercial concerns. The use of pesticides mirrored practices in agriculture and commercial horticulture, where control was central to economic success and the cost of pesticides (and artificial fertilizers too) was built into the profit and loss account. When it became clear that DDT was toxic to fish, difficult for animals to metabolize and probably carcinogenic to humans, its days were numbered. One of the fastest growth areas in amateur gardening during the closing years of the twentieth century was an awareness of organic practices and their potential. Perhaps more than any other chemical, DDT gave rise to the organic movement and the emphasis upon conservation which accompanies it.

Specialist Societies

The sort of event which went from strength to strength during the second half of the twentieth century was the traditional flower show. County agricultural and horticultural shows prospered. Exhibition organizers offered to set up new shows and run plant sales where a score or more of specialist nurserymen would bring their wares to a common site and members of the public would pay a fee for the opportunity to buy. The Royal Horticultural Society's annual Chelsea Flower Show in May was so oversubscribed that the society began to launch a series of national shows in the provinces, starting with an annual show for Londoners at Hampton Court in July.

Indeed, all the activities of the Royal Horticultural Society grew apace, as did its membership and turnover. The society remained at the heart of English gardening, producing a constant stream of membership benefits and embarking on a substantial expansion of its commercial activities through its subsidiary companies. From the 1970s onwards, it also sought a more popular membership, and although most of its new members were decidedly middle class, the RHS successfully managed its own transformation from an aristocratic and learned society into a broad-based organization which was not only concerned with the science and art of horticulture but also reflected the preoccupations of all 'serious gardeners'. Back in 1938, the Duke of Portland recalled how his brother-officer Lord Lambourne, later President of the Royal Horticultural Society, had said to him, 'When you were lucky enough to win the Derby twice, you achieved one of the ambitions of your life. I also did so, a few days ago, when I won the first prize for orchids at the RHS's show. Let's have a glass of wine together … we have both brought new honours to the Coldstream Guards.'[16] Such a remark would have been unthinkable by the end of the twentieth century.

Although the Royal Horticultural Society sought always to be comprehensive and to cater for the interests of all amateur horticulturists, it began to find during the latter half of the nineteenth century that it could not always offer a focus for specialist interests. This was most notable when the National Rose Society was founded in 1876. Always more popularly based than the Royal Horticultural Society, the National Rose Society was spectacularly successful during the middle years of the twentieth century, but its membership shrank to fewer than 15,000 in the 1990s.

Four important specialist plant societies which still exist were founded in the nineteenth century: the National Chrysanthemum Society in 1846, the National Dahlia Society in 1881, the

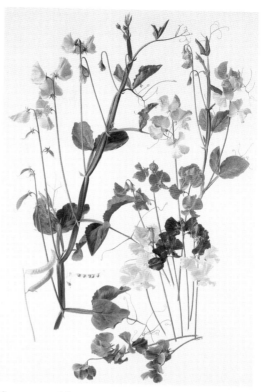

Sweet peas (these were painted by Raymond Booth) became popular during the twentieth century: the National Sweet Pea Society was founded in 1900.

British Pteridological Society in 1891 and the Daffodil Society in 1898. Some of the societies grew out of earlier regional associations: the London Dahlia Society, founded in 1858, was the precursor of the National Dahlia Society, just as the Royal Horticultural Society itself grew out of the Horticultural Society of London. During the first half of the twentieth century, many more societies were founded: the National Sweet Pea Society in 1900, the National Viola and Pansy Society in 1911, the British Iris Society in 1922, the British Gladiolus Society in 1926, the Herb Society in 1927, the Delphinium Society in 1928, the Alpine Garden Society in 1929, the British Fuchsia Society in 1938, the National Begonia Society in 1948 and the British National Carnation Society in 1949. Pre-eminent among them has been the Alpine Garden Society. Rock gardening and alpine cultivation has always been the province of the enthusiast, often middle class, scientific and intellectual, and certainly the interest of the richer gardener. Enthusiasts display remarkable skills in cultivation and are passionate in their acquisition of plants. The popular association between alpine gardeners and hearty walking or climbing in the mountain ranges of the world is not without foundation. The professionalism and knowledge which they display in the society's studies and publications are a constant source of wonder. Sometimes, when these are compared to the greedy enjoyment of horticultural variety which comes naturally to most plant-lovers, the alpine gardeners resemble the last of the puritans after the restoration of the monarchy.

Listing the specialist plant societies founded in the second half of the twentieth century provides a useful guide to the relative popularity in recent years of the specialist interests they represent: the British Pelargonium and Geranium Society in 1951, the Orchid Society of Great Britain in 1951, the Hardy Plant Society in 1957, the National Association of Flower Arrangement Societies in 1959, the National Vegetable Society in 1960, the Heather Society in 1963 and the British Hosta and Hemerocallis Society in 1981. The three strongest societies by the end of the twentieth century, judged by their steady growth and solid expansion, were undoubtedly the Alpine Garden Society, the Hardy Plant Society and the organic gardening society the Henry Doubleday Research Association. But the size of some of these societies is often surprisingly small: the British Iris Society and the Daffodil Society are now down to about 700 members, the British Gladiolus Society to 400, and the National Viola and Pansy Society to about 150. Only in three areas of specialist interest has the Royal Horticultural Society been able to found groups which are, in effect, the specialist plant societies: the Rhododendron, Camellia and Magnolia Group, the Fruit Group and the Lily Group of the Royal Horticultural Society. None has a membership of more than 1,000.

Publishing & Broadcasting

The growth in horticultural shows, gardens to visit and plants to buy – and the money to enjoy all three – was accompanied by an expansion of dedicated broadcasting and publishing. *The Gardener's Chronicle* passed through a number of vicissitudes and was finally absorbed into a trade periodical. The top end of the market was filled principally by the Royal Horticultural Society's *Journal*, which changed its name in 1975 to *The Garden*. Long seen as the principal benefit of membership of the society, it was content for many years to mirror those members' interests, but during the 1980s it began to be developed as a means of attracting new members. It remains peerless and faultless. At the bottom end of the market were weekly magazines like *Amateur Gardening* and *Garden News*, always a good read in the potting shed with a no-nonsense hands-on approach and lots of readers among allotment-holders. *Amateur Gardening* has a particularly distinguished history. It was founded in 1884 with a distinct market focus – the owners of small gardens in towns and cities – and has remained true to its readership throughout its unbroken history.

In between these examples of 'high' and 'low' gardening, a mass of magazines, new and old, took up their market positions in the 1980s and 1990s. Some were oriented towards information on techniques of cultivation – among them, *Practical Gardening* and *Garden Answers*. Best and most enduring of the titles which gave information on how to get the greatest value out of everything concerned with gardening was *Gardening Which?*. A series of lifestyle mag-

Graham Thomas dominated English horticulture from 1950 to 2000, first as Gardens Adviser to the National Trust and later as a prolific and profoundly original writer.

azines catered for the socially aspirational; *Gardens Illustrated* was set apart by its international coverage, distinguished writing and stylish photography. Not all magazines cut themselves a distinct place in the market, and there were a number of failures – as indeed there had been when horticultural publishing first got under way in the 1830s and 1840s. The nearest rival to *The Garden* – albeit a poor shadow of the Royal Horticultural Society's flagship monthly – was *BBC Gardeners' World Magazine*, a good-looking, lavishly illustrated mid-market monthly with a wide readership. Launched in March 1991 to provide a mixture of practical advice, ideas and inspiration, the main contributors were the current gardening presenters from BBC radio and television.

These dedicated gardening magazines were matched by much-read gardening correspondents in the national newspapers and leading magazines. The top end of the market was dominated by Christopher Lloyd's stylishly written and digressive column in *Country Life* and the classic articles on gardens and plants which have made it a journal of record for over 100 years. Robin Lane Fox's thoughtful and idiosyncratic column, first published on Wednesdays but latterly in the Saturday edition of the *Financial Times*, also had a marked influence among the money-wise and their spouses. Lane Fox claimed to be interested only in the cultivation of plants, but was widely thought to write best when his analytical skills were put to work on broader issues. But other magazines had their own following among garden-owners, notably *Country Living* and the *Daily Telegraph*. And a spate of specialist titles arose with names like *Organic Gardening*, *Plant Talk* and *The Water Gardener*, so that it seemed that every conceivable garden interest was satisfied by either general gardening magazines, articles on gardening in newspapers and magazines, or the specialist publications of garden societies.

The same could not be said of gardening programmes on television and wireless. Almost every interest and enthusiasm was at some point indulged by the new media, but there were never enough slots to satisfy all of the people all of the time. The first broadcasts were made in 1923 by Marion Cran, a popular novelist who also wrote highly personal gardening books with such titles as *The Garden of Ignorance* (subtitled *The Experiences of a Woman in a Garden*) and its sequel, *The Garden of Experience*. During the 1930s, and throughout the important war years, the BBC's garden broadcaster was C. M. Middleton (always known as

'Mr Middleton'), a county horticultural adviser in Surrey. His weekly programme, *In Your Garden*, acquired a tremendous following until his death in 1945, just after the end of the war. He was followed by Fred Streeter, whose strongly rural accent and slow manner masked a keen intellect which had been put to good use as head gardener to Lord Leconfield at Petworth. Roland Smith, who was head gardener to the Earl of Bradford at Weston, was another early broadcaster, who worked in both wireless and television. All these broadcasters – and indeed all pro-

Radio Allotment *was a popular and informative wartime programme. Here the Royal Parks gardener Tom Hay imparts his wisdom to an effete BBC journalist while Land Girls labour beyond.*

grammes up until the 1970s – concentrated upon giving practical advice to listeners on how to become better gardeners, and practical demonstrations to viewers of gardening tasks and techniques.

The cult of the television personality gardener took off in 1951 when Smith was joined by Percy Thrower in a regular weekly programme called *Gardening Club*. Thrower was a natural communicator who realized that the best way to succeed as a broadcaster was to promote himself as a personality. For twenty-five years he dominated the screen; the introduction of colour television in the late 1960s gave a great boost to gardening programmes and *Gardening Club* changed its name to *Gardener's World*. Other programmes were now possible which emphasized the beauty of flowers, plants and gardens rather than listing the jobs that had to be done to make such beauty possible. Histories of gardens, gardens abroad, royal gardens and a series on the history of the rose were typical of the 1980s and 1990s, until garden make-overs took the potential of programmes to new levels of popular appeal. A string of presenters were turned into media personalities by the power of television: Roy Lancaster, Geoffrey Smith, Geoff Hamilton and Alan Titchmarsh. But one wireless programme never changed its format and never ceased to attract large audiences: *Gardeners' Question Time*, which started in 1947

Garden make-overs are not so different from show gardens. This design won a gold medal at Chelsea in 2001 – the best by far, and relying in large measure upon natural plantings.

and takes a panel of experts every week, usually to a local gardening club somewhere in England, and tries to answer the questions which members put to them.

The garden make-overs which television programmes promoted so effortlessly and with such convincing results gave rise to a desire for instant effects. The area around a house should be decorated to express the personality and the aspirations of the owners just as much as the interior of the house itself. The designers supplied large mature plants, grown in containers and often imported from specialist growers in Italy, to create an immediate impact. Stately exotics like tall Australian tree-ferns would be planted out in summer and then abandoned to winter's mercy. Fashion statements never come cheap, but garden make-overs were only for the affluent. Of course they cost a lot of money, but they also promised instant gratification. Indeed, that was the whole point of them: they were statements of wealth and status.

In truth, there is little of substance to distinguish these suburban seekers after glory from the show-offs of Elizabethan or Victorian days. All gardens serve the purpose of the people who make them. They are part of the lifestyle which everyone creates – part of the myth which people build up around themselves. A garden is a social statement and a declaration of the owner's taste. Time and again we have seen that taste is no more than fashion. Fashions are top-down and transient. They are intended to bind some people together and to divide them from others. Fashions for garden design and plants are tyrannical, illogical and capricious.

The general expansion of English garden-making over the last 500 years reflects an improvement in our educational, technological and political conditions but, above all, in our social and economic circumstances. The interruptions to that progress have generally been the result of war and taxation. The changing fortunes and ambitions of successive generations are there to see in individual gardens. The story of gardening has always been a tale of aspiration and self-fulfilment. But the design and management of gardens have altered, above all, in direct response to social and economic transformations in English society itself.

References

INTRODUCTION

1 Mark Girouard, *Life in the English Country House*, London, 1978.
2 John Sales, *National Trust Magazine*, Spring 1998, p. 23.
3 John Loudon, *Landscape Gardening and Landscape Architecture of the late H. Repton*, London, 1840. This view is expressed in Loudon's introduction.
4 George Sheeran, *Landscape Gardens in West Yorkshire, 1680–1880*, Wakefield, 1990, p. vii.
5 Girouard, *Life in the English Country House*, p. 3.
6 Benjamin Disraeli, *Sybil*, London, 1845, Ch. VII.
7 Canon H. N. Ellacombe, *In a Gloucestershire Garden*, London, 1896.
8 Alfred Austin, *The Garden That I Love*, London, 1905, p. 126.

CHAPTER ONE
Early English Gardens

1 Quoted in W. G. Hoskins, *The Making of the English Landscape*, ed. Christopher Taylor, London, 1988.
2 Roy Strong, *The Renaissance Garden in England*, London, 1979, p. 11.
3 Ibid., p. 22.
4 Ibid., pp. 42–3.
5 *LCC Survey of London. The Parish of St Margaret, Westminster, ii, Neighbourhood of Whitehall*, I, London, 1930, p. 90.
6 This is lucidly explained by John Schofield in 'City of London Gardens, 1500–c. 1620', *Journal of the Garden History Society*, Vol. 27, No. 1, 1999, pp. 73–88.
7 But note that gardens did not begin to be symmetrically aligned on a house until the early 1600s.

8   Quoted by Christopher Thacker in *The Genius of Gardening*, London, 1994, p. 45.

9   John Harvey, *Early Nurserymen*, London, 1974, p. 45.

10 Ibid., pp. 60–61.

11 Schofield, 'City of London Gardens'.

12 Keith Thomas, *Man and the Natural World: Changing Attitudes in England, 1500–1800*, London, 1983, p. 224.

13 Harvey, *Early Nurserymen*, p. 60.

14 Thomas Fuller, *Worthies of England etc.*, London, 1662, p. 419.

15 Melvyn Barnes, *Root and Branch: A History of the Worshipful Company of Gardeners of London*, London, 1994, p. 31.

16 Stephen Switzer, *Ichnographia Rustica*, London, 1718, Vol. 1, p. 273.

17 Fynes Moryson, *An Itinerary*, London, 1617, p. 147.

18 'The King's Forrests have innumerable heards of Red Deare, and all parts have such plenty of Fallow Deare, as every Gentleman of five hundreth or a thousand pounds rent by the yeere hath a Parke for them inclosed with pales of wood for two or three miles compasse. Yet this prodigall age hath so forced Gentlemen to improve their revenews, as many of these grounds are by them disparked, and converted to feed Cattell': ibid., p. 148.

19 *Richard II*, Act 3, Scene 1.

20 Tristram Risdon, *Survey of the County of Devon*, London, 1811, pp. 6–7.

21 Quoted in Vita Sackville-West, *Knole and the Sackvilles*, London, 1922. Lord Dorset inherited in 1652, so this may be associated with raising funds to pay fines and compositions during the Commonwealth.

22 James Lees-Milne, *Ancestral Voices*, London, 1975, p. 232.

23 Elisabeth H. Whittle, 'The Renaissance Gardens of Raglan Castle', *Journal of the Garden History Society*, Vol. 17, No. 1, 1989, p. 83.

24 Quoted in Stewart Harding and David Lambert, *Parks and Gardens of Avon*, Bristol, 1994, p. 14.

25 Daphne Bath, *Longleat from 1566 to the Present Time*, Longleat, 1949, p. 13.

26 Moryson, *An Itinerary*, p. 147.

27 Henry Peacham, *The Complete Gentleman*, London, 1622, p. 11. Peacham was here discussing excellence and the qualities of nobility to which all well-bred men should aspire.

28 *Viscount Montagu's Household Book*, 1595, p. 132.

29 William Lawson, *The Country House-wife's Garden*, London, 1618.

30 Harvey, *Early Nurserymen*, p. 27.

31 John Harvey, 'Fritillary and Martagon – Wild or Garden?', *Journal of the Garden History Society*, Vol. 17, No. 24 (1), 1996, p. 36.

32 This list comes from John Schofield's fascinating and well-researched article on the garden of the Carpenters' Hall in London Wall, 'City of London Gardens', p. 79.

33 This point is well made by Judith Roberts in 'The Gardens of the Gentry in the Late Tudor Period', *Journal of the Garden History Society*, Vol. 27, No. 1, 1999, pp. 89–108.

34 Schofield, 'City of London Gardens', p. 75.

35 Lisa Jardine and Alan Stewart, *Hostage to Fortune: The Troubled Life of Francis Bacon*, London, 1998, p. 187.

36 J. Sprat, *Voyage to England with Observations on Sobière's Voyage to England*, London, 1709, p. 64.

37 Quoted by Hilary Spurling in her delightful *Elinor Fettiplace's Receipt Book*, London, 1986, pp. 96–7.

38 Thomas, *Man and the Natural World*, p. 231.

39 Vicky Basford, *Historic Parks and Gardens of the Isle of Wight*, Newport, 1989, p. 25.

40 Quoted in Sackville-West, *Knole and the Sackvilles*.

41 Ibid.

42 Schofield, 'City of London Gardens'.

43 Barnes, *Root and Branch*, p. 30.

44 Thomas Percy (Bishop of Dromore), *The Regulations and Establishment of the Household of Henry Algernon Percy, the Fifth Earl of Northumberland, at his Castles of Wresill and Lekinfield in Yorkshire. Begun anno domini M.DXII*, London, 1770.

45 Royal Historical Society Camden (fifth series), Vol. 6, *Household Accounts and Disbursement Books of Robert Dudley, Earl of Leicester, 1558–1561, 1584–1586*, Cambridge, 1995. See also Harvey, *Early Nurserymen*, p. 60.

46 David Jacques, 'The Chief Ornament of Gray's Inn: The Walks from Bacon to Brown', *Journal of the Garden History Society*, Vol. 17, No. 1, 1989, pp. 66–7.

47 In his *Herball* (1597), John Gerard says that the sycamore is 'a stranger to England'.

48 See William Harrison's *Description of England* in the 1587 edition of Holinshed's *Chronicles*.

49 See Prudence Leith-Ross's excellent account of the Tradescants' achievements, *The John Tradescants: Gardeners to the Rose and Lily Queen*, London, 1984, p. 105, on which I have relied heavily.

CHAPTER TWO

The Rise and Fall of the Formal Garden

1 John Rea, *Flora; seu de Florum Cultura etc.*, London, 1665, p. 2.

2 Paul Stamper, *Historic Parks and Gardens of Shropshire*, Shrewsbury, 1996, p. 13.

3 Steven Pugsley, *Devon Gardens: An Historical Survey*, Stroud, 1994, p. 34.

4 Samuel Hartlib, *His Legacy of Husbandry*, 1655, p. 93.

5 Ibid., see in particular pp. 4 and 10.

6 William Lawson, *A New Orchard and Garden*, London, 1618, p. 8.

7 See William Lawson, *The Country House-wife's Garden*, London, 1618.

8 Michael Jermin, *A Commentary upon ... Ecclesiastes*, London, 1639, pp. 35–6.

9 Thomas Fuller, *Worthies of England etc.*, London, 1662, p. 543.

10 Ibid., p. 419.

11 Ibid., p. 543.

12 Quoted in Dorothy Hartley, *Food in England*, London, 1954, p. 424.

13 Sir William Temple, *The Gardens of Epicurus*, 1685, London, p. 45.

14 Theological teaching was not so comfortable with controlled hybridization. When Thomas Fairchild bred his 'mule' between *Dianthus caryophyllus* and *D. barbatus*, some commentators 'questioned whether they did not amount to blasphemy. Did they not deny the biblical account of the Creation, which credited God as the creator of all things, and had until now been taken to mean that His scheme was not subject to alteration?' See Michael Leapman, *The Ingenious Mr Fairchild*, London, 2000, especially p. 12.

15 Alan MacFarlane, ed., *The Family Life of Ralph Josselin, a Seventeenth-Century Clergyman*, Cambridge, 1970, p. 70.

16 Pugsley, *Devon Gardens*, p. 35.

17 John Rea, *Pomona*, London, 1665, p. 193.

18 Quoted from Hertford-Pomfret correspondence (Vol. 1, pp. 245–8) in Peter Martin, *Pursuing Innocent Pleasures: The Gardening World of Alexander Pope*, Hamden (USA), 1984.

19 Daniel Defoe, *A Tour thro' the Whole Island of Great Britain*, London, 1738, Vol. II, p. 195.

20 Mark Girouard, *Life in the English Country House*, London, 1978, p. 145.

21 Tom Williamson and Anthea Taigel, eds., *Gardens in Norfolk*, Norwich, 1990, pp. 14–15.

22 Moses Cook, *The Manner of Raising, Ordering, and Improving Forrest-Trees & etc.*, London, 1676, p. 137.

23 H. J. Todd, *The History of the College of Bonhommes, at Ashridge etc.*, London, 1823, p. 76.

24 Martin Lister, *A Journey to Paris in the year 1698*, London, 1699, pp. 202–3.

25 Rea, *Flora*, p. 3.

26 Temple, *The Gardens of Epicurus*, p. 43.

27 Cook, *The Manner of Raising ...*

28 'J W Gent' (John Worlidge), *Systema horti-culturae*, 1682, p. 146.

29 Rea, *Flora*, p. 3.

30 'J W Gent', *Systema horti-culturae*, p. 21.

31 Temple, *The Gardens of Epicurus*, p. 44.

32 'J W Gent', *Systema horti-culturae*, p. 22.

33 See Barry Doyle, 'The Kitchen Garden in Norfolk', in Williamson and Taigel, eds., *Gardens in Norfolk*, pp. 54–5.

34 This was not published until 1664.

35 Stephen Switzer, *Ichnografia Rustica*, 1718, p. 50.

36 Defoe, *A Tour thro' the Whole Island of Great Britain*, Vol. II, p. 193.

37 John Evelyn, *Acetaria, a Discourse of Sallets* (The Dedication), London, 1699.

38 This view is well expressed by Joseph Levine in his essay 'Between the Ancients and the Moderns', in Therese O'Malley and Joachim Wolschke-Bulmahn, *John Evelyn's 'Elysium Britannicum' and European Gardening*, Washington, 1998, pp. 76–7.

39 In *The Royal Society: Concept and Creation*, London, 1967, Marjorie Purver debunks many old myths about the origins of the Royal Society.

40 Thomas Sprat, *History of the Royal Society*, London, 1667, pp. 61–2.

41 Cook, *The Manner of Raising . . .*

42 Purver, *The Royal Society*, p. 235.

43 Rea, *Flora*, p. 3.

44 William Hughes, *The Flower Garden*, London, 1672, pp. 6–9.

45 'J W Gent', *Systema horti-culturae*, p. 1. Worlidge's own tips, based on observation, include sifting ashes around a plant to protect it from snails and keeping the roots of tender plants like rosemary, sage and wallflowers dry to make them hardier.

46 John Aubrey, *Brief Lives*, ed. Oliver Lawson Dick, London, 1949, p. 145.

47 Edward Nicholas, *Diary of John Evelyn*, London, 1879, 11 March 1690.

48 Switzer, *Ichnografia Rustica*, Vol. 1, pp. xxiv–xxv.

49 Keith Thomas, *Man and the Natural World: Changing Attitudes in England, 1500–1800*, London, 1983, p. 225.

50 Williamson and Taigel, eds., *Gardens in Norfolk*, p. 55.

51 Ibid., p. 56.

52 Batty Langley, *Pomona*, London, 1729, p. ix. See also Switzer, *Ichnografia Rustica*.

53 C. H. C. and M. I. Baker, *The Life and Circumstances of James Brydges, First Duke of Chandos*, Oxford, 1949.

54 See Vita Sackville-West, *Knole and the Sackvilles*, London, 1922.

55 Melvyn Barnes, *Root and Branch: A History of the Worshipful Company of Gardeners of London*, London, 1994, p. 41.

56 Temple, *The Gardens of Epicurus*, pp. 38–9.

57 Ibid.

58 Ibid.

59 'J W Gent', *Systema horti-culturae*, p. 5.

1 Benjamin Rand, ed., *The Life, Unpublished Letters and Philosophical Regime of Anthony, Earl of Shaftesbury*, London, 1900, p. 247.

2 Tom Williamson, 'The Landscape Park: Economics, Art and Ideology', *Journal of Garden History*, Vol. 13, Nos. 1 and 2, 1993, pp. 49–55.

3 Batty Langley, *New principles of Gardening*, London, 1728, pp. viii–xi.

4 Ibid., pp. 21–4.

5 This is quoted from *Elysium Britannicum*: see Therese O'Malley and Joachim Wolschke-Bulmahn, *John Evelyn's 'Elysium Britannicum' and European Gardening*, Washington, 1998, p. 17.

6 George Vertue, *Note Books*, Oxford (Walpole Society), 1934, p. 140.

7 See Alan Fletcher, *Journal of the Garden History Society*, Vol. 19, No. 2, 1991, p. 146 *et seq.*

8 Quoted from Mavis Batey, 'Horace Walpole as Modern Garden Historian', *Journal of the Garden History Society*, Vol. 19, No. 1, 1991, p. 8.

9 Richard Pococke, *Travels through England*, ed. James J. Cartwright, The Camden Society, 1888.

10 Humphry Repton, *Observations on the theory and practice of Landscape Gardening*, London, 1803, p. 93.

11 The best account of Wooburn is by R. W. King, 'The "Ferme Ornée": Philip Southcote and Wooburn Farm', *Journal of the Garden History Society*, Vol. II, No. 3, 1974, pp. 27–60.

12 Christopher Thacker, *The Genius of Gardening*, London, 1994, p. 215.

13 Repton, *Observations . . .*, p. 266.

14 The Hon. John Byng, *Travel Journals*, 1781.

15 Richard Bacon, *Report on the Agriculture of Norfolk*, London, 1844, p. 39.

16 G. E. Mingay, *A Social History of the English Countryside*, London, 1990, pp. 118–19.

17 Bacon, *Report on the Agriculture of Norfolk*, p. 39.

18 The Hon. John Byng, *Travel Journals*, 1792.

19 Daniel Defoe, *A Tour thro' the Whole Island of Great Britain*, London, 1738, Vol. I, pp. 114–15.

20 Thomas Whately, *Observations on Modern Gardening*, London, 1770, p. 1.

21 Edwin Morris Betts, ed., *Thomas Jefferson's Garden Book*, Philadelphia, 1944, p. 111.

22 Joyce Godber, *The Marchioness Grey of Wrest Park*, Bedford, 1968, p. 45.

23 Humphry Repton, *An Enquiry into the changes of taste in Landscape Gardening*, London, 1806, pp. 116–17.